MW01614577

Brown

# Coaching Football's Special Teams

## Kenny Ratledge

©2005 Coaches Choice. All rights reserved. Printed in the United States.

No part of this book may be reproduced, stored in a retrieval system, or transmitted, in any form or by any means, electronic, mechanical, photocopying, recording, or otherwise, without the prior permission of Coaches Choice.

ISBN: 978-1-58518-914-4
Library of Congress Control Number: 2004112502
Cover design: Jeanne Hamilton
Book layout: Jeanne Hamilton
Front cover photo: Craig Jones/Getty Images

Coaches Choice
P.O. Box 1828
Monterey, CA 93942
www.coacheschoice.com

# Dedication

I would like to dedicate this book to my family: my wife, Debbie, and my children, Patrick and Laura. I love you all more than anything!

# Acknowledgments

I would like to thank official Lee Hedrick for his help in reviewing kicking game rules. His help was invaluable on the rule and regulation portions of the book. I would also like to thank Dixon Brown and Bryan Atchley for their computer expertise. Special thanks go to Darlene Metcalf for typing the manuscript.

# Contents

# Introduction

*Special*: "distinctive, peculiar, or unique…highly regarded or valued."
*Team*: "a group of people working together in a coordinated effort."

When you combine the two words, special team, you are describing a group of people who are highly regarded or valued, distinctive, and work together for a common goal. In football nomenclature, special teams involve various groups of players who perform during kicking plays, either on the kicking or receiving teams. In some cases, these units have the option to try to block a kick instead of receiving the ball (i.e., punt block).

Historically, special teams have been a major part of football games. George Allen noted that the kicking game is a full one third of a team's season. Former great coaches such as Alonzo Stagg, Knute Rockne, Bobby Dodd, and General Robert Neyland have espoused the virtues of good special teams play. The kicking game can decide the outcome of a game, often on a single play. However, it was not until the late 1960s and early 1970s that special teams play became specialized and compartmentalized.

George Allen has been called the father of modern special teams play and is considered the best special teams coach in the history of football. He was a true visionary and established the special teams coordinator position. After Allen's Los Angeles Rams team failed to get to the divisional championship game in 1968 because of poor special teams play, he decided to create a new coaching position. This attempt was an effort to improve his special teams' effectiveness. Allen hired Dick Vermeil, who was then coaching quarterbacks at Stanford, to be the first NFL special teams coordinator. When Vermeil left for UCLA, Allen became the head coach of the Washington Redskins and hired Marv Levy to be his special teams coach. Levy would later introduce the Canadian Football League to the special teams coordinator concept. During Allen's stay with the Redskins they became dominant on special teams and went 67-30-1 in regular season play.

The Redskins reached Super Bowl VII, in part, because of their kick blocking prowess and by allowing an astounding total of only 39 punt return yards for the season. History has borne out Coach Allen's premise to his team in 1971 when he said, "The offense doesn't set the tempo! The defense doesn't set the tempo! Special teams set the tempo!" Later, Dick Vermeil (the former coach of the Philadelphia Eagles and St. Louis Rams, and presently head coach of the Kansas City Chiefs) was quoted as saying: "I think special teams are the biggest dimension in winning and losing football games today."

Special teams play has directly, or indirectly, won or lost championships on all levels of play. In the NFL, many examples exist of special teams failures that have adversely affected a team's chance to win, or advance to a championship. The Buffalo Bills lost Super Bowl XXV when Scott Norwood missed a field-goal attempt at the end of the game. Some people place part of the blame for Norwood's miss on the holder for not turning the laces away from Norwood. In the 1985 NFL playoffs, Sean Landeta of the New York Giants foul tipped his punt, which allowed the Chicago Bears to score a touchdown on their march to the World Championship. In 1991, Ian Howfield of the Houston Oilers missed a 31-yard field-goal attempt that cost Houston the home-field advantage in the playoffs – and Howfield his job.

Special teams played a crucial part as the Buffalo Bills successfully executed an onside kick at a crucial time, which enabled the Bills to erase a 35-3 deficit in a comeback win. This comeback occurred in a wildcard game in 1993 against the Oilers, and marked the erasure of the largest lead in a comeback win in NFL history. A prime example of a special teams meltdown occurred during the 2002 AFC Championship game. The New England Patriots upset the heavily favored Pittsburgh Steelers 24-17, due in large measure to a punt return for a touchdown, and a blocked field-goal attempt that was returned for a touchdown. Pittsburgh allowed four touchdowns during the playoffs. Of those four touchdowns, three were given up by Steeler special teams. Lee Flowers, of the Steelers, was quoted after the game as saying, "We're not taking [special teams] seriously enough to be a dominating team. We dominated most teams on defense and offense, but to have the game before you go the Super Bowl come down to two returns on special teams is very disappointing."

College football also has been dramatically affected by special teams failures. In the early 1990s, "wide right" entered sports lexicon as a result of failures by Florida State kickers. These blunders probably cost Bobby Bowden two national titles. On the other hand, excellent special teams play, especially the punt team, enabled Oklahoma to win the 2001 National Championship Game. In the title game, against Florida State, Oklahoma's punter left three punts inside the Florida State seven-yard line. Two of these punts were pooch kicks and the third punt was a 52-yard effort that rolled dead at the Florida State six-yard line. These kicks tilted field position in favor of Oklahoma, which went on to win a low scoring game by a 13-2 score. More recently, two blocked punts and an onside kick by Stanford cost Oregon a chance at the 2002 Rose Bowl game for the national championship.

Two kickoff returns have a permanent place in football lore and legend. "The Play" occurred in 1982 at the end of the game between Cal and Stanford. Cal won the game 25-20 on a five lateral kickoff return with no time left on the clock. Kevin Moen started the play, ended up with the ball as he evaded Stanford's coverage team and band as he ran into the end zone, and had a collision with a Stanford trombone player. John Elway had just led Stanford to the go-ahead touchdown for an apparent win. The NFL equivalent of "the play" occurred during a wildcard game in 2000 between the Tennessee Titans and the Buffalo Bills. The "Music City Miracle" occurred with 16 seconds on the clock when the Titans ran "Homerun Throwback." The call involved a lateral from Frank Wycheck to Kevin Dyson, who went 75 yards for the winning touchdown. As luck would have it, Dyson had not practiced the play; he was inserted into the game at the last second because of an injury to the assigned recipient of the lateral. Additionally, the Titans had not practiced the play versus a sky or pooch kick. The Titans improvised and executed a play that is considered to be in the same category as "The Drive" and the "Immaculate Reception" in NFL folklore.

Statistics show that the average NFL game will have 145 plays. Of those total plays, 17 percent are special teams plays. In addition, 34 percent of all points scored come during special teams plays. Field goals, extra points, punt blocks, punt returns, and kickoff returns all have potential to score. In many cases, field position is lost or gained by special teams plays. Some pundits estimate that two NFL games a week are decided by the kicking game. Special teams plays account for one play in six, and most involve considerably more yardage than most scrimmage plays. It has been estimated that gains and losses on special teams can account for more than 1,000 yards per team per season. This equals having a thousand-yard rusher.

A review of Super Bowl records can give insight on how teams who win the special teams' battle often win the game. The three teams who are tied for the most successful points after touchdown (PAT) won their respective Super Bowls. San Francisco kicked seven extra points in 1990 and 1995. Dallas also kicked seven extra points in 1993. The significance of this statistic is a no-brainer. You have to score a lot of touchdowns to be in a position to kick that many extra points. The significance of other statistics, however, is subtler.

Green Bay and San Francisco are tied at four each for the most field goals made. Green Bay kicked its four against Oakland in 1968 during Super Bowl II, while San Francisco's Ray Wersching kicked four against Cincinnati in 1982. Brad Maynard has the dubious honor of having the most punts in a Super Bowl game. He had a total of 11 punts for the Giants in a losing effort against the Baltimore Ravens in 2001. The Washington Redskins hold the record for the lowest per punt average with a mark of 31 yards per punt in a losing effort against the Dolphins in Super Bowl VII. The record for the most punt returns, which in turn signals a good defensive effort, is held by the Redskins and Packers – who both had six punt returns in winning efforts. Green Bay holds the record for the most punt return yardage with 90 yards in a winning effort against New England in Super Bowl XXXI in 1997.

An effective kicking game will allow a team to have a smooth transition in ball possession. It can provide positive field position for the offense or defense. The offense benefits from a good return or a punt block. A defense can gain an advantage with a good punt, or good kickoff coverage. Successful teams succeed in protecting their kicks while blocking or pressuring their opponent's kicks. Just as there are more ways to score on defense than on offense, the same is true for special teams. A team can score points in a variety of ways: points after touchdowns, field goals, kickoff returns, punt returns, blocked kicks returned for touchdowns, and stripped balls for touchdowns.

Field position can be dramatically altered by good special teams play. Coverage teams can cause and recover fumbles. Great coverage and blocked kicks can result in advantageous field position. Pooch kicks can cause gain or loss of field position. Properly executed punts and field goals, as well as surprise onside kicks, can psychologically damage an opponent. Solid special teams play can positively affect offensive or defensive calls. Faith in special teams allows offensive or defensive coordinators to be more aggressive. Tennessee Volunteers' coach Philip Fulmer is quoted in his book *A Perfect Season* (about his team's rise to the National Championship in 1998), that a big part of their game plan against the Florida Gators was to throw the ball downfield and over the top, because he felt his team had an advantage in the kicking game. The result was a 20-17 overtime win for the Volunteers.

This book will benefit those programs that seek to take their special teams play to a higher level. Teams can gain a decided advantage through effective special teams play. Included within the scope of this book are offensive and defensive kicking strategies, placekicking techniques, holding techniques, punting techniques, scouting techniques, and special teams drills. Kicking game rules for high school, college, and NFL are also included. Coaches who subscribe to the philosophy that the kicking game is essential for success, and who truly feel that the kicking game is a third of the total game, will benefit from this book.

# 1

# Coaching Special Teams

> **Wanted**: a workaholic coach to work with self-centered athletes, who, in many cases, do not want to play on special teams. He should be able to deal with temperamental kickers. He should be mentally capable of making strategic and tactical decisions during times of bone-crushing pressure. This position requires a coach who likes to live on the edge. He should also possess a maniacal desire to succeed. Last, but not least, the special teams coach should possess an evangelist's fervor toward special teams play.

As this make-believe want ad shows, coaching special teams is a daunting task. In fact, many football experts agree that the most pressure-packed coaching position is that of the special teams coach. In most cases, he has to perform his job with limited resources (such as practice time, personnel, and input and support from other coaches). Special teams play is usually a hit-or-miss, feast-or-famine proposition. Unlike offensive or defensive play calling, no mulligans exist for special teams play. Mentally, and physically, the pressure can be unbearable. Dallas' Bruce DeHaven has said of special teams jobs, "On game day, it is the worst job in the league. When things go bad, there is no one else to blame. The special teams guy is hanging out there all by himself." Seattle's Pete Rodriguez has been quoted as saying, "Every play is like the single most important play in your life. All heck breaks loose."

A special teams down is not like an incompletion or a sack. A bad play on special teams can mean disaster. Everything and everybody is focused on that one play. The Patriots' Brad Seely has said, "You only have a few plays to shine out there. You want it to be perfect and sometimes it isn't. It's frustrating and nerve-racking." Joe Marciano of the Houston Texans has noted that coaching special teams can take a physical toll on coaches. Marciano is quoted as saying that just before a kickoff, he will have a resting pulse rate of 140 to 150.

Notwithstanding all the mental and physical pressure of coaching, special teams can be a great track to a head coaching position. Many current and former NFL head coaches were special teams coaches at some point—Dick Vermeil, Marv Levy, Bill Cowher, Bobby Ross, Dennis Green, Bruce Coslet, and Mike Ditka, to name a few.

Successful special teams coaches must be proficient in many areas. Especially important are the areas of motivation, organization, and technical knowledge.

# Motivation

Motivation may be the single most important component of successful special teams play. In many cases, the coach needs to overcome the perception that special teams are an afterthought or drudgery, or that they are a form of punishment, or even purgatory. Even some good programs attach a stigma to special teams players. Often, special teamers are down-the-line players. They may be second- or even third-teamers on offense or defense. Coaches should understand that great special teams play begins with great special teams players. These players are easily recognized in practice. They are the ones who leave their feet to make a play. They are the players going full-speed in a half-speed drill. These players like contact. They hustle and do not let up until the whistle blows. They do these things irrespective of speed, size, or ability level. A successful coach should first find these people and impart the feeling that they are indeed starters. They *start* on special teams.

Non-special teamers should also be educated on the importance of special teams play. In high school, the down-the-liners are usually not very talented. Smaller programs may have to play their offensive and defensive starters on special teams. Coaches may not be able to give their front line players much rest on kicking downs. Larger schools have an easier job because they may have more players from which to choose. Top-notch programs that do not have to play a lot of underclassmen offensively and defensively have a broader talent base from which to select.

Motivation on the collegiate level should be somewhat easy. Talented underclassmen should look at special teams as an opportunity to get playing time. Starters can be motivated to play hard and well on special teams because their effort could result in a better chance of being drafted. Players with exceptional snapping skills can earn a good living in the pros. Returning kicks in college can enhance the prospects of making an NFL team. The pros are looking for people who can come in and immediately make a contribution to the team. Special teams coaches also have to develop a sense of urgency in their players, which is paramount to good special teams play since it is a one-play series. One play can determine the outcome of the game.

Special teams members should be ready when they are called upon to perform. Again, no mulligans exist for special teams play. For the special teams coach, motivation includes instilling within his charges the principles of hard work, maximum effort, staying positive (especially kickers), and accountability.

# Organization

As with any other phase of a football game, special teams organization is a prerequisite to success. The special teams coach has to be part magician to get everything covered in a limited amount of time. Many different situations exist in the kicking game, and overlooking any potential situation could cost the team a game. A special teams coach should be able to put his players in the right place, just as offensive or defensive coordinators do.

Special team practice schedules should be as well-planned and well-executed as an offensive or defensive practice schedule. Game management involves a wide variety of organizational skills. A good coach should:
- Constantly monitor the game situation, time, and field position.
- Communicate with players who, in many instances, have offensive or defensive responsibilities.
- Know whom he can talk to at any given time.
- Remain in constant contact with trainers concerning injuries that could affect a myriad of special teams.
- Be a weather prognosticator. He should be aware of and have a plan for a variety of weather conditions.
- Be aware of, and react to, any changes in the opponent's special teams game plan, or personnel changes.

# Technical Knowledge

A special teams coach must have a strong and varied field of knowledge in order to effectively coach all the various special teams. He should plan for, and teach, a varied assortment of skills and movements, including the following:

- Catch a kickoff
- Cover the kickoff
- Return the kickoff
- Punt
- Snap for a punt
- Catch a punt
- Cover a punt

- Block for a punt
- Block a punt
- Kick an extra point
- Snap for an extra point
- Hold for an extra point
- Block for an extra point
- Block an extra point

- Kick a field goal
- Snap for a field goal
- Hold for a field goal
- Block for a field goal
- Cover a field goal attempt
- Block a field goal

Additionally, the coach should convey to his players the rules and nuances for each situation. Teams that are well prepared on special teams can go into any game with a high level of confidence. They know they will have a decided advantage over most teams since not all teams expend the necessary energy on special teams. Many teams are lax concerning special teams play, but teams willing to spend valuable practice time on special teams reap the benefits. Organizations strong on special teams feel they are at an advantage because of the team's highly-practiced and well-prepared special, or trick, plays.

Success or failure in special teams play starts at the top with the head coach. For a team to be successful in the kicking game, the head coach should realize how important special teams play is to the overall success of the team. The head coach should be committed not only to give sufficient practice time, but he should provide that time during prime practice slots. Time at the end of practice, in many cases, is counter-productive because it gives the impression that the practice is only an afterthought.

The head coach should also be open to the use of starters on special teams. However, for many coaches, this decision is difficult. Many coaches extol the importance of special teams, but their actions indicate otherwise, only paying lip service to special teams play. Not only should the head coach make a decision on practice time and the availability of players, he should also decide how to approach the kicking game philosophically. Some head coaches are satisfied with a conservative approach. These coaches see special teams play as simply an interval between gaining possession of the ball and kicking the ball to the opponent. They only want the kicking game to be sound and not get them beat. They do not see the unlimited possibilities in the kicking game, nor do they see special teams as a way to attack the other team. They would rather react than initiate. These teams simply seek to have a smooth transition of ball possession. On the other hand, some teams choose an aggressive approach to special teams play. These teams attack with their special teams, seeking and scheming to create big plays. They game plan and scheme to gain field position by blocking and pressuring kicks, as well as gaining ground with their return game. Teams who are imaginative with all three phases of the game—defense, offense, *and* special teams—are hard to beat.

# 2

# Kickoff Team

The kickoff, which starts the game or the second half, is the prime time to gain momentum. The results of these plays can affect the score and field position for the duration of that particular half. Good results from the opening kickoff can give a great psychological boost to the kicking team. If the receiving team has to go 80 plus yards for a score, their chances of scoring are dramatically reduced. Statistics have shown that a team starting from its own 20-yard line has a one-in-thirty chance of scoring on that drive. While opening kickoffs offer a great chance to set the tone and tempo of a half, kickoffs that occur after a score can help the team that just scored build on the momentum they have gained.

Kickoffs are also used in very crucial stages of a game. When a team has given up a safety, they must free kick from their own 20-yard line. Poor execution can cause their opponent to score another seven or eight points in a very short period of time. Adding the two points for the safety, a team can give up nine or 10 points in very short order. Additionally, the kickoff team can be called upon to execute an onside kick. Obviously, an onside kick can determine the outcome of the game.

The special teams coordinator has a varied assortment of kickoffs from which to choose. Not only can he vary the type of kick, he can also choose from a wide array of kickoff formations. The following is a list of potential kickoff types:

- Deep right - middle - left
- Squib right - middle - left
- Sky right - middle - left
- Surprise onside kick - right - middle - left
- Obvious onside kick - right - middle - left
- Overload onside kick - right - left

Deep kicks have an emphasis on distance and hang time. Deep right kicks should be placed just outside the right numbers, while deep left kicks should be targeted just outside the left numbers. Directional kicks serve to narrow the field available for a return, and coverage schemes can load up in that particular area.

Squib kicks are used to neutralize a good returner late in the second half, or any time the coach desires sure coverage. The objectives are to take the ball out of the hands of the skilled athletes, and place the ball in the hands of players who are usually blockers. It may also be used to disrupt the timing of returns. This type of kick will give up some field position to insure good coverage. A squib kick may also be used when time is a prime consideration. A squib kick may result in burning time off the clock by making it difficult for the receiving team to field the ball and get out of bounds to conserve time. Sky kicks, which sacrifice distance for hang time, have gained popularity in recent years. Common reasons for using the sky kick are to insure good coverage, attack a dead area, or place the ball in the hands of an inferior return man.

The kickoff team can set the tone for the game or the half with a big hit, field position, or a turnover. One of the prime objectives of the cover team is to not allow the return to get past the 20-yard line. Turnovers on a kickoff return are very damaging to the return team's psyche, especially considering that in most cases the return team has just given up points to the kicking team.

Strategically, several questions should be asked before a kickoff is executed: Do we use multiple launch points? Should we kick deep or short? How much elevation should be used on the kick? Varying launch points can serve to limit the field available to the return team, and can limit the amount of area the cover team has to defend. Multiple launch points can also limit the number and types of returns available to the opponent. Varying the length and height of a kickoff can also serve to disrupt kickoff return schemes.

## Qualities of Kickoff Cover Personnel

To be a member of the kickoff team, a player should possess some recklessness. The most violent collisions usually occur on kickoffs. To be successful in covering kickoffs, a player should be able to defeat a block, and make an open field tackle. To be a member of this elite team, a player should possess the following qualities:

- Toughness
- Ability to function in space
- Good tackling
- Speed
- Determination

Cover men should be able to sprint downfield and tackle a returner who is usually an exceptional athlete. The returner has the advantage of space, since he is working in an area 160 feet wide. Solid tackling is essential; arm tackling will be ineffective on a back who has a running start. Speed is also essential; only the fastest men should be used if they fit the other criteria. Usually defensive backs are good candidates. The coach might choose to place bigger players in the center of the line versus wedge return teams.

# Seven Phases of Kickoff Coverage

The kickoff is broken down into seven distinct phases. The following seven phases or parts are essential to good kickoff coverage:
- Pre-kick
- Take-off
- Lane placement
- Safeties
- Zones
- Block protection
- Tackle

### Pre-Kick

The special teams coach has the advantage of huddling the cover team on the field or on the sideline. Either procedure has its advantages. When the cover team huddles on the sideline, the coach should count the number of players, and make the call as to the type of kick and the coverage to be used. When the team huddles on the field, someone should be designated to make the kick call, and count the number of players; the designee is usually the kicker. When the referee signals ready for play, the kicker should check both sides to see if everyone is ready. R1 and L1 should be given the assignment of reminding everyone to be onsides. It is beneficial that the cover men look inside to the kicker and ball so they can better time up with the kicker's approach to the ball. Some teams choose to cover from a two-point stance, while some prefer a three-point takeoff. Varying the amount of time the receiving team gets their hands on the ball is highly beneficial because it disrupts the return team's timing; varying the launch point and height of the kick distorts that timing.

## Take-Off

When the kicker starts forward, the cover men should also start their approach. They should be full speed at the time of the kick, and half a yard behind the kicker when the kicker contacts the ball. It is imperative that no one be offside. The takeoff is an all out mad dash. The coverage should gain as much ground in as little time as possible, which starts with a great takeoff.

## Lane Placement

As the coverage team sprints and adjusts to the ball, they should maintain a constant spacing. A player out of his lane creates a seam the returner can exploit. Defenders should never follow the same color. As they sprint downfield, they should be aware of the depth and direction of the kick. Cover men should take a peek early to locate the flight of the ball. Also, the coverage should locate the return man and note his reaction to the ball. Initially, the coverage team should defend the field by staying in their prescribed lanes. Once the type and direction of the return has been analyzed, they should adjust to, and defend, the returner.

After a cover man is in his lane for approximately 35 yards, he should start to converge on the ball. If a man is knocked down, the teammate to his outside should move in and fill that lane. The man who was knocked down should get off the ground as quickly as possible and replace to the outside to fill in for the man who replaced him.

Proper containment is a very important element of lane placement, and involves maintaining outside leverage on the returner. Contain responsibilities involve keeping the ball on the inside shoulder; contain men should never allow the ball to gain a head-up position. Containment involves taking on blocks with the inside arm, keeping the outside arm and leg free. Contain men should close to the blocker aggressively, and then soft play him by using hands and shielding his feet. Should the ball go away from the contain man, he should be aware of possible trick plays, such as reverses, throwbacks, and fake reverses. Whenever the ball goes away, the contain man should get as deep as the ball and trail.

## Safeties

Assigning safety responsibilities to one or more people is one of the components to successful return defense. Good safeties should close to within 10 yards of the coverage. They should not allow the ball carrier to have an abundance of open field in which to make his moves if he breaks through the coverage. A safety should be able to get off blocks quickly, use head and foot fakes, and be athletic enough to use the open field to his advantage. A safety should force any breakthroughs to the sideline or to the other safety.

## Zones

The coverage team should be aware of three distinct zones, which will be transversed as they cover the kick.

### Speed Zone

This 15- to 20-yard segment is the sprint stage. In this area, the coverage team should close the distance to the returner as rapidly as possible. In this zone, the cover team should read the type and direction of the return the opponent is using. Cover men should outrun any block in this zone. Blocks should be beaten with speed and hands. Avoid blocks to the ball side and do not slow down; speed will defeat angle or cross type blocks.

### Avoid Zone

In this area, the cover men will have to avoid the primary blocks in the return scheme. Kick team members should work to the butt of potential blockers if they see an angle block. After avoiding the block, cover men should get back into their proper lane. Defenders should go through the shoulder of the second line of blockers to the ball side.

### Contact Zone

This area is defined as a 10-yard zone from the ball carrier. No avoidance techniques should occur in this zone. Cover men should attack and run through any block. The coverage should not take a side on a blocker until the returner declares himself, as well as pressuring the blocker by controlling him with hands. When the ball carrier commits, the defender should disengage and make the hit. The coverage team should come to balance five yards from the ball. The first man to a wedge should take out as many men as he can, taking on the wedge with the same leverage he would have on the ball carrier (outside in). Defenders may come out of their assigned lanes 15 yards from the ball. Coverage men should always replace the man to the inside if he beats him downfield; inside players should always replace the teammate to the outside if the outside man crosses his face. The coverage team should never assume that the ball would not be brought out of the end zone; thus, the kickoff team should be coached to cover all the way into the end zone.

## Block Protection

Pre-kick organization, good takeoff, and correct lane placement will all be for naught if the defender cannot defeat a block and make the tackle. Defenders should be able to ward off blocks if the cover team is to be successful. Following are ways to defeat the various types of blocks.

*Head-Up Block*

Defenders should avoid to the ball side. They should use head and foot fakes, and at the point of contact, they should use a club and rip to disengage.

*Kick-In/Kick-Out Block*

Avoiding them in the direction from which they are coming best defeats the kick-in and kick-out blocks. These blocks should be beaten with speed, so when defenders see this type of block, they should close fast and zero in on the blocker. When the blocker settles to execute the block, the cover man should burst by him to his butt side. Defenders can foot fake opposite the direction he wants to go, plant, and drive in the desired direction.

*Double-Team Block*

Coverage men should take on the blockers and try to neutralize them. The defender should not trade one for one.

## Tackle

The end result of the kickoff is to tackle the returner as close to his own goal line as possible. The cover team should have the goal of gang tackling and stripping the ball each time they kick off. Cover men should possess good open field tackling skills, with the ultimate objective of the cover team being getting the ball carrier on the ground.

# Types of Kicks

The following section describes a variety of free kicks. Included are deep middle, deep right, deep left, kicks with lane exchanges, and a free kick following a fair catch. Obvious and surprise onside kicks are also illustrated. For better communication, the field is divided into seven areas or zones (Diagram 2-1). These zones are as follows:
- Right and left sideline: Area from the out of bounds line to the numbers
- Right and left numbers: Area through the middle of the numbers
- Right and left alley: Area from the top of the numbers to the hash
- Chute: Area from hash to hash

NFL dimensions have been used for the diagrams and landmarks. NFL hashmarks are 70 feet, 9 inches from each sideline. College hashmarks are 60 feet, while the dimensions for high school hashes are 53 feet, 4 inches. Adjustments in applying these kickoffs may be necessary, depending upon the level of play. As a basic rule, five cover men are placed on either side of the kicker. These men are tagged with a number in ascending order from one to five counting toward the ball.

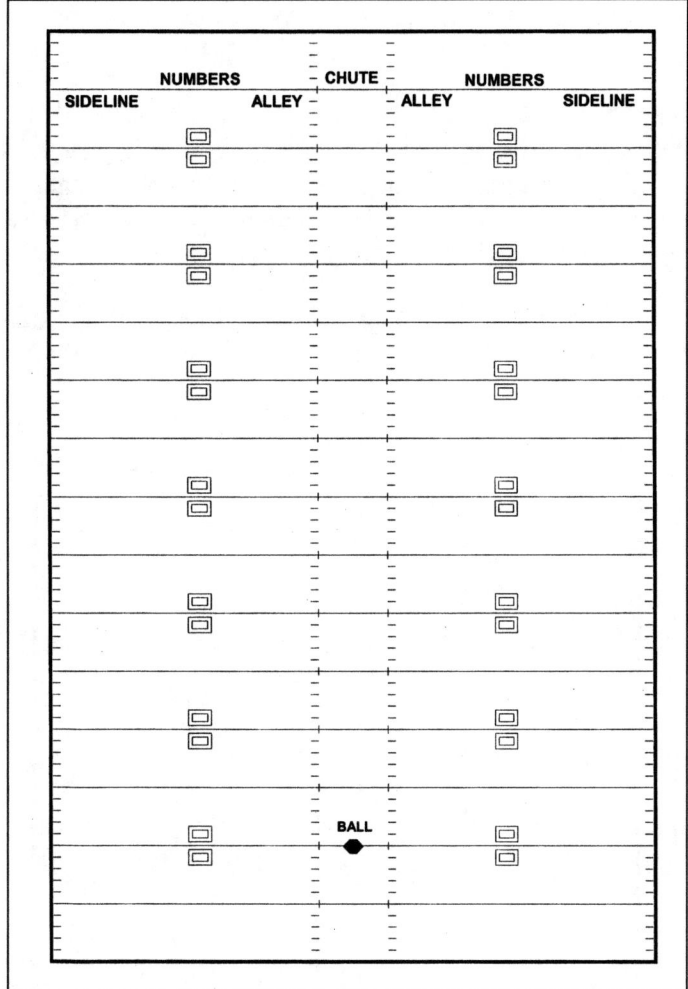

Diagram 2-1. Seven areas or zones.

To keep the return team off balance, change up the safety responsibilities with a cover 1, 2, or 3 call, which will identify who has safety responsibility. If #1 has safety responsibilities, #2 will have contain; if #2 has safety responsibilities, #1 will have contain. A #3 call places #1 on contain.

## Deep Middle Cover 1 (Diagram 2-2)

The ball will be kicked deep to the chute area.

*L1/R1:* Align four yards from the sideline. They have contain. #1 will keep his original spacing with #2 until he gets near the +35 yard line. At this point, he pulls out. He should look past the ball to the opposite side for anyone coming toward his side, which would be a tip-off on a possible reverse. He should feel any players hanging around the alley, numbers, or sideline areas, and should keep the ball on his inside shoulder.

*L2/R2*: Align three yards outside the numbers. His assigned lane is the sideline area. A Cover 1 call gives #2 contain responsibility. He should play as deep as the ball with seven yards width, keeping the ball on his inside shoulder. Versus a wedge return, he has the option of going around the wedge if there is separation between the wedge and the ball. He is also allowed to fold inside on the wedge with outside in leverage.

*L3/R3*: Alignment is the top of the numbers. Their primary job is to maintain leverage on the ball by keeping the ball on their inside shoulder. Their assigned lane is the numbers area.

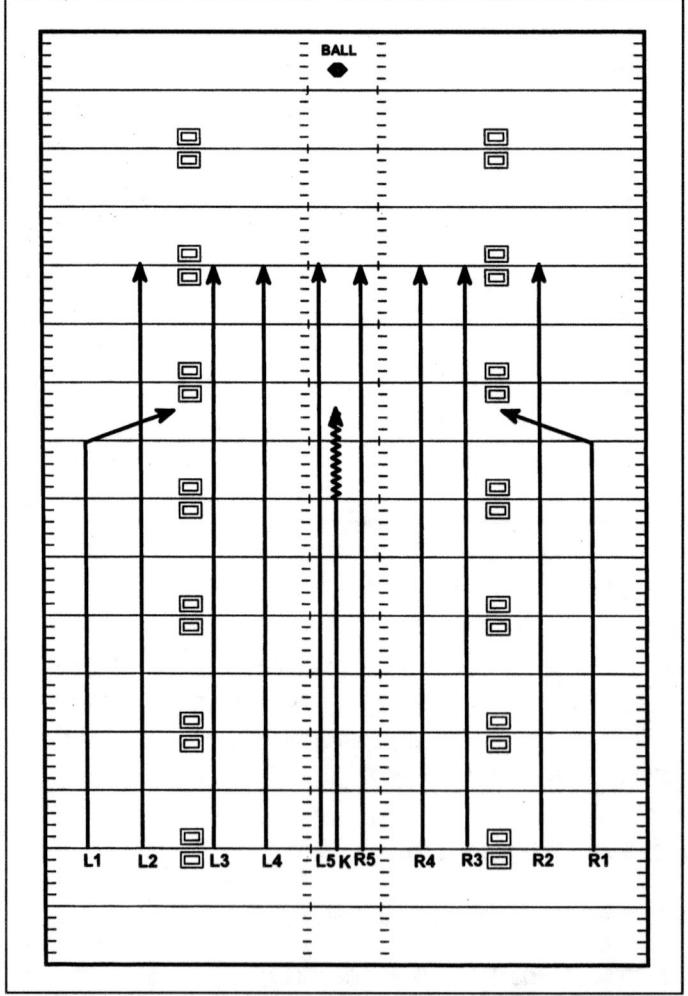

Diagram 2-2. Deep middle cover 1

*L4/R4*: Align four yards outside the hash. Basically, they split the distance between the hash and the numbers. Their assigned lane is the alley, keeping the ball on their inside shoulder. They should sprint to the ball and come to balance, and should squeeze the ball vertically and horizontally.

*L5/R5*: Align inside the hash. These men should be larger and more physical than the other cover men because they are designated as wedge busters. Their assigned lane is the chute area. They keep the ball on their inside shoulder and squeeze from the outside. They should attack blockers from outside in.

*Kicker*: The launch point can vary by game plan. The kicker can be a safety. After the kick, he gives a directional call and squeezes to the +40 keeping leverage on the ball. He should leverage the ball to one of the other safeties; should the ball break through, he should leverage the ball to the sideline.

## Deep Right (Diagram 2-3)

This kick is a directional kick. By game plan, the ball will be kicked to the numbers. Alignment is the same as for the deep middle kick. Assignments are given for a deep right kick. Deep left kick assignments would simply be reversed.

*L1*: Squeezes one lane to the kick side. At the +30 or +35 yard line he will roll over and become a safety. He is the left safety.

*R1*: He has an automatic force assignment, maintaining the sideline lane all the way to the ball.

*L2*: Squeezes one lane to the kickside. He has force responsibility. He contains the ball, and should keep 21 men inside him. He keeps the ball on his inside shoulder, and assumes the numbers lane initially before he squeezes.

*R2*: Maintains the sideline lane all the way to the ball. Should the ball go away, he trails.

*L3*: Squeezes one lane to the kickside. He fills the alley.

*R3*: Covers all the way through the numbers.

*L4*: Squeezes over one lane. He fills hash to the chute.

*R4*: Normal lane responsibility. He fills the alley.

*L5*: Goes directly to the ball. #5 has no field lane assignment, and keeps the ball on his right shoulder.

*R5*: Covers down the hash all the way to the ball.

*Kicker*: His first and most important job is to place the kick to the target area. An off-target kick could compromise coverage. The kicker is a safety. He goes to the numbers at the +35. He is the right safety.

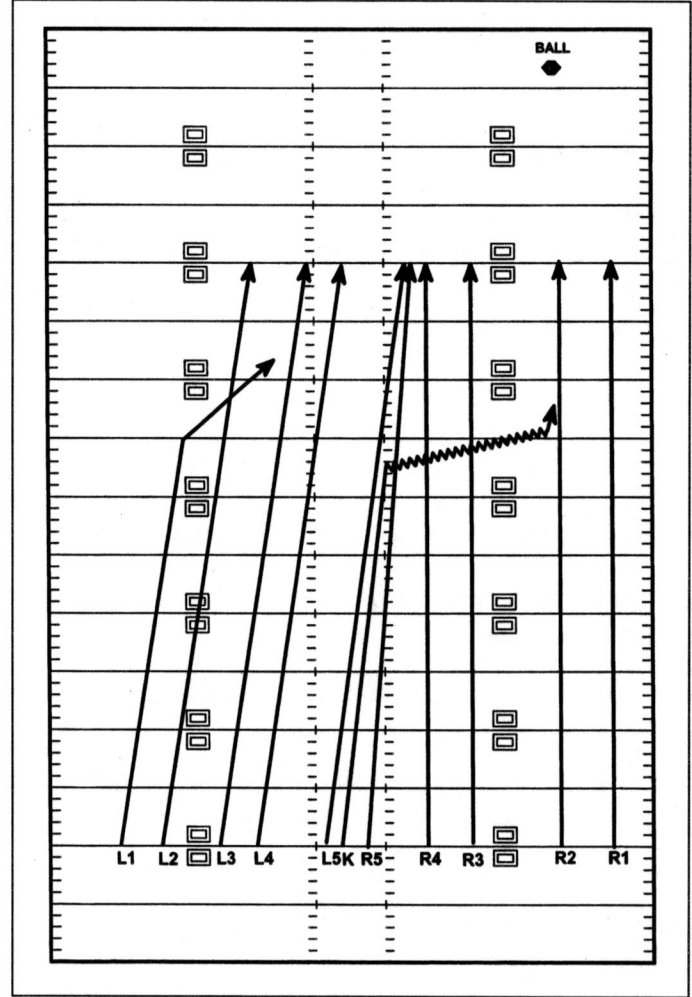

Diagram 2-3. Deep right

As was stated previously, it is imperative that the kickoff team use change-ups to give return teams recognition and execution problems. Following are some change-ups in coverage.

## Deep Middle 55 Twist Cover 1 (Diagram 2-4)

*L1/R1*: Have the same responsibilities as the deep middle kick. They have safety responsibility.

*L2/R2*: Same responsibilities as deep middle.

*L3/R3*: Same responsibilities as deep middle.

*L4/R4*: Same responsibilities as deep middle.

*L5/R5*: They will cover in their basic field lane initially, and as they cover, they will read the center. Should the center block R5 or L5, the cover man will twist across the center's face and assume the opposite #5's cover lane; if the center blocks away from #5, he should twist off his butt into the opposite #5's cover lane. They still defend the chute. In essence, all they have done is exchange lanes when the center tips his hand as to whom he will block.

*Kicker*: Same responsibilities as deep middle.

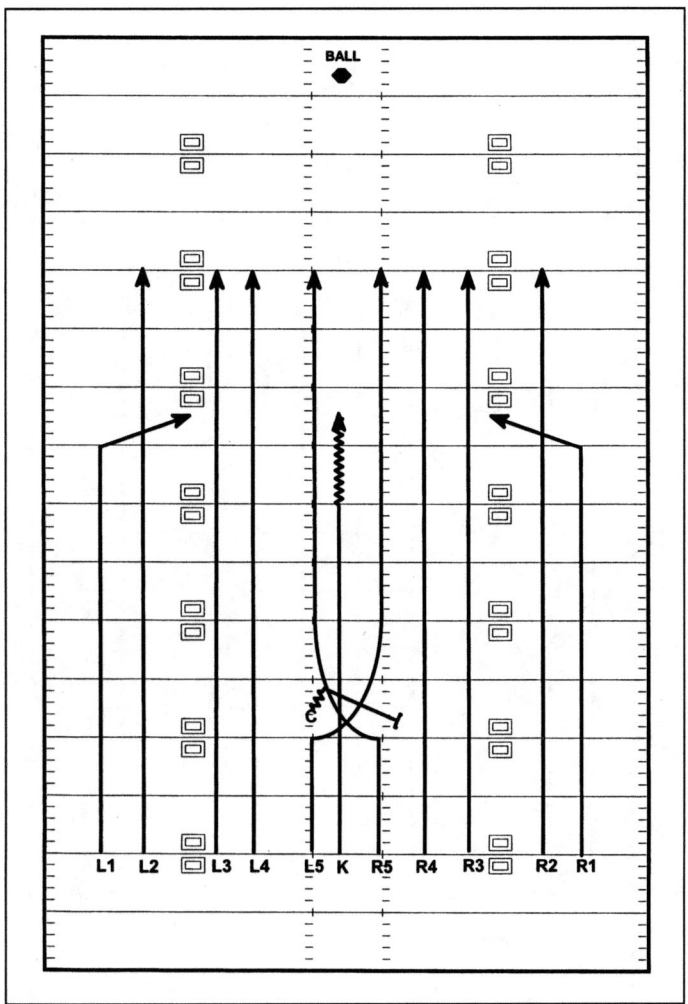

Diagram 2-4. Deep middle 55 twist cover 1

## Deep Middle 34 Twist Cover 1 (Diagram 2-5)

This exchange is a twist or lane exchange between #3 and #4, and occurs on both sides. Unlike the 55 Twist, this exchange is not predicated by the blocking scheme.

*L1/R1*: Same responsibilities as deep middle.

*L2/R2*: Same responsibilities as deep middle.

*L3/R3*: They maintain the numbers lane until the +30- or +35-yard line. At this point, they dip inside and assume the alley. #3 initiates the twist.

*L4/R4*: They maintain the alley until #3 crosses their face. When #3 commits, #4 will slide outside to protect the numbers. If #3 never crosses on the exchange, #4 should stay basic and defend the alley.

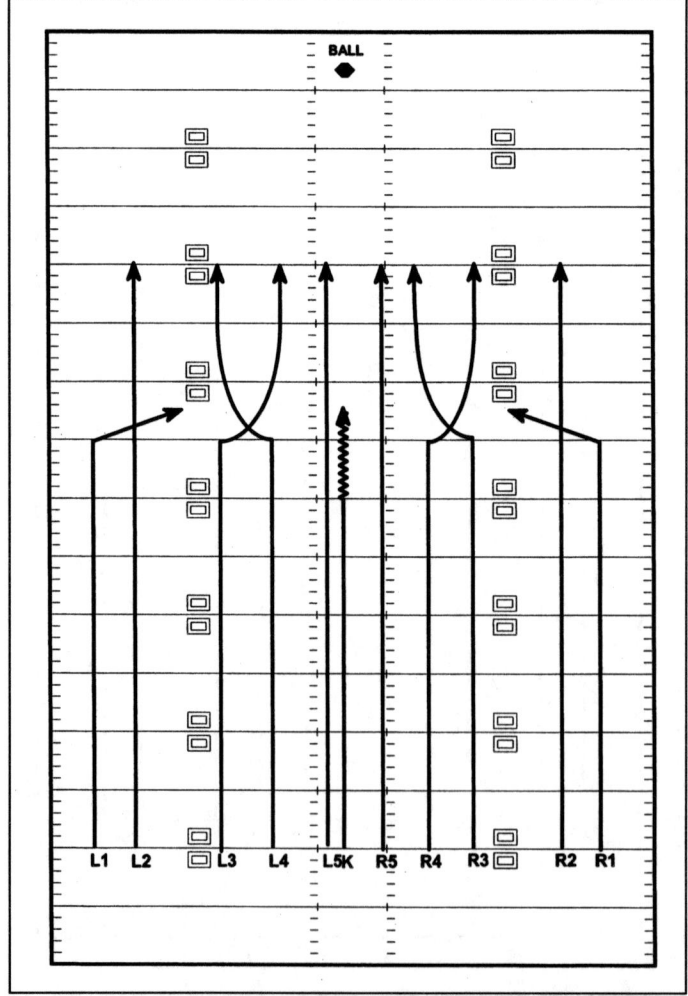

Diagram 2-5. Deep middle 34 twist cover 1

*L5/R5*: Same responsibilities as deep middle.

*Kicker*: Same responsibilities as deep middle.

Any of the illustrated kickoffs can be executed with a squib style kick instead of an airborne kick. The coverage would be the same in either case.

## Onside Kicks

Various situations exist when an onside kick should be considered. Some teams use an onside kick as a surprise tactic. In rare instances, a team will start the game with an onside kick. Some coaches use surprise onside kicks in order to establish momentum, or to change momentum. Onside kicks are sometimes used when a team is mismatched against a vastly superior team; a successful onside kick can catch the better team unaware and could supply the spark needed for an upset. On the other end of the spectrum, a strong team can demoralize a weaker opponent with a surprise onside kick. A successful onside kick could lead to a quick touchdown that would undermine the opponent's psyche.

Through scouting techniques, a coach can determine the mental alertness of the return team's front line. Many front lines are susceptible to an onside kick. They may leave their spot too quickly to get to their assigned area on a kickoff return. Following are three onside kicks. Two of these three kicks are overload schemes, used in obvious situations. The other onside kick is an unexpected onside kick. The kicker should experiment as to the best type of kick for him. He can choose to bloop, bounce, or knuckleball the kick. The mechanics of the kick should be beneficial to the total scheme.

## Surprise Onside Kick (Diagram 2-6)

This kick is disguised, and is used as a surprise tactic. From all appearances, it is simply a basic kick off. The kick attacks the areas between the center and the guards. During the pre-kick phase, the kicker finds the area with the most space and places the ball in that space. Most return teams will offset the center so he does not get hit with a low line drive, or squib type kick. The space opposite the offset usually offers the space needed to place the kick, which must travel at least 10 yards.

*L1 /R1*: On the kick, they sprint laterally to the middle of the field. L1 is the left safety, while R1 is the right safety.

*L2/R2*: They sprint and cut off the tackle to their side. They assume contain when they are in position.

*L3/R3*: They identify the hole and then sprint to recover the ball.

*L4/R4*: #4 to the hole must angle block the center. He takes the center on, with his inside shoulder on the center's near shoulder. The other #4 sprints to the hole and recovers the ball.

*L5/R5*: Align with good inside out angles on the guards. They attack and block the guards, placing their outside shoulder(s) on the guard's inside shoulder and shielding them from the ball.

*Kicker*: The kicker's first and most important job is to identify the hole. He then directs his kick to that hole. The kicker should follow the kick and expect a rebound or ricochet. The ball must travel at least 10 yards.

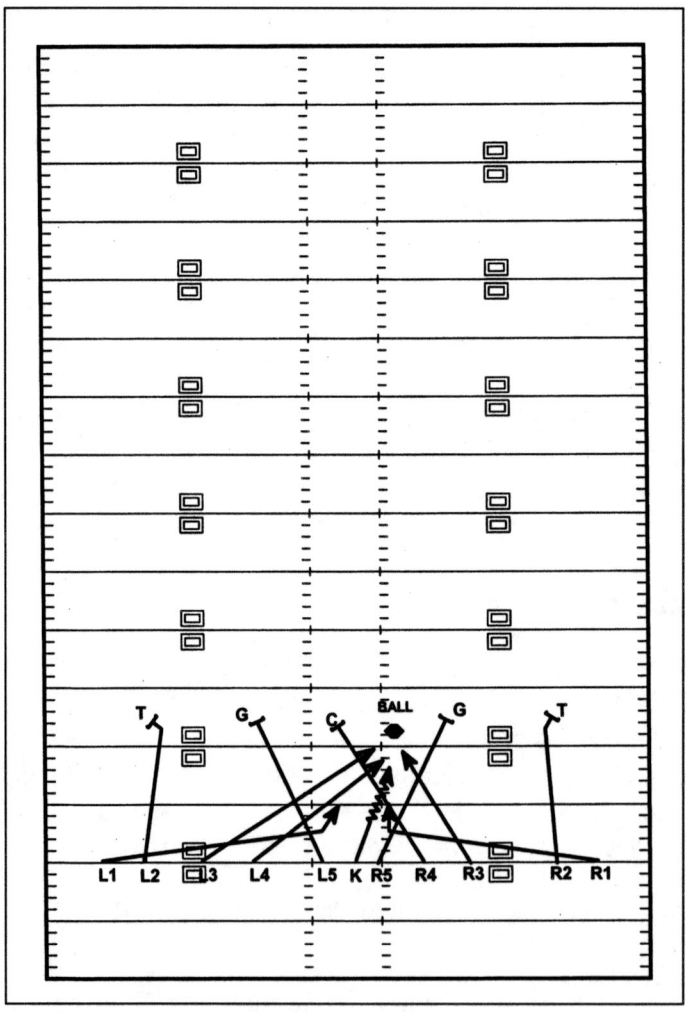

Diagram 2-6. Surprise onside kick

## Obvious Onside Kick (Overload) (Diagram 2-7)

The obvious onside kick, with an overload, can also be used as a surprise onside kick with a late shift to the overload. The overload limits the return team's reactions and alignments with late movement. This onside kick has a built-in read by the kicker. If the return team's adjustment against the late movement leaves them shorthanded to the backside, the kicker has the option to place the kick in that area.

*L1*: Aligns two yards from the sideline. He looks for the ball on a high bounce, or squirting from the pack. He should keep the ball in bounds.

*R1*: He is the deep safety when the ball is kicked to the left. He should expect the ball carrier to pop through if the receiving team fields the ball. He should be alert to the ball being kicked to his side if the numbers favor the kicking team.

*L2*: His assignment is to run through #1 (counting outside-in). L2 will block him chest high.

*R2*: He has contain when the ball is kicked to the left. He should be alert to the ball being kicked to his side if the numbers favor the kicking team.

*L3*: Recovers the ball after it has gone 10 yards or hits a return man.

*R3*: He is the short safety if the ball is kicked to the left. He should be alert to the ball being kicked to his side if the numbers favor the kicking team.

*L4*: His assignment is to run through #2 (counting outside-in). L4 will block him chest high.

*R4*: Goes in motion and fills between L4 and L5. He tries to recover the ball after it has gone 10 yards or hits a return man.

*L5*: His assignment is to run through #3 (counting outside-in). L5 will block him chest high.

*R5*: He goes in motion and fills between L5 and the kicker. He tries to recover the ball after it has gone 10 yards or hits a return man.

*Kicker*: He should decide where to kick the ball. He should go to the called side, unless the return team is outnumbered three-to-one, or three-to-two to the backside. After executing a proper kick, he follows the ball and anticipates the ball ricocheting back to him. An onside kick to the right would reverse everyone's assignment. Note: College rules require at least four members of the kicking team to be aligned on either side of the ball when it is kicked.

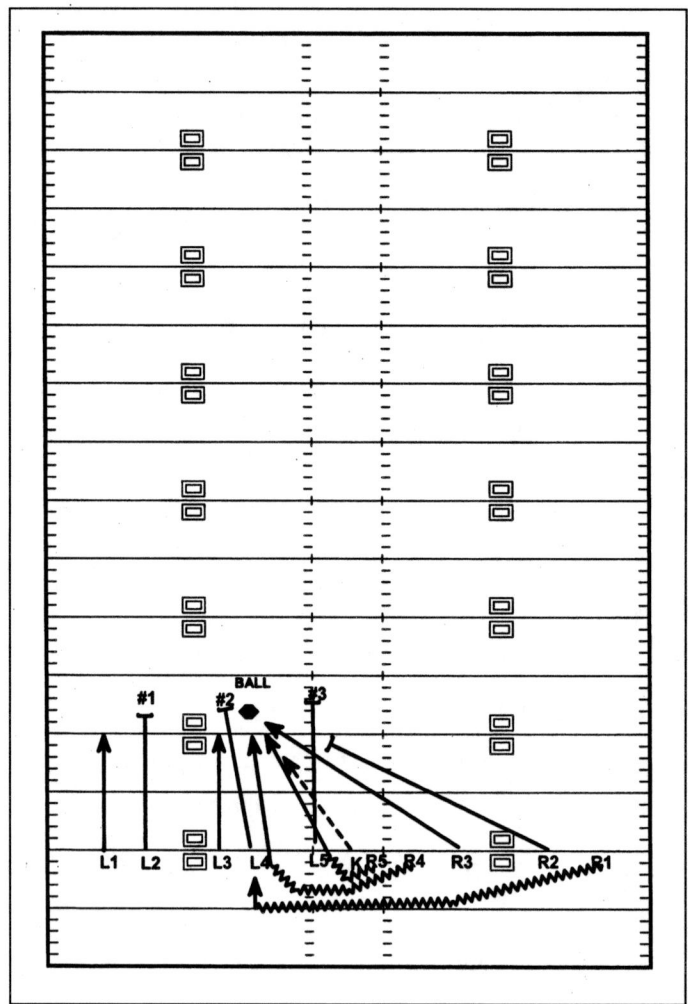

Diagram 2-7. Obvious onside kick (overload)

## Onside Kick (Overload) (Diagram 2-8)

This type of onside kick can be executed in one of two ways. In an obvious onside situation, the kick team can align in the final formation. If subterfuge is desired, the kicking team can align in a basic five on either side alignment, and jailbreak to the final formation.

*L1*: Aligns in a three-point stance crowding the line. He attempts to recover the ball after it has gone 10 yards or hits a return man.

*R1*: Becomes the deep safety on the kick. He should expect the ball carrier to pop through if the receiving team fields the ball.

*L2*: Aligns in a three-point stance crowding the line. He attempts to recover the ball after it has gone 10 yards or hits a return man.

*R2*: Has contain responsibility.

*L3*: Aligns in a three-point stance crowding the line. He attempts to recover the ball after it has gone 10 yards or hits a return man.

*R3*: Aligns or shifts to a position five yards from the line. R4, L4, R5, and L5 get their alignment off R3. His movement sets off the coverage of R4, L4, R5, and L5. His assignment is to run through the return team's #4 (counting outside-in). He should block #4 chest high. If the ball is kicked to #4, he should fight for the ball.

*L4*: Aligns or shifts to a position between L1 and L2. He gets his alignment off R3. L4 runs through #2 (counting outside-in). He should block #2 chest high, and should fight for the ball if it is kicked to #2.

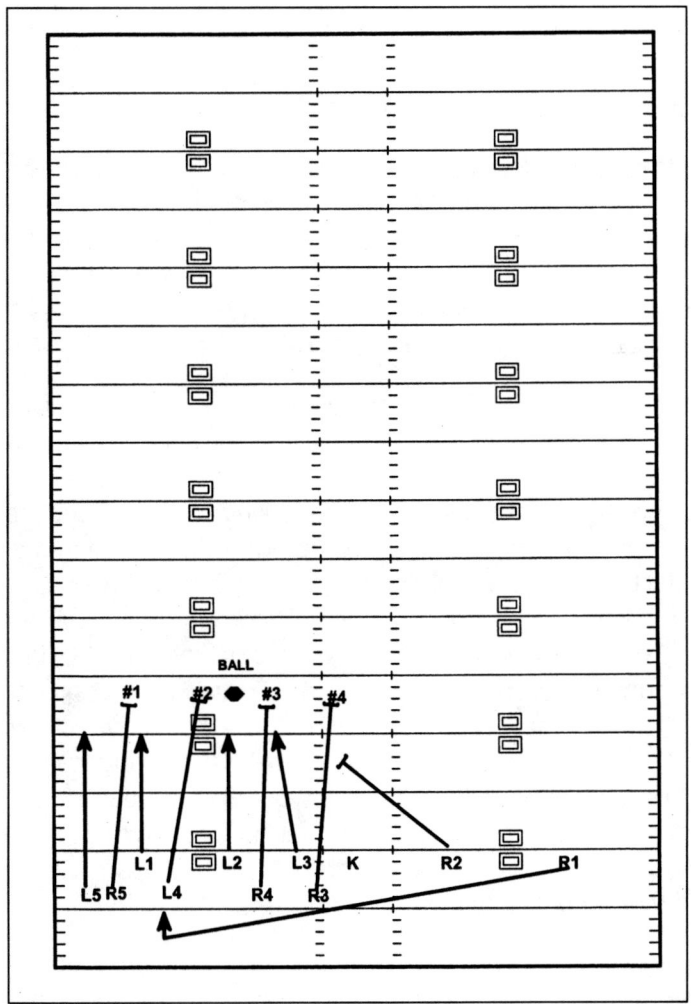

Diagram 2-8. Onside kick overload

*R4*: Aligns or shifts to a position between L2 and L3. He aligns five yards off the line, and gets his alignment from R3. R4 runs through #3 (counting outside-in). He should block #3 chest high, and should fight for the ball if it is kicked to #3.

*L5*: Aligns or shifts to a position two yards from the sideline. He aligns five yards off the line, and gets his alignment from R3. He should look for the ball on a high bounce or squirting from the pack, and should keep the ball in bounds.

*R5*: Aligns or shifts to a position just outside L1. He aligns five yards off the line, and gets his alignment from R3. R5 runs through #1 (counting outside-in). He should block #1 chest high, and should fight for the ball if it is kicked to #1.

*Kicker*: If a late movement is used, the kicker gives the move call. After the kick, he follows the ball and anticipates the ball ricocheting to him. An onside kick to the right would reverse everyone's assignment. Note: College rules require at least four members of the kicking team to be aligned on either side of the ball when it is kicked.

## Safety Kickoff

When faced with a safety kick situation, the team which has given up the safety is on the brink of giving up anywhere from 5 to 10 points in short order. If a field goal is scored after the safety, the kicking team will have given up five points. If a touchdown is scored after the safety and then a two-point play is converted, the kicking team will have given up a total of 10 points in a very short time span. Needless to say, this short period of time can drastically affect the outcome of the game.

Another crucial time to use a safety kickoff might occur toward the end of the game, when the team ahead finds it is advantageous to give up a safety. Regardless of the reason for a safety kickoff, a team can decide how it wants to kick the ball. A safety kick will occur from the -20 yard line and the kicking team can choose either to punt the ball or to kick the ball. The overriding objectives in this situation are to kick the ball deep, and to effectively cover the kick to turn around the bad field position. Most teams choose to punt the ball as opposed to using a traditional kickoff. A punter who has a 40-yard average on his punts will be kicking the ball closer to the line of scrimmage, as opposed to punting from a depth of 12 to 13 yards on a conventional punt. This change in the launch point means a punter with a 40-yard average will actually punt the ball 50 yards. If the punter has good hang time, the punting team can obtain good field position. Regardless of the preferred type of kick, the kicking team should understand that the same rules apply to the safety kick as they do with a normal kickoff. The same coverages illustrated earlier in this chapter can be used in a safety kick scenario with either a punt or traditional kickoff.

Various ways exist for a team to give up a safety. A team may *choose* to give up a safety. However, most safeties are unintentional. The following is a list of actions that would cause a loss of two points:

- A blocked punt that goes out of a team's end zone.
- The punter steps on the end line unintentionally.
- A ball carrier carries the ball into his own end zone and is downed.
- The offensive team commits a foul and the spot of enforcement is in the end zone.
- A player on the receiving team muffs a kick and then creates the impetus that forces the ball into the end zone where he is tackled, or falls on the ball.

**Fair Catch Kick**

When a high school or pro team fair catches a punt, or is awarded a fair catch, they can choose to put the ball in play with a scrimmage snap, or they may elect to execute a free kick. The team possessing the ball can decide to dropkick, or placekick. If the fair catch is close enough, the kicking team can elect to dropkick or placekick the ball through the uprights for three points (NFHS-NFL). The player who made the fair catch must ask the official for a free kick. The ball can be placed anywhere between the hashes through the spot of the catch (NFHS). A fair catch kick would probably occur near the end of the first half with time running out, or at the end of the game with a team behind by three points or less and time running out.

When attempting a free kick, a team will align in a basic kickoff formation. However, there are a couple of subtle differences in a free kick attempt. The ball kicked downfield is treated as a field-goal attempt (NFHS), not a free ball as it is on a kickoff. The kicking team cannot gain possession of the ball unless the receiving team touches it first. The other difference is caused by the proximity of the ball to the end zone. The kick should, at the very least, reach the end zone. The chances of a coordinated return are close to nil, so coverage is not a prime consideration. Nevertheless, the kick must be covered just as any field-goal attempt. On a fair catch attempt, the cover team should align five yards deeper and should not move to cover until the ball is kicked. Any chance of an offside penalty must be eliminated.

# Kickoff Checklist

The following are situations that should be discussed, coached, and understood for the kickoff team to be truly prepared to do the best job possible. Each of these situations can arise during the game:

- Base kickoffs
- Directional kickoffs
- Squib kickoffs
- Pooch kickoffs
- Various onside kickoffs
- Fair catch kick
- Safety kick
- Lane change-ups
- Various safety designation calls
- Kickoffs that carry into the end zone (ball impetus)
- Kickoffs that are carried into the end zone (player provides impetus)

- Muffs
- Fumbles
- Kicks with a holder
- Kicks versus good/poor returners
- Kicks after a penalty (+15, -15, +5, -5)
- Kickoff that goes out of bounds
- Kickoff when the ball does not go 10 yards
- Kickoff that is touched by the receiving team before it goes 10 yards
- Kickoffs during various weather conditions
- Safety techniques
- Lane integrity
- Pursuit angles
- Tackling

# Kickoff Rules and Regulations

- A place kick, while the ball is in a fixed position on the ground or on a kicking tee, may be used for a scrimmage kick, a kickoff, a free kick following a safety, or for a free kick following a fair catch, or awarded fair catch (NFHS-NFL).
- The kickoff shall be from the kicking team's 30-yard line (NFL), 35-yard line (college), or 40-yard line (high school). A kickoff is used to start each half, and after a team scores a touchdown or field goal. A kickoff is considered a free kick.
- A kickoff may be initiated from any point between the inbounds lines and on the kicking team's free kick line. Once the kicking team designates the spot, they must kick from that spot. No material or device may be placed on the ground to improve the kicker's footing.
- After the ball is ready for play – and until it is kicked – no player other than the kicker or the holder (if used) may be beyond the free kick line. If the ball falls off the tee for any reason, the official will immediately blow the ball dead. The ball may not be kicked until it is reset and again marked ready for play.
- All members of the kicking team must be inbounds and must have at least four players on each side of the kicker when it is kicked (college). In college, all players have to be inside the numbers until the ready for play signal is given; no such provision exists in high school and the NFL.
- A tee may be used on a kickoff. The NFL allows a one-inch tee, and two-inch tees are permissible in high school and on the collegiate level.
- A kickoff may not score a field goal.
- A member of the cover team may not go out of bounds and participate during the kick, unless he was pushed or blocked out of bounds and attempts to return in bounds immediately.
- A kickoff is off limits to the kicking team, unless it travels 10 yards, or is touched by the receiving team. Once the ball has gone 10 yards, or is touched by the receiving team, it is a free ball. The receiving team may recover the ball and advance it. The kicking team may recover but not advance the ball, unless the receiving team had possession (no muff), and then lost the ball. If the kicking *and* receiving teams jointly recover the ball, it will be awarded to the receiving team.

- When a kickoff goes out of bounds between the goal lines without being touched by the receiving team, the ball belongs to the receiving team 30 yards from the spot of the kick, or the receiving team can choose to take the ball at the out-of-bounds spot (NFL). Collegiate rules state that the receiving team can decide to put the ball into play 30 yards from the spot of the kick, or take a five yard penalty and have the ball re-kicked or put in play at the out of bounds spot. High school rules allow the receiving team to accept a five-yard penalty from the previous spot and have the ball re-kicked, put the ball in play 25 yards beyond the previous spot, or decline the penalty and put the ball in play at the out-of-bounds spot. If the ball goes out of bounds after touching the receiving team, it is the receiver's ball at the out of bounds spot.
- A ball kicked through the end zone, or that goes out of bounds behind the goal line, belongs to the receiving team. In the NFL, a returner may choose to return a kick out of the end zone. He may also choose to down the ball in the end zone for a touchback. The ball will be put in play on the receiving team's 20-yard line. If the impetus of the kick carries the ball into the end zone, the returner does not have to carry the ball out of the end zone. However, if the receiving team provides the impetus of the ball into the end zone, they must bring it out or the result will be a safety. The ball becomes dead and belongs to the receiving team when a kickoff touches the ground in the end zone and is untouched by the receiving team. Collegiate rules read the same. High school rules declare the ball dead when it crosses the goal line.
- Any member of the kicking team may use his hands or arms to ward off blockers or to push him out of the way in an attempt to recover the ball. The cover team cannot block an opponent below the waist.
- A member of the kicking team can catch a pooch kick in the air. If the receiving team signals for a fair catch, the cover team may not interfere with that catch. NFHS rules do not allow the kicking team to catch a free kick in flight.

## Timing During a Kickoff

NFL rules state that the game clock will start with the kickoff, except during the last two minutes of each half when a player of either team in the field of play touches the ball. High school and college rules state that on any kickoff, the clock does not start until the ball is touched or brought onto the field of play (NCAA). It also does not start on first touching by the kicking team.

# Onside Kick Rules and Regulations

- The ball must travel at least 10 yards, or be touched by a member of the receiving team, before the kicking team can touch it.

- Other than the kicker and/or holder, the kicking team may not cross the kick line before the ball is kicked.
- A member of the receiving team may cross the receiving line to field an onside kick after the ball has been kicked, and the kicking team cannot contact him until the ball goes 10 yards, or he touches the ball.
- A pooch onside kick may be fair caught. The kicking team must give the returner the opportunity to make the catch.
- If the receiving team recovers a legal onside attempt, they may advance the ball; however, the kicking team may not.
- If the kick is ruled a simultaneously recovery by two opposing players, the ball will be awarded to the receiving team.
- If an onside kick goes out of bounds in the NFL, it will result in a five-yard penalty and a re-kick. If the second kick goes out of bounds, the ball is awarded to the receiving team at the spot. This rule is in effect only in the last two minutes of the game. College or high school rules allow the receiving team to take the ball at the spot.
- College rules declare that the kicking team must have at least four men on each side of the kicker. NFL or high school rules have no such provision.
- If any member of the kicking team touches the ball before it crosses the 10-yard mark, or is touched by the receiving team, it is referred to as "first touching." The return team may take the ball at the spot of the first touch, or they may choose to have the ball put in play as determined by the action that follows first touching.
- A member of the return team blocked into the ball is deemed not to have touched the kick. If the ball is batted into a return team member, he is deemed not to have touched the ball. If the kick comes to rest inbounds and no player attempts to secure it, the ball becomes dead and is awarded to the return team at the spot.

## Onside Kick Axioms

- The ball must go 10 yards or be touched by the receiving team.
- Do not be offside.
- Know the call and direction of the kick.
- Know who has safety responsibility.
- Each player should know his role. Members will be divided into blockers and recoverers. Blockers attempt to recover only if the ball is kicked to their assigned man.
- Do not try to pick up the ball. The kicking team may not advance the ball. Possession is all-important.
- Fight for the ball if in a pile. Leverage the ball out. When possession is in doubt, the official will give it to the man who ends up with the ball. As on any loose ball, unless directly involved with the recovery, help the officials by pointing toward the opponent's goal.

# 3

# Kickoff Return Team

A kickoff return is a big aspect of special teams play, and happens for one of four reasons: the start of the game (or the second half of the game), the return team has just given up a field goal or a touchdown, and the return of a safety kickoff. Receiving the kickoff to start the game or half is a great way to set the tempo for the first or second half, to continue momentum, or to regain momentum after giving up a score. A good return is an effective way to re-establish tempo and quiet a hostile crowd. A coach with an aggressive mindset treats a kickoff as the first down of a new offensive series. This chapter deals with various types of kickoff returns; middle, right, left, and wedge returns are diagrammed. Personnel characteristics are also discussed.

Return teams should have a goal of returning the kick at least 20 yards, the equivalent of two first downs. Obviously, the longer the return, the better chance the offense has to score on that particular drive, or on a subsequent drive because of advantageous field position. Conversely, a poor return (or a penalty on the return) can put the offense in a position where play-calling is limited and conservative. The following set of statistics shows the chances for a score, depending on where a drive begins:

- 20-yard line  –  1 out of 30 possessions
- 40-yard line  –  1 out of 8 possessions
 50-yard line  –  1 out of 5 possessions
+40-yard line  –  1 out of 3 possessions
+20-yard line  –  1 out of 2 possessions

# Personnel

Most kickoff return team personnel can be broken down into three parts, or groups: blockers exclusively, blockers who have receiving skills, and receivers who can block. Additionally, this third group can have a sub-group. In this case, the return scheme calls for a single returner. This individual may be a player who lacks football skills, per se (for example, a track man who only returns kickoffs).

The front line should possess good open field blocking abilities, and should be able to correctly leverage cover men who have the advantage of space. Speed should be a consideration. They should be able to run to the block point quickly, and have the footwork to successfully engage their assigned man. Since the cover team is predicated on speed, the return team should match speed with speed. Members of the return team should be aggressive and like contact.

# Middle Return

A middle return with cross blocking can be used against teams that twist or lane exchange as they cover the kick, or teams that stack the cover men before they declare their lane assignment. Kickoff teams who use these tactics make identification very difficult. Return teams who number cover men for blocking purposes have a difficult time coping with these disguises. This return, instead of assigning a blocker to a particular man, involves blocking areas or zones. See Diagram 3-1.

### (C) Center

The center aligns off-center 11 yards from the ball. He should not line up directly in front of the kicker, rather in the gap between the kicker and the first man to his kicking leg side. He has the responsibility of reminding the front line to watch out for an onside kick. Once he is sure the ball has been kicked, he drops 10 to 15 yards deep, depending upon the depth of the kick, and blocks the first man downfield.

The front line on all kickoffs will line up around 10 yards from the kick spot. The front line should be in a two-point stance, facing the ball with their arms loose at the sides, with a good bend in the knees and the hands placed lightly on the thigh boards. The deeper players can use a more erect stance, since distance from the ball allows them more time to react.

### (G) Guards

The guards line up 11 yards from the ball. When the ball is kicked, they drop 5 to 10 yards deep, depending on the kick, and run for the opposite hash. Once they pass each

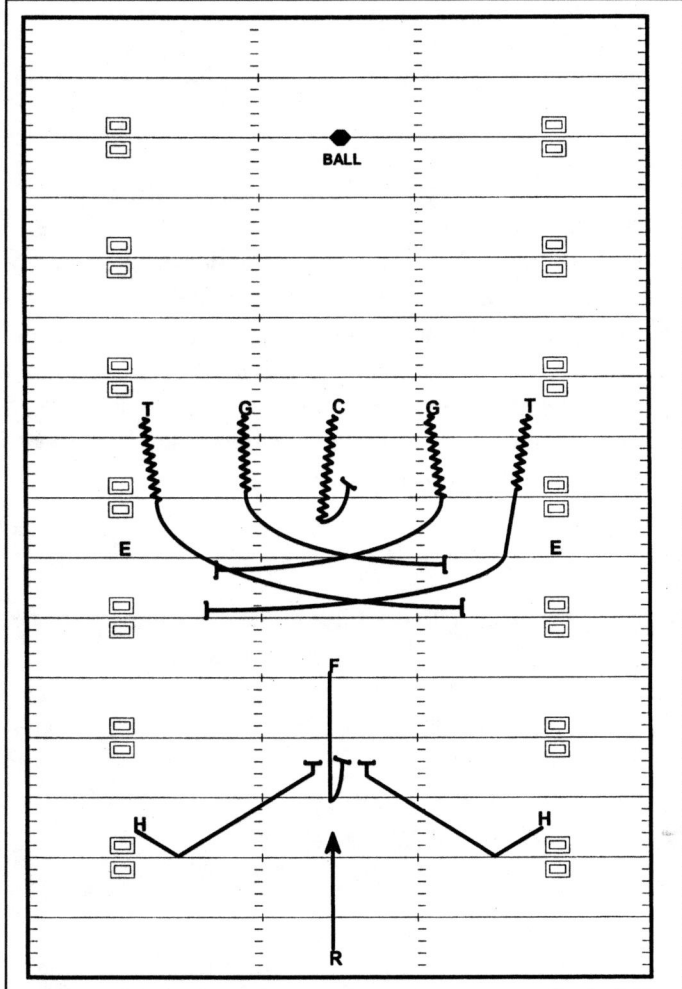

Diagram 3-1. Middle return

other, they should start looking for the first opposite color to block. The right guard should be given the right of way; the left guard has the responsibility of avoiding him.

## (T) Tackles

The tackles line up 11 yards from the ball. When the ball is kicked, they drop 10 to 15 yards deep, depending on the kick, and run for the opposite hash. Once they pass each other, they should start looking for the first opposite color to block. The right tackle should be given the right of way, with the left tackle given the responsibility of avoiding him.

## (E) Ends

The ends usually line up 15 yards behind the front line. They first should be aware of any kick coming to their area. Once they are sure the ball will clear their area, they drop five yards and head for the opposite hash. Once they pass each other, they should start looking for the first opposite colored jersey. The right end should have the right of way, with the left end given the responsibility of avoiding him.

### (F) Fullback

The fullback should align 10 yards behind the ends in the middle of the field. He should first make sure the kick is not coming to him; however, he should field the ball, if the kick *does* come to his area. He can be coached either to return the ball himself, or lateral the ball to the returner. The fullback should *never* back up to catch a ball. If the fullback is coached to return a short kick, the return man will replace him in the wall. The fullback becomes the apex of the wedge, if the ball is kicked deep. He drops to within five yards of the catch. He will head straight upfield, shoulder-to-shoulder with the halfbacks, blocking the first man he encounters.

### (H) Halfbacks

The halfbacks' alignment is determined by the game plan. Obviously, they adjust to the leg strength of the kicker. They should field the ball and get to the wall, if the ball is kicked to them, and, like the fullback, should not back up to catch the kick. When the return man fields the ball, the halfbacks will drop to within five yards of the ball and fit shoulder-to-shoulder with the fullback. They should scan outside-in, and not try to find work wide. It is the returner's responsibility to close the gap to the wall and allow outside pressure to splash off the edge. The wedge should be kept compact and solid. The halfbacks should not drift from the core of the wedge.

### (R) Returner

The returner should concentrate on the catch first. The returner is similar to a center fielder in baseball. He is in charge of the situation. He must verbally call for the ball with a "me" call. If a halfback is in a better position to field the ball, he should give a "you" call. Once the returner fields the ball, he will give a "go" call, serving to time up the wedge. With a "go" call, the fullback and both halfbacks start upfield. The returner wants to stay with the wedge as long as possible. If he sees daylight in the wedge, he should hit it north and south. He should be careful to secure the ball.

## Wedge Return

This return is a double wedge. The first wedge involves the front five, while the second wedge is comprised of the five deep men. This return assigns areas, or zones, to each blocker, as opposed to a numerically tagged individual. The return team should discretely compact the width of its alignment. A more condensed alignment is beneficial to this type of return. See Diagram 3-2.

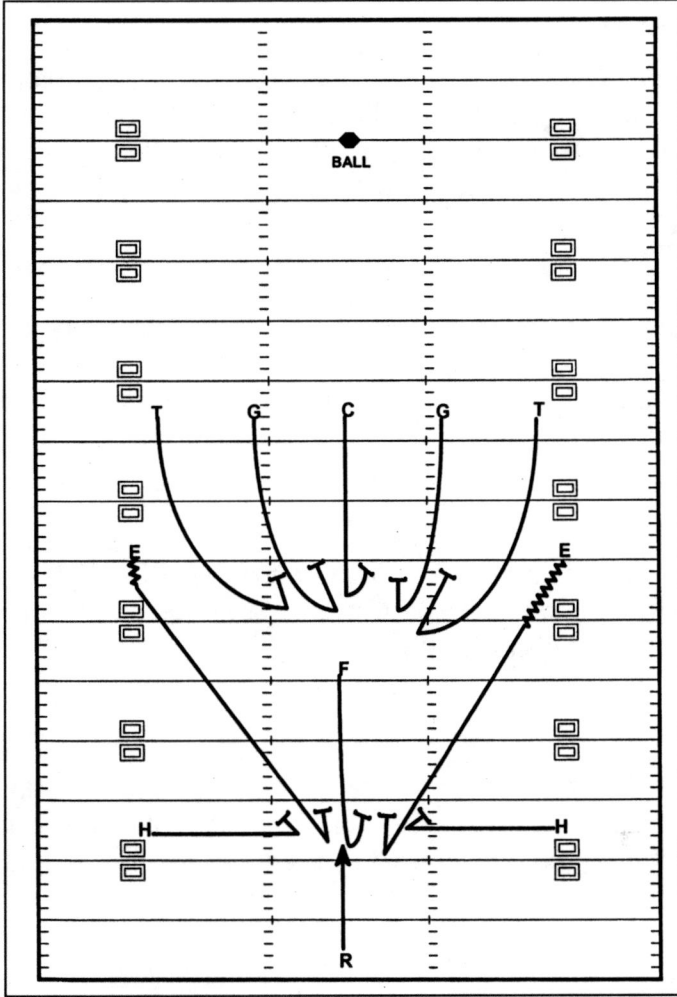

Diagram 3-2. Wedge return

## (C) Center

The center aligns off-center, not head-up on the kicker. Once he is sure the ball is launched deep, the center drops until he hears a "go" call. He should drop in a direct line between the kick and the spot where the returner will catch the ball, positioning the center of the wedge with the returner. When he hears the "go" call, he will square up and become the apex of the first wave. He runs upfield and blocks the first opponent he encounters.

## (G) Guards

When the guards are sure the kick has been made, they drop back and inward toward the center, turning inside as they drop so they can see the center. They drop to the outside shoulder of the center. When the center starts upfield, the guards run with him, staying shoulder-to-shoulder.

### (T) Tackles

The tackles' assignment is similar to the nearby guard. They also drop inward and fit with the guard. When the guards start upfield, the tackles follow suit and stay shoulder-to-shoulder with the guards. They should not drift wide in search of work, nor should they open up a lane between the guard and themselves.

### (F) Fullback

The fullback is the apex of the second wall, taking the wall within five yards of the catch. When he receives a "go" call, he leads the ends upfield. When he hears the "go" call, he should echo the call for the second wall. The fullback blocks the first off-colored jersey he encounters.

### (E) Ends

The ends close inward as they gain depth, to within five yards of the catch. Each end will fit with the fullback to their respective side. When the fullback starts upfield, the ends run with him staying shoulder-to-shoulder.

### (H) Halfbacks

The halfbacks should first look for the ball. If the ball is kicked to the returner, the halfbacks close to the shoulders of the ends. They should hold the compact nature of the wedge and not drift outside. When they get a "go" call, they should work upfield.

### (R) Returner

He must first catch the ball. He then gives a "go" call, and runs behind the wedge.

## Sideline Return

This return attacks the area between the hash and the numbers. It can be run to the right or the left. Diagram 3-3 shows a right return. A left return would reverse everyone's responsibilities.

### (RT) Right Tackle

Once the ball has been kicked deep, the tackle takes the wall to the returner, down a line between the hash and numbers. He is the first man in the wall.

### (RG) Right Guard

The right guard follows the right tackle to the returner. When the right tackle starts to

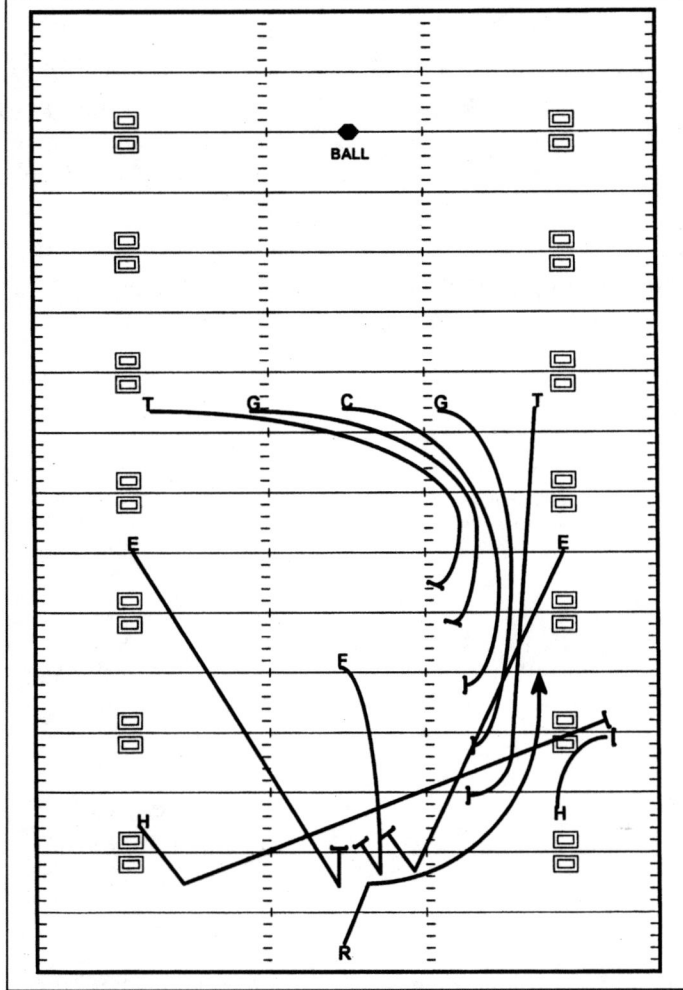

Diagram 3-3. Sideline return

come to balance, he too will start to settle. He should keep a five-yard spacing from the tackle. He is the second man in the wall.

## (C) Center

The center follows the right guard to the returner. When the right guard starts to come to balance, he too will start to settle. He should keep a five-yard spacing with the guard. He is the third man in the wall.

## (LG) Left Guard

He follows the center to the returner. When the center starts to come to balance, he too will start to settle. He should keep a five-yard spacing with the center. He is the fourth man in the wall.

### (LT) Left Tackle

The left tackle follows the guard to the returner. When the guard starts to come to balance, he too will start to settle. He should keep a five-yard spacing with the guard. He is the fifth man in the wall.

### (F) Fullback

He is the apex in the wedge. He drops to within five yards of the catch. Once he gets a "go" call from the returner, he leads the ends straight upfield.

### (E) Ends

The ends sprint to the fullback. The right end will fit his left (or inside) shoulder with the fullback's right shoulder. The left end will fit his right (or inside) shoulder on the fullback's left shoulder.

### (H) Halfbacks

*Right half* attacks the widest man (contain man) inside-out, if the kick does not come to him. He should attack the man down the middle. The contain man should be forced wide and outside.

*Left half* attacks in conjunction with the right halfback. He places his right shoulder on the contain man's inside shoulder. The contain man should be forced wide and outside.

### (R) Returner

The returner should concentrate first on securing the ball. Once he has the ball safely tucked away, he yells, "go." This command signals the wedge to start upfield. He follows the wedge to draw the cover team to the middle of the field. After four or five steps, he should veer to the wall side looking for the left halfback to flash across his face. He should hug the kick-out block and get north.

## Kickoff Returner

The kickoff return man should look at each kickoff as a chance to score a touchdown, or break a long run. Speed is a must at this position. A kick returner is apt to be a pure sprinter, and many teams choose to use a trackster at the position. Comparatively speaking, fielding a kickoff is easier than fielding a punt, which is why raw talent can be more readily used at this position.

The kickoff return man can easily see the ball from the moment it is kicked. His view is not blocked, as is that of a punt returner. A kickoff return artist can easily discern the direction and depth of the kick because of the end-over-end action of the ball. He does not have to read the nose of the ball as a punt returner does. Unlike a punt returner, who must decide whether or not to field a punt, the kickoff returner *must* field each kick because a kickoff is a free ball. The actual catch of a kickoff is very similar to that of a punt. The kickoff return man should form a pocket by placing his hands together with the little fingers touching and the palms up. The pocket should be extended upward toward the ball with elbows kept in and the forearms and chest used to expand the pocket. The ball should be engaged first near the shoulder area and the ball drawn into the returner's chest. On contact with the ball, the return man should give slightly at the knees to cushion the ball. The return man should look the ball all the way into the tuck, since a bobble or drop can disrupt the timing of the return. On sideline returns, the returner should start straight ahead to draw the coverage in then hit the wall to the called side.

Correct positioning of the returner is essential to an effective return. Many variables determine his alignment. Leg strength of the kicker is probably the most important consideration. Weather conditions also influence the depth of the returner. A head wind usually indicates the need for a deeper alignment, a shorter alignment for a tail wind. An astute returner will observe the kicker in pre-game warm ups to get a feel for leg strength and how the wind is affecting his practice kickoffs. Rain, obviously, can affect the depth of the kickoff – not only rain that is falling at that moment, but also earlier rain that causes the ball to be wet. The kicker's footing may also be poor due to the moisture.

An experienced returner will line up slightly deeper than where he expects the kicker to kick the ball, which allows the returner to attack the ball with a running start. After the catch is secured, he should attack the coverage at full speed, scanning the coverage for a crack or seam and hitting it full speed without hesitation. With a ball kicked into the end zone, the returner should make a decision as to whether to down the ball or bring it out. The returner should understand, however, if he carries the ball into the end zone, he must run it out of the end zone or give up a safety. Some coaches give their returner a rule that allows them to bring the kick out of the end zone if it is no deeper than two yards. Other coaches give extremely talented athletes permission to bring out kicks that go halfway into the end zone. When faced with a squib kick, the returner should first focus on fielding the ball and not look up at the coverage. Kickoff returners should be coached to secure the ball and never ever fumble.

# Onside Prevent (Hands) Team

Undoubtedly, this special team is very important, and will be used at a very crucial time in the game. Victory or defeat is usually determined on this one play. Possession of the ball by the return team is the goal of the hands team; therefore, only sure-handed players should be used on the hands team. Players who are comfortable with handling the ball (i.e., backup quarterbacks, receivers, running backs, and defensive backs) should be used as prime candidates for this team. The hands alignment is typically front-loaded, usually having nine men within 18 to 20 yards of the kickoff. Twin safeties are commonly used. The alignment in Diagram 3-4 is a 5-4-2 arrangement.

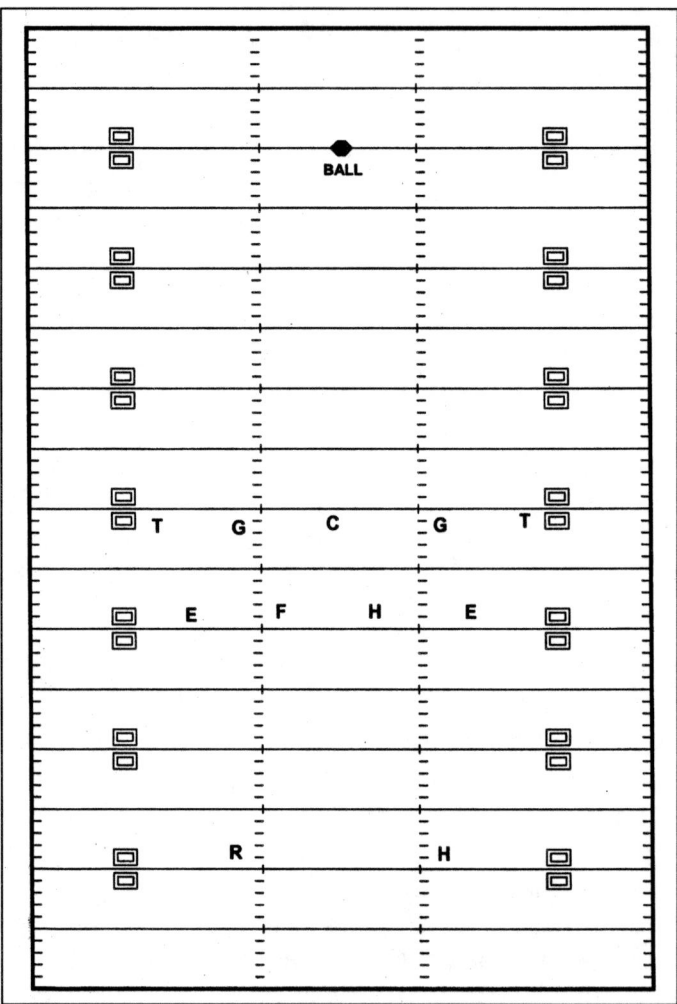

Diagram 3-4. 5-4-2 alignment

Possession of the ball is the objective. Rules allow the return team to advance the ball. However, return yards should not be a consideration. Possession of the ball usually signals victory. The ball must travel 10 yards, or be touched by the return team, before the kicking team can touch the ball. Just prior to the kick, the receiving team should echo the term "baseball," as a reminder that they should assume a baseball infielder's stance – with good knee bend, the hands held knee high, and the palms facing the kick. The front line will not try to field a kick that is kicked hard at them. It is better to let the second line field these types of kicks. The added depth of the second line will serve to slow the kicked ball. Additionally, any miscue or ricochet by the second line is less damaging than a front line blunder. The receiver of the kick should use a simple fall on the ball technique. He should fold his top leg over the ball with his back to the cover team if possible. He must secure the ball by covering both tips of the ball. In a pile up, the cover team will try to leverage the ball loose.

Other members of the hands team should cover and protect the man who has secured the ball. If the hands team's man has to jump to field a high bounce he should immediately fall to the ground. A kick that is airborne and has not touched the ground should be fair caught. If the ball is kicked deep, the front nine should gain depth quickly and wedge return. The safeties should also understand that return yardage is not the goal of the hands team. They should field any deep ball and get what they can without taking a hit. They should fall down before the cover team contacts them. The safety who does not catch the ball should become the point man and block. Communication is very important, so it is best to designate one of the returners to be in charge. He should give a "you" or "me" call to the remaining safety.

## Adjustment to Overload

Adjustments should be made if the onside attempt is made from an overloaded alignment. The overload may occur on the kick team's original alignment, or it may entail a shift. The front line will slide to the overload. The onside end will move forward and outside the tackle. The fullback, halfback, and offside end slide and stack in the appropriate gap. The returner away from the overload moves forward into the gap between the guard and tackle. The remaining returner becomes the single safety. He should align over the ball and must field a deep kick or a sky kick away from the overload. It is best to leave a one-man advantage to the side away from the overload. Diagram 3-5 shows a 3-on-2 advantage on the backside. This kick alignment is not legal in college. If #9 on the kick team is to the overload, the guard would cross the ball to the loaded side and the halfback would move up to replace him, leaving a 2-on-1 advantage.

## Kickoff Return Checklist

- Hash kick
- Middle kick
- Squib kick
- Onside kick
- Shift

- Safety kick
- Reverse
- Possession Rules
- Sky kick

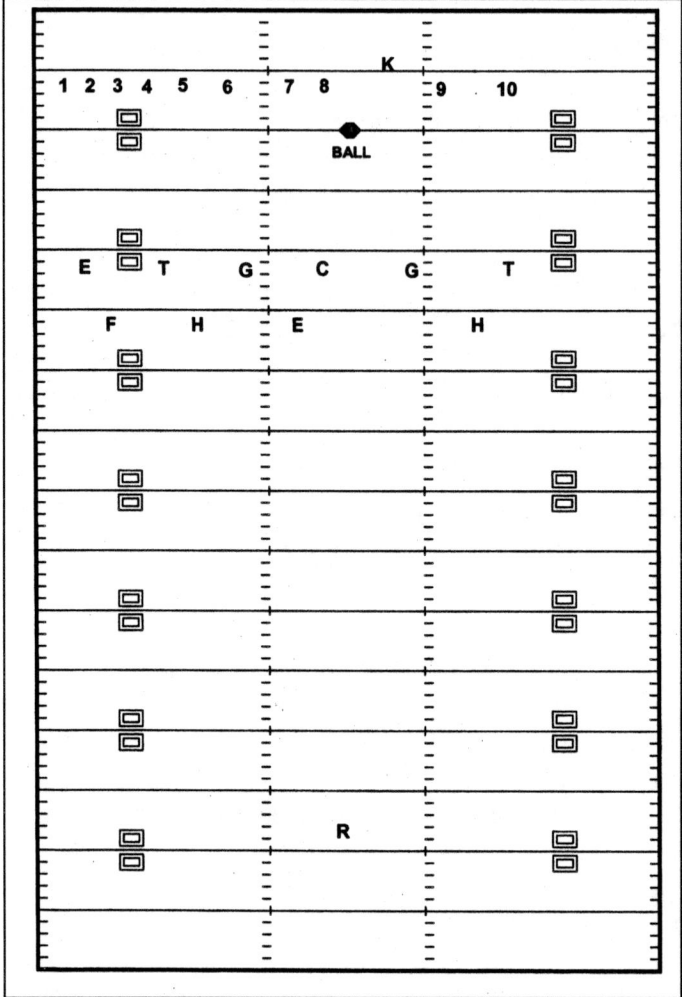

Diagram 3-5

# Kickoff Return Rules and Regulations

- The receiving team cannot be within 10 yards of the kickoff spot. As a basic rule, NFL teams have to align behind the +40-yard line; college teams line up behind the +45-yard line. High school teams observe the 50-yard line as their alignment area.
- The kickoff team can touch the ball after it has traveled 10 yards or a member of the return team touches the ball before it goes the required 10 yards.
- An ungrounded airborne kick can be fair caught.
- All blocks must be above the waist and in front.
- NFL rules state that a kickoff that goes out of bounds can be put into play at the spot where it went out of bounds or 30 yards from the spot of the kick. College rules state

that an errant kick can also be put into play 30 yards from the spot of the kick, or a five-yard penalty can be accepted followed by a re-kick. They can also take the kick at the out of bounds spot. High school rules provide for a five-yard penalty and re-kick, or the offended team can put the ball in play 25 yards from the previous spot. A third option would allow taking the ball at the out of bounds spot. If the ball touches a return team member before it travels out of bounds, the ball is spotted for play where it went out of bounds.

- If the impetus of the kick carries the ball into the end zone, NFL and collegiate rules permit the kick to be brought out by the returner. High school rules declare the ball dead as soon as it crosses the goal line. If the returner provides the new impetus that carries the ball into the end zone, it must be brought out or a safety will be awarded.

# Kickoff Return Axioms

- Know the assignment given.
- Avoid mental errors. No mental busts on alignment or assignment.
- Avoid physical errors. No illegal blocks.
- Line up onsides.
- Expect an onside kick at any time. Receive and echo a "watch the onside kick" call.
- Time up the block. Blocking too early or too late damages the return.
- Return the kick at least 20 yards.
- Cleanly field all kicks that are returnable.
- Use good judgment as to whether or not to bring a kick out of the end zone.
- Fair catch a short pooch kick.

# 4

# Punt Team

Many football coaches think that the most important special team is the punt team. Superior punt teams have the potential to gain at least 10 yards of field position on every punt, which equates to one first down; five punts would equal 50 yards, or five first downs. Good punting moves the offense closer to the opponent's goal line, while pushing the opponent away from the offense's own goal line. Many experts think that punting the ball is the most dangerous phase of the kicking game. The complexion of many games has hinged on a blocked kick or a long punt return. Many coaches believe that 80 percent of the teams that score off a blocked punt will win the game.

Punt team effectiveness depends upon an effective blend of protection and coverage. Protecting the kick is, without a doubt, the most important aspect of the punt team; however, without effective coverage, a long return can be devastating as well. An effective punt game must balance these two parts. By the same token, a fake punt can also be a game breaker.

## Personnel

A good way to find snappers and punters is to have tryouts in pre-season camp. It is a good idea to test everyone on the squad, since help can be found in unlikely places. No matter how or where you find a snapper, he must fit into a certain mold because a snapper should possess certain qualities. With the advent of spread-punt formations, the center must be able to be a primary blocker. Because he controls the tempo of the snap, he controls the tempo of the punt team. He should have nerves of steel to be able to perform in crucial situations, as a bad snap can mean defeat. He should be able to cover punts and tackle in the open field, although these two skills are not as important as making an accurate pass.

Punters can also be discovered in a team-wide tryout. Players with a strong leg are good candidates. Consistency is a must in order to have a good punting game. A punter who follows up a good kick with a shank is a liability; it would be more beneficial to use a punter who kicks consistently, rather than a more talented kicker who is erratic. Height consistency is also desirable. Hang time and net return yardage are two important statistics, since they give an insight on how effective the punt team is performing. The prime choice for a punter is a player who consistently has the best combination of height and distance. Accuracy is paramount, especially if the coach prefers directional kicks. The prospective punter should possess some athletic ability, and coordinated enough to field stray snaps. Size is desirable but is not a requirement. A tall punter does make a better target for the snapper, but it is not essential that the punter be physically large.

Linemen should have the ability to block, run, and make an open field tackle. Obviously, defensive backs are prime candidates for these positions. Defensive backs possess tackling skills and have the necessary speed to play at that position; however, their blocking skills may not be as polished. If the punt team uses a spread type formation, gunners should be able to run, as well as possess the ability to defeat single- or double-team holdups. Hand and foot skills are a requirement, and they should be excellent open field tacklers.

The personal protector should possess intelligence, since he is the quarterback of the punt team. He counts the number of defenders in the box, makes protection calls, is usually the main ingredient on any fakes, and thus should possess throwing as well as running skills. The personal protector should also be an effective blocker, given that he is the last line of defense for the punter.

# Formations

A wide and varied assortment of punt formations exists. The following are some commonly used sets with a list of their strengths and weaknesses.

**Formation #1** (Diagram 4-1)

*Advantages*:
- It is the most commonly used punt formation.
- Four quick receivers.

- The defense cannot put more than eight men in the box.
- It is a great formation for fakes.
- Gunners are in good position to go to the ball.
- When the defense doubles the gunners, they can only put six men in the box.

*Disadvantages:*
- Since this is a spread-type formation, it might be vulnerable up the middle.
- The center must be used as a primary blocker.
- Most fakes from this set will have to be passes. This formation is not very strong with off-tackle runs.

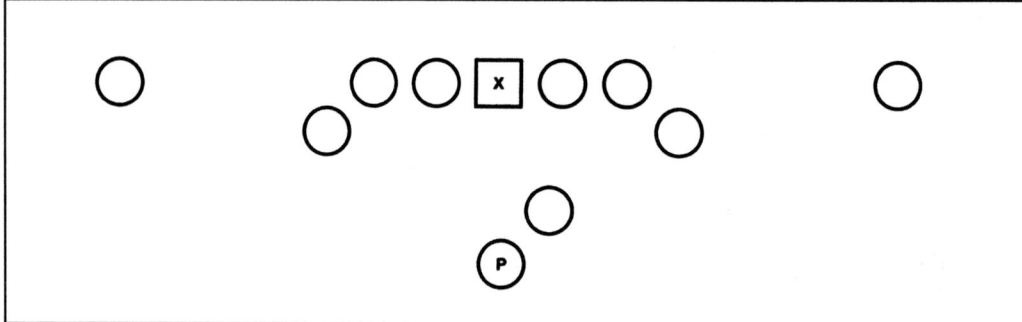

Diagram 4-1. Formation #1

**Formation #2** (Diagram 4-2)

*Advantages:*
- This formation can be a changeup of Diagram 4-1. The offense simply backs the gunners off the ball, and moves the slots up on the ball.
- The gunners are in a position to motion. This would help them avoid hold up blocks.
- Four quick receivers.
- The defense cannot put more than eight men in the box.
- The gunners are in good position to cover the kick. When the defense doubles the gunners, they cannot have more than six men in the box.
- This is a good formation for run fakes. Because of the two tight ends, the off-tackle run areas are strong.

*Disadvantages:*
- Since this is a spread type formation, it might be vulnerable up the middle.
- The center must be used as a primary blocker.
- The slots can be held up easier, since they are on the line of scrimmage.

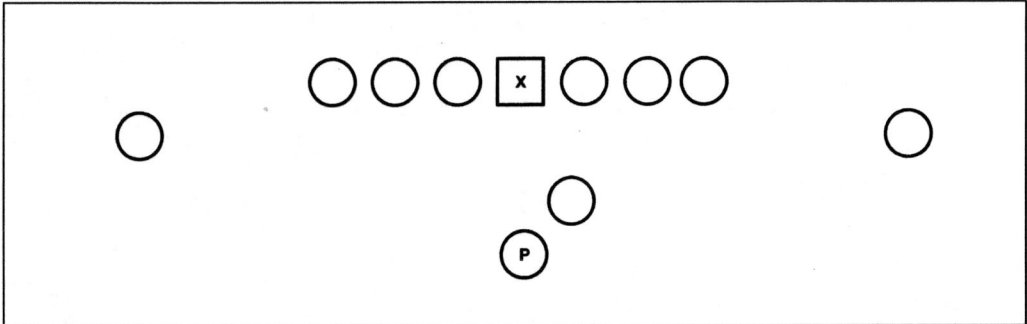

Diagram 4-2. Formation #2

## Formation #3 (Diagram 4-3)

*Advantages*:
- With four quick receivers, a variety of pick- or rub-type pass routes are available.
- A very good formation for fakes; the off-tackle run area is strong.
- Reverse possibilities are enhanced because of the positioning of the wings.

*Disadvantages*:
- With a more compact punt alignment, the defense can put 9 or 10 men in the box. With all that clutter, it is harder to distinguish between rushers and droppers.
- The wings are not as effective in coverage when aligned this close to the core of the formation.
- The center must be used as a primary blocker.
- The compressed nature of the formation could make it harder to expand the punt coverage.

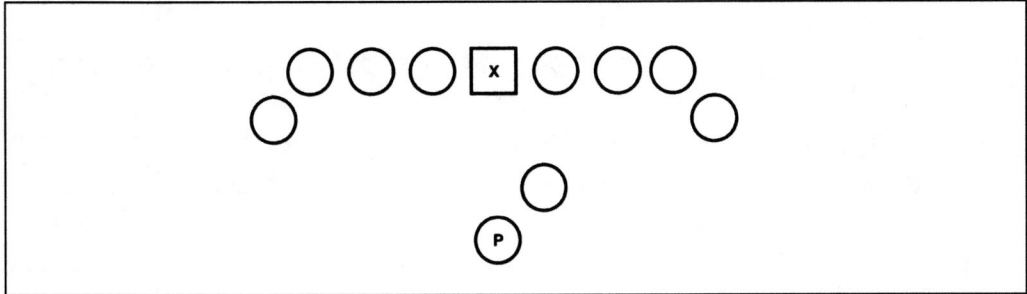

Diagram 4-3. Formation #3

## Formation #4 (Diagram 4-4)

*Advantages*:
- Four quick receivers.
- The defense can have no more than six men in the box.

- With four gunners, the defense cannot double all of them.
- The offense can nullify double teams with motion.
- Cross motion can result in a trips formation, which would be very beneficial when directional kicking.
- The possibility exists for an uncovered receiver.

*Disadvantages*:
- It is a very poor formation for run fakes.
- Wide slots allow shortened corners for rushers.
- Any pass fake would require a pass of some distance.
- The center must be used as a primary blocker.

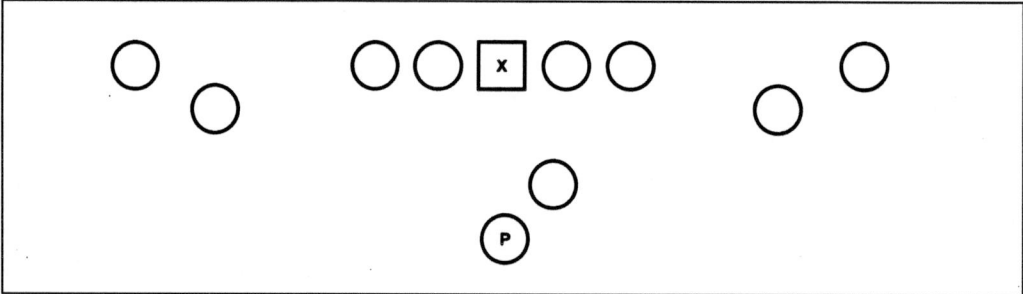

Diagram 4-4. Formation #4

## Formation #5 (Diagram 4-5)

*Advantages*:
- The defense will have problems distinguishing the eligible receivers when receivers shift on or off the ball.
- This formation disrupts any planned block attempt because defenders should cover all the eligibles.
- The possibility exists of having a numbers advantage on either side, or in the middle.
- Some teams will decide to play it safe and cover eligibles instead of pressuring the kick.
- A great formation for fakes, since everyone on the punt team (except the center) are potential eligible receivers.
- This formation causes the opponent to spend practice time defending the formation and all of its possibilities.

*Disadvantages*:
- Run fakes are limited.
- The punt team can be outnumbered in the middle.
- Opponents with an aggressive mindset can be successful with pressure.

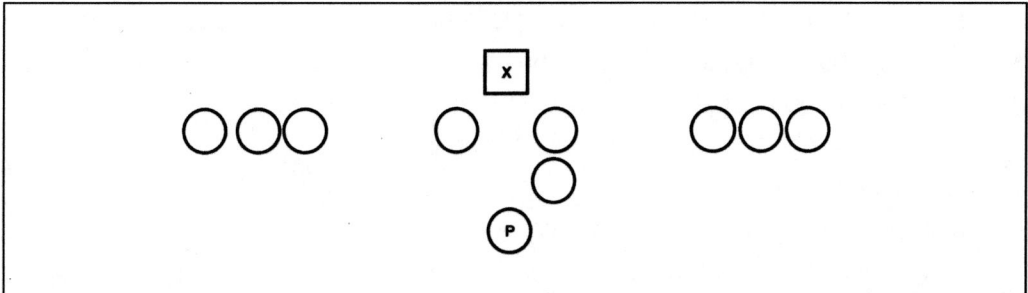

Diagram 4-5. Formation #5

## Formation #6 (Diagram 4-6)

*Advantages*:
- A good formation for maximum protection.
- A more compact formation allows for additional blockers.
- The center can be covered up with the addition of two upbacks.
- The center of the formation is strong.
- A good run fake formation with two tight ends.
- The two upbacks are in good position to block off-tackle on a run fake.

*Disadvantages*:
- No gunners.
- Because of the packed nature of the formation, cover men can be held up more effectively.
- Only two quick receivers .
- The upbacks are not effective pass receivers because they can be held up more easily.

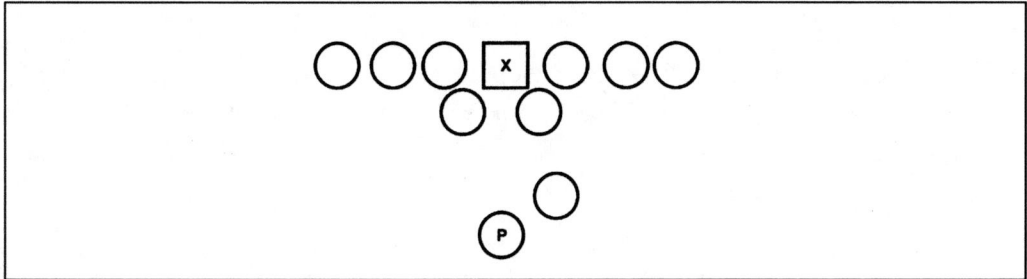

Diagram 4-6. Formation #6

## Formation #7 (Diagram 4-7)

*Advantages*:
- Gunners are able to release more easily.

- The center can be covered up with the placement of two upbacks.
- The center of the formation is very strong.
- Upbacks are in good position to block off-tackle on run fakes.
- The defense cannot put more than eight men in the box.

*Disadvantages*:
- Two shortened punt block corners exist.
- Pass fakes will cover substantial ground.
- The upbacks can be held up more easily on pass fakes or when covering the punt.

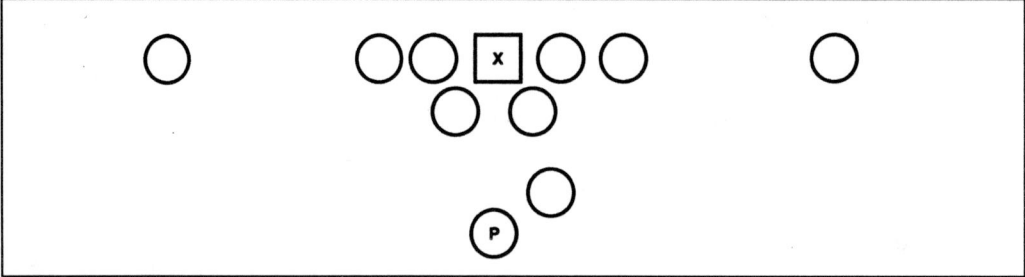

Diagram 4-7. Formation #7

**Formation #8** (Diagram 4-8)

*Advantages*:
- Great for maximum protection.
- Good for backed up punts.
- The center is not required to be a primary blocker.

*Disadvantages*:
- The two ends can be easily held up.
- No gunners.
- This formation is not a good for kick coverage.
- The defense can focus on holding up the front line because of the depth of the second line.

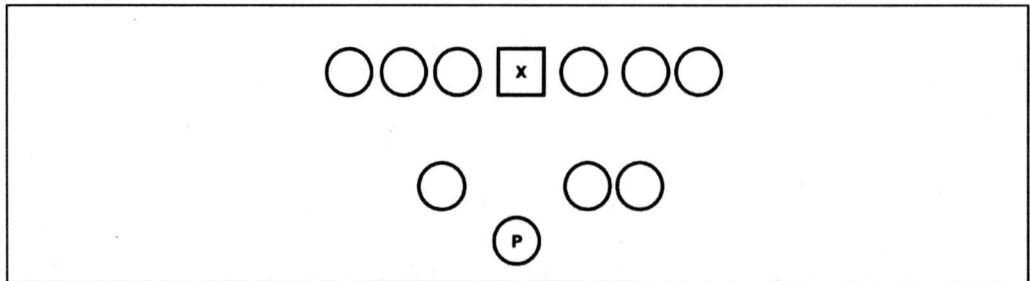

Diagram 4-8. Formation #8

**Formation #9** (Diagram 4-9)

*Advantages*:
- Protection is solid.
- Combo or rub routes are viable options.
- With the gunners tight, the off-tackle area is widened.
- The off-tackle area is strengthened.

*Disadvantages*:
- Gunners can be held up more easily.
- Coverage is more compacted.
- The center must be used as a primary blocker.

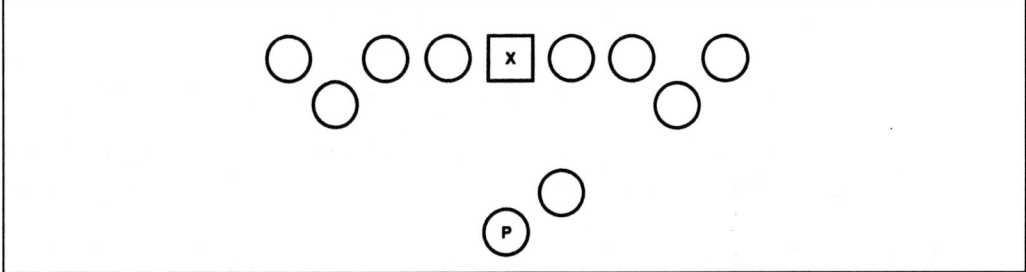

Diagram 4-9. Formation #9

The remainder of this chapter will cover information on positions, stances, alignments, protections (man and zone), coverage, directional kicks, and coverage changeups. Situational punts such as clock punts, delayed punts, taking a safety punt, tight punts, and pooch punts are detailed, including punting in windy conditions. Since the most widely used punt formation is the spread formation (Diagram 4-10), it is used when illustrating the material covered in the remainder of this chapter.

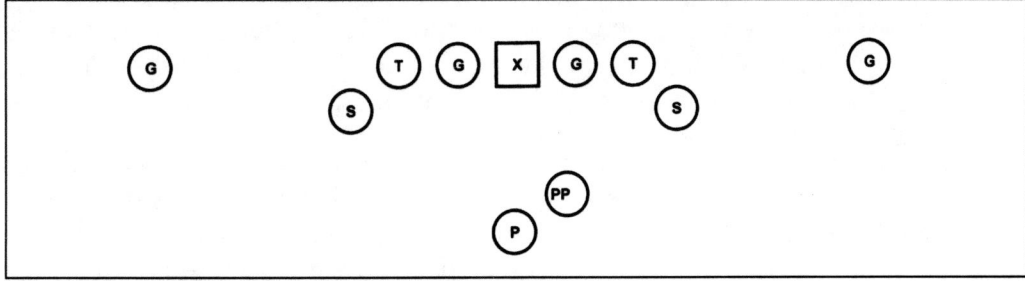

Diagram 4-10. Spread formation

# Personnel

X - snapper

G - guards

T - tackles

S - slots

G - gunners

PP - personnel protector

P - punter

# Stance and Alignments

*X*: Aligns on the ball, using a basic square stance.

*G*: Align in a two-point stance with their hands on their thigh boards, bent at the knees and their back kept straight. Weight should be on the balls of the feet, and the feet should be shoulder width apart with the inside foot forward. Guards should take a six-inch split from the snapper. Vertical alignment should be as far off the ball as legally possible. Rules state that their helmet must break the snapper's numbers.

*T*: Should use the same stance as the guards. Horizontal alignment should be one foot from the guard; vertical alignment should be off the ball as far as legally possible.

*S*: Should use the same stance as the guards and tackles, aligning with their inside foot on the outside foot of the tackle. Vertical alignment should be one yard deeper than the tackle. Shoulders should remain parallel to the line of scrimmage.

*PP*: Uses a square two-point stance. He may align directly behind either guard, depending upon many variables (game plan, the punter's foot, overloads, etc.). As a basic rule, he should place his heels at six yards.

*G*: Should use a two point staggered stance. Takeoff is paramount when playing this position, so they should look in toward the ball to see the snap. Horizontal alignment varies according to ball position. With the ball in the middle of the field, the gunners should be one yard outside the numbers; as the ball moves toward the gunner, he will widen his alignment the distance the ball is from the middle of the field. He will plus his alignment if the ball moves toward him; if the ball moves away from him, he will minus his alignment the same distance the ball is from the middle of the field.

*P*: As a basic rule, he lines up 15 yards deep from the ball, and should be assigned to count the number of players on the punt team. If there are too many or not enough players on the field, he should take a delay of the game penalty if the game situation allows it. Some situations may dictate that the punter call time out. The punter should be coached on how to react to the various situations he may encounter.

The personal protector is the punt team quarterback. Since he is in charge of the punt team, he should be able to communicate and count the number of potential rushers, make any changes needed in the protection scheme, be aware of the clock, and be athletic enough to run or throw the ball on planned fakes. His blocking assignment usually involves blocking #4 away from the protection call. If he has no rusher, he will check from his side to the offside for leakage. He also should give a directional call after the kick.

The personal protector will give three calls on each punt. The first call communicates how many men are in the box. This number designates the number of potential punt rushers. For example, an "eight up" call signals that eight men are in a rush position. The second call tags the protection. Protection calls are normally denoted by colors. For example, a "red" call tells the center to block to his right; a "blue" call instructs the center to block left. The protector will block opposite the center's block. The third call will be "set." With this call, the punt team must become stationary and the center can snap the ball at any time after the call. The center should vary the time between the "set" call and the snap. He does not want to allow the defense to get a feel for the timing of the snap.

# Steps

The same steps are used whether man or zone protection schemes are used. The punt team must keep a constant split relationship, while executing their vertical sets. Each blocker will place his weight on his inside foot, kick back with the outside foot, and slide step with the inside foot. They should retreat straight back. These steps are used whether performing zone or man protections. Zone and man protections are basically the same; the only difference is that with zone protection the blocker will basically block man or area with a deeper set. Man protection involves a shorter set. The personal protector should step up on each snap. He should never work straight back.

# Zone Protection

Each blocker should key the ball and get off on the snap. They should gain depth quickly and get as deep as possible. The blocker does not make a stand until he can "smell their breath." Zone protection requires inside out protection. The blocker should stay square and focus on an area, and not a particular man. Each blocker punches inside to outside. Versus stacks, each blocker should zone set and protect his area. Blockers cannot focus on a particular rusher and allow one of the other rushers to run past him. Blockers in zone protection are able to allow stacks to divide and block whomever shows in their assigned areas. Blockers should understand that anyone aligned in the box is a potential rusher; however, rushers in a down alignment should be handled first. Blockers should be alert for shoulder pulls that are designed to tie up blockers while teammates run through (see Diagram 4-11).

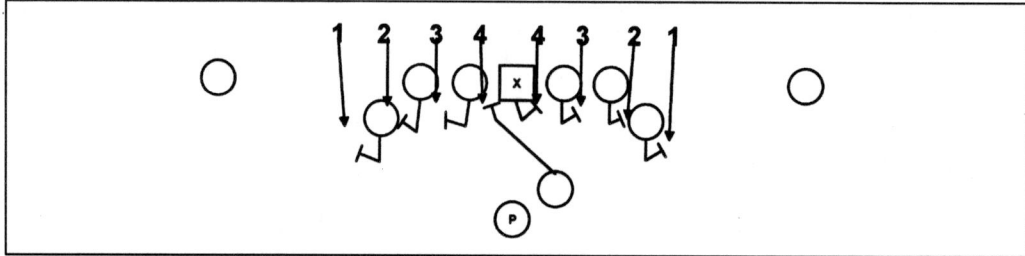

Diagram 4-11. Zone protection with a red call

# Man Protection

In the protection scheme, the defenders will be given a number, counting outside in.

*X*: Blocks #4 right or left according to the call given by the personal protector; "red" means right, "blue" means left. He should take time to get comfortable in order to make a good snap. He should change up the interval between "set" and the snap, preventing the defense from timing up the snap. After the release of the ball, he should basketball shuffle at a 45-degree angle with his hands to his assigned side, and keep his head up. He should strike the rusher, and push him laterally.

*G*: Zone drop and block #3. If possible, he should bump from #4 to #3 if the snapper is working toward him, which helps the snapper.

*T*: Zone drop and block #2.

*S*: Zone drop and block #1.

*PP*: Will block #4 away from the snapper's block. He has #4 right with a "blue" call, and #4 left with a "red" call.

*G*: Key the ball for the snap. The gunner should keep the defender's hands off his body with quick feet and violent hands. Gunners must get vertical quickly. A good tactic is to fake opposite the desired release. When faced with a 2-on-1 bracket, he should attack one man and react to the second, rather than try to split them. He should try to beat the inside man with an inside release, or the outside man with an outside release. After the release, he should go to the ball (see Diagrams 4-12 and 4-13).

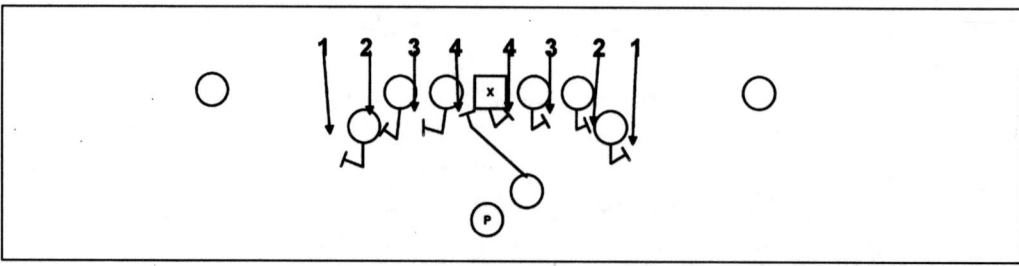

Diagram 4-12

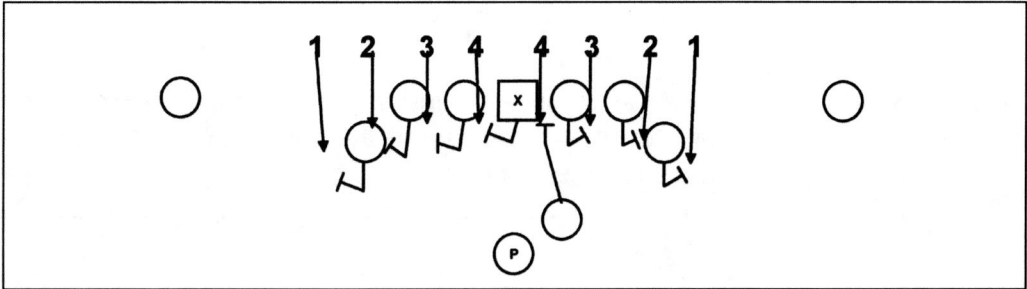

Diagram 4-13

Blockers should not chase their assigned man, even when a man protection scheme is used. In Diagram 4-14, #2 becomes #3 and #3 becomes #2, whether the called protection was zone or man (see Diagram 4-14). Diagram 4-15 shows a stack where either man in the stack can be #3 or #4, which is why depth in the set will give the blockers time to sort it out (see Diagram 4-15).

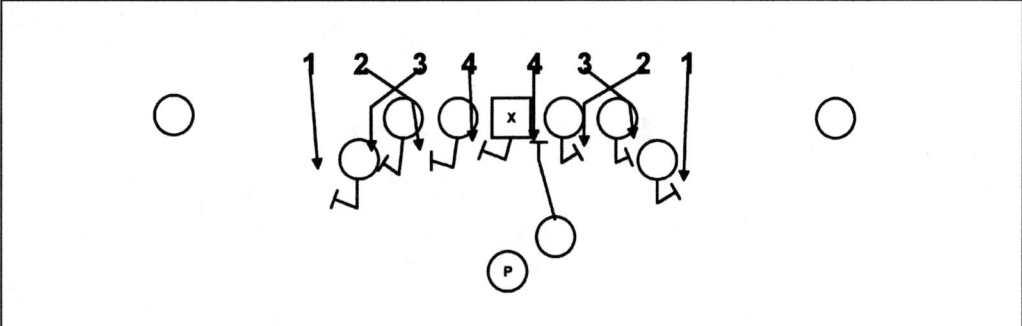

Diagram 4-14

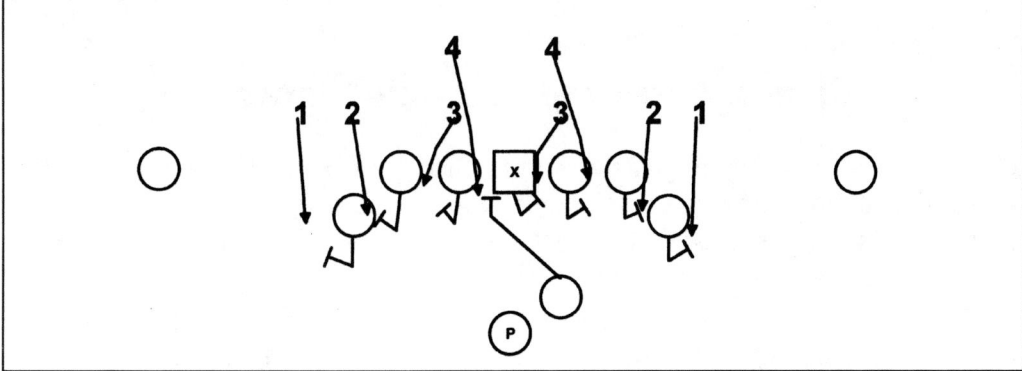

Diagram 4-15

# Max Call

This call can be used whenever a big gap exists between #3 and #4 on one side, and triggers a switch in blocking responsibilities between the personal protector and the guard away from the center's block (see Diagrams 4-16 and 4-17).

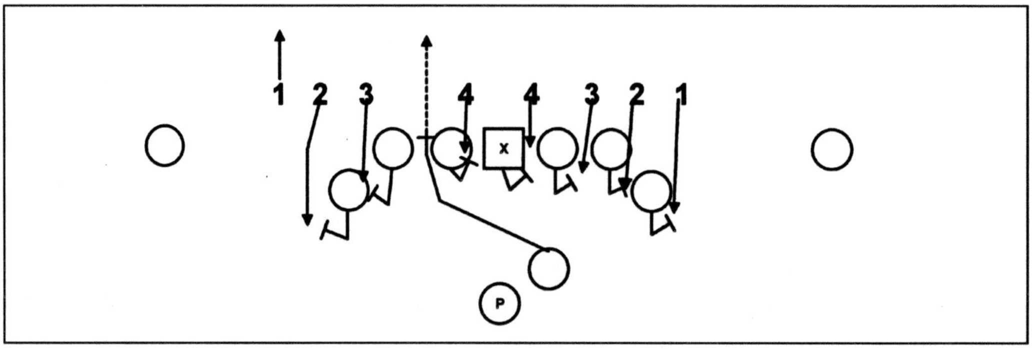

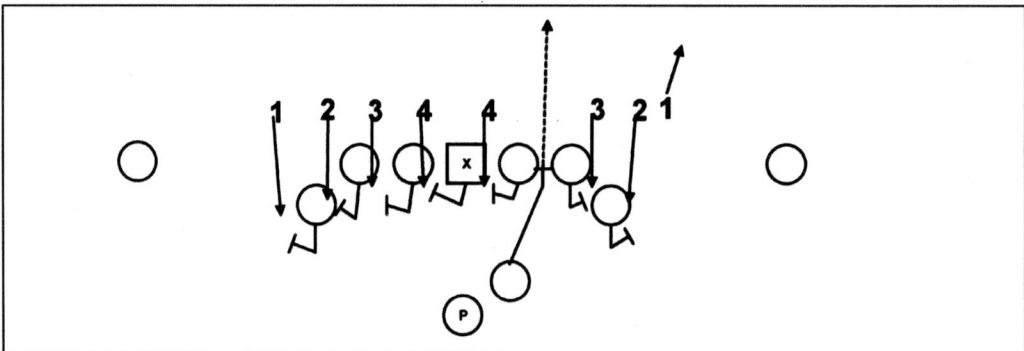

Diagram 4-16. Red Max

Diagram 4-17. Blue Max

# Coverage Principles and Progression

Once the punt has been adequately protected and the kick is airborne, the punt team should get into the coverage phase. Good coverage is a must for effective punt team play. The elements are important no matter what formation is used. The following are coverage principles and progressions:

- Protection is the number one priority. The punt team should maintain its poise and composure against return teams that move around and scramble a lot.
- Cover men cannot be held up or forced out of their assigned lane. Covering punts is mostly hustle and desire.
- Coverage should run through its assigned release point, and then assume the assigned lane. Players should not follow the same colored jersey.

- Coverage should sprint through the assigned lane, then converge on the ball. A five-yard spacing between players should be maintained, with the ball kept on the inside shoulder with outside-in leverage.
- Coverage should keep leverage and come to balance five yards from the ball. Gunners, however, should run through the ball, taking a shot at the returner. They should seek to make a big hit. Gunners should never allow the ball to split them, or bounce outside them. Contain men should be the widest men on the field, alert for trick plays. They should keep 21 men inside them.
- Coverage should tackle and strip the ball. The first man should ensure the tackle (gunners are excluded), while later arrivals should try to strip the ball. Cover men should avoid contact when a fair catch is signaled. If the punt is a pooch type kick, the first man should run by the return man and turn his back to the goal line; the second man should face up the returner. Even with a fair catch signal, the cover team should still hustle and anticipate a muff of the kick. Cover team members should call out "fair catch" when they recognize that the ball is being fair caught, which serves to inform cover men who have not seen the signal.
- The punter and personal protector should give directional calls.
- "Hatch" the ball. On any punt, the ball should be picked up and handed to the official. If the return team does not attempt to catch the ball, the coverage team can catch the ball (inside the 10-yard line). When the opponent makes a "Peter" call, the cover team should locate the ball and anticipate the ball hitting a member of the return team.

# Lane Assignments

Coverage assignments for the following punts are based upon college hashes, which are 60 feet from the sidelines. NFL hashes are placed at 70 feet, 9 inches, and high school hash marks are 53 feet, 4 inches. Adjustments to different landmarks should be made accordingly.

*X*: Has no lane responsibility. He goes directly to the ball.

*G*: Their assigned landmark is two yards outside the hash. They start to the assigned landmark and then react to a directional call from the punter. Once the ball has been located, they work toward it keeping a five-yard spacing between teammates.

*T*: Their assigned landmark is two yards inside the numbers. They start to the assigned landmark, and then react to a directional call from the punter. Once the ball has been located, they work to it keeping a five-yard spacing between teammates.

*S*: Their assigned landmark is two yards outside the numbers. Slots, as a rule, have contain. Coverage changeups can occur where contain responsibilities are switched. If slots have contain, they will be the widest men horizontally on the field. Their job is to

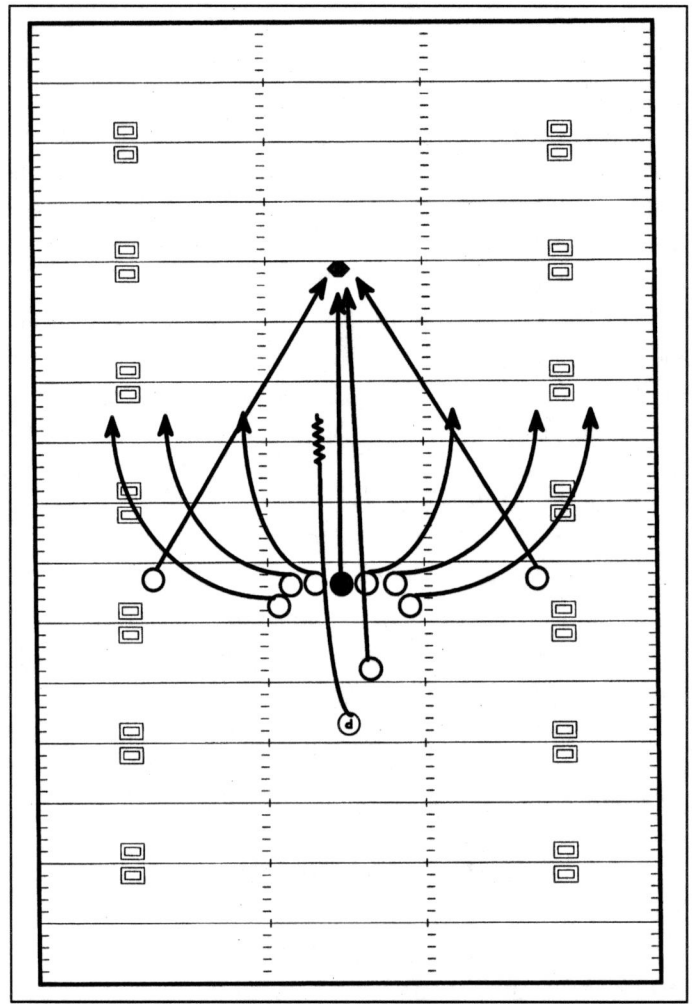

Diagram 4-18. Lane assignments

keep 21 men inside them, so they should be alert for kick-out blocks, reverses, throwbacks, and so forth.

*PP*: Like the center, he has no assigned track to the ball, so he should go directly to the ball.

*G*: Go to the ball. They have no lane responsibility, should not allow the ball to split them or bounce outside them, and attack outside in. The gunner should come off low and hard. He may have to use a rip, swim, or karate technique to get the defense's hands off him.

*P*: He is the safety, and should close the distance so he can make a tackle as the ball pops through the coverage, and not in an open field situation. He should expect a crack block from the side, and must leverage the ball to a teammate or the sideline.

# Coverage Change-Ups

Coverage variations can be productive. Sowing doubt as to who has contain by changing lane responsibilities can cause recognition and assignment problems for the return team. One effective deviation is to put the personal protector on contain to one side, and allow the slot to that side to go directly to the ball. Everyone else follows his normal deep middle rules (see Diagram 4-19). Another coverage change up is to move a slot up on the line of scrimmage, back the gunner off the line, and then send him in motion, which would serve to give the gunner a chance to beat a double team holdup (see Diagram 4-20).

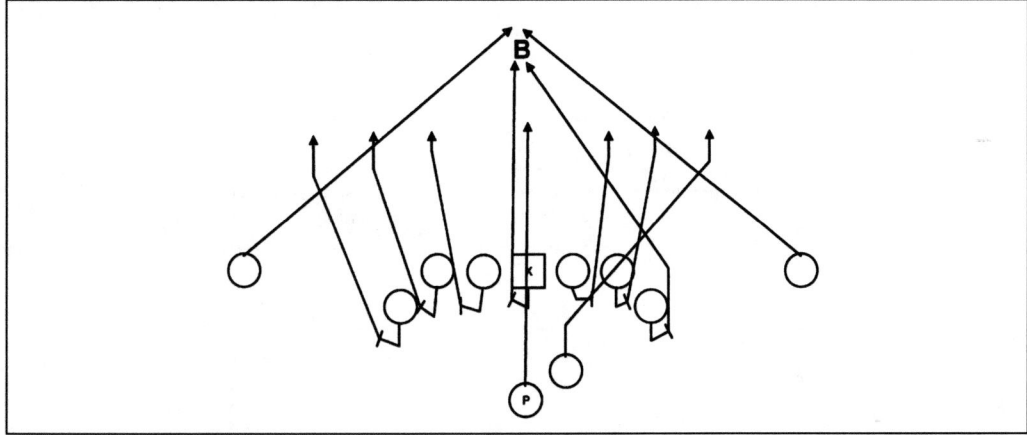

Diagram 4-19

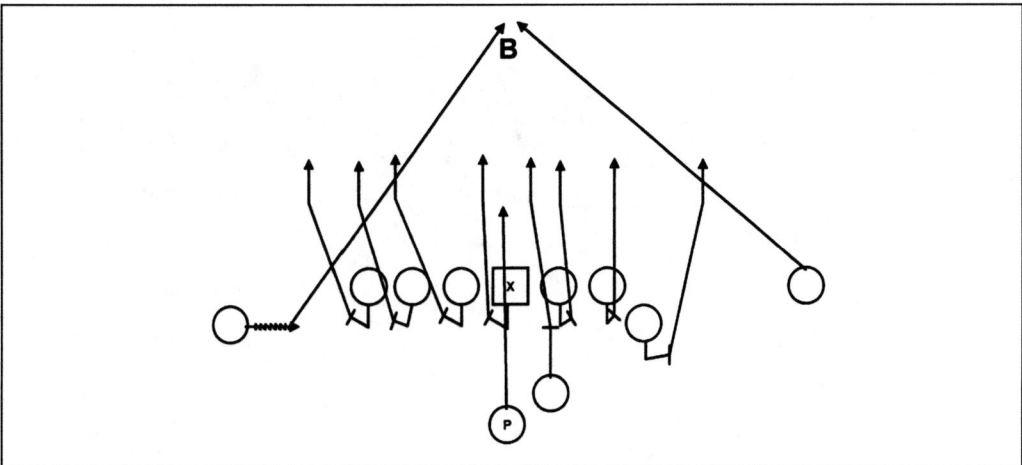

Diagram 4-20

# Directional Punts

In some cases, the coach may want to kick the ball in a particular direction, and not down the middle of the field. Directional kicks can cause problems for the return team. Punt teams will directional kick for a variety of reasons: to pin a receiver into the boundary, to kick the ball away from a particularly dangerous return man, or to take advantage of a crosswind. When a punter is called upon to execute a directional kick, he should turn his hips and body in the desired direction. Aiming his body pre-snap, his alignment and first step establishes the direction of the kick. Diagram 4-21 shows an example of a deep right punt.

*C*: Assigned landmark is two yards outside the right hash.

*LG*: Assigned landmark is the middle of the field.

*RG*: Assigned landmark is two yards inside the numbers.

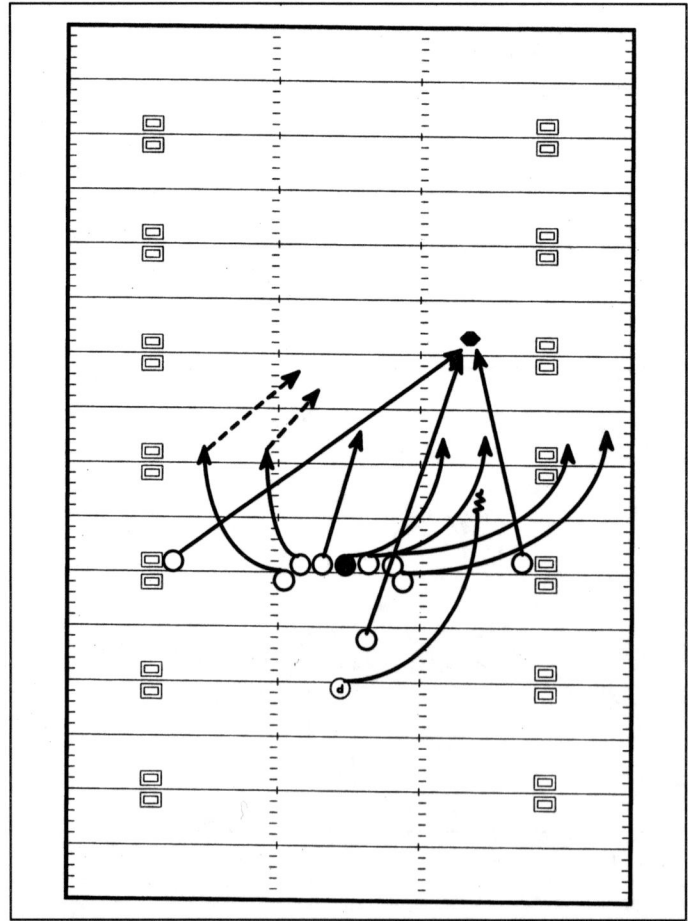

Diagram 4-21. Deep right

*LT*: Assigned landmark is two yards outside the hash.

*RT*: Assigned landmark is two yards outside the numbers.

*LS*: Assigned landmark is two yards inside the numbers.

*RS*: Assigned landmark is five yards from the sideline.

*PP*: Goes directly to the ball. He has no assigned lane responsibility.

*LG*: Goes directly to the ball. He has no assigned lane responsibility. He should minus his split without giving away the directional kick.

*RG*: Goes directly to the ball. He has no assigned lane responsibility.

*P:* Makes the desired directional kick. He becomes the safety. A deep left punt would simply entail the positions to exchange responsibilities.

# Coffin Corner Kicks

The coffin corner kick is a highly effective punt that has gone out of vogue in recent years. This type of kick does not allow a return, since the ball is purposely kicked out of bounds. Obviously, the punter must be within range of the opponents' end zone. This kick is usually launched from the gray area where a successful field-goal attempt is not a good bet. Also, the coach should favor a coffin corner kick over a pooch kick. A pooch attempt that goes into the end zone would result in the ball coming out to the 20-yard line; whereas, a successful coffin corner kick would spot the ball inside the five- or-10-yard line. The kicker does not have to play the bounce or roll with a coffin corner kick. A bouncing or rolling ball does not leave much room for error. One reason for the disappearance of the coffin corner kick is that the punter must change or adjust the mechanics of the kick.

The punter tries to kick a line drive on a coffin corner attempt. The drop is lower, and the contact point is below the knee. The punter should aim the ball by turning his body pre-snap and kick to a target. Most coffin corner kicks are kicked to the short side of the field. For example, if the ball is on the right hash the punter will kick the ball to the right; a ball on the left hash will be kicked to the left. Most punters will aim for the five-yard line when kicking to the right. The ball should sail out of bounds between the 5- and 10-yard line. A really proficient punter can aim for the goal line. This would place the ball between the goal line and the five-yard line. The punter should aim for the 10-yard line when the ball is placed on the left hash. The kick should go out of bounds between the 10- and 5-yard lines. The theory behind these targets is that a punter will usually miss toward the kick leg side. A right-footed kicker will miss to the right, while a left-footed kicker usually misses to the left. Obviously, coverage should be tailored to cover in the direction of the kick.

# Situational Punts

## Clock Punt

Situations occur when clock considerations enter into a punt down. A good example is when the offense wants to use up time on the clock toward the end of the half or the game before the ball is punted. In this situation, the punt team will use as much clock as possible before the snap. The offense wants to run as much of the clock as possible, but not incur a delay of the game penalty. The personal protector controls the timing of this kick. The snap in this situation, unlike other punts, will be initiated by sound. He will give the snap command with two seconds left on the clock, and the center will snap the ball on command.

## Delay Punt

The ball will not be snapped on a delay punt. A delay of the game penalty is the immediate goal, so this strategy is used in a situation when the clock is more important than five yards of field position. In this case, the punt team trades five yards for time off the clock. A delay punt can also be used when setting up a pooch kick. In this scenario, the loss of five yards gives the punt team a little more field with which to work when attempting to pin the return team with a pooch kick.

## Pooch Punt

This punt is an attempt to pin the return team near its own goal line, so distance is not a requirement. The punter strikes the ball so it travels less distance than a normal punt, and has a longer hang time. In this case, less is more. On a pooch kick, at least one gunner and the center should be assigned to sprint to the goal line and turn around to face the incoming kick; their primary job is to keep the ball from going into the end zone. The remainder of the cover team covers exactly like a normal punt with the same landmarks. Cover men sprint to assigned areas and then find the ball. The cover team should not trust the actions of the punt returner, since he may try to fool the coverage. Each player must locate the ball!

## Take a Safety Punt

This punt usually occurs near the end of a game when a deliberate safety works to the advantage of the kicking team. The head coach may call this play, or it may result from a bad or mishandled snap. The kick team should use a tight formation when executing the safety punt. The punt team will block solid, and not release to cover. The punter will usually set up with his heels just inside the end line, and should completely concentrate on the snap, watching the ball all the way into his hands, secured high and tight. To use some of the clock, he can move around and step out the back of the end zone just before he gets hit. The punter should not take a hit on the field of play. If a bad snap occurs, the punter should allow the ball to go out of bounds; he should not try to catch an errant snap. If the punter muffs or drops the ball, he should immediately fall on it; he must not try to pick up the ball!

## Tight Punt

This punt is commonly used whenever the ball is inside the minus five-yard line. The guards take a normal six-inch split from the snapper. The tackles adjust their alignment from one foot from the guard to a six-inch split. The wing's alignment is the same as on a regular punt. The gunners can either align tight or wide. If they line up wide, they should shift to tight if eight in the box exists. If the personal protector gives the gunners a "move" call, they should minus their split to a position two feet from the wing. Everyone's blocking assignments are the same as for a deep middle punt. If the gunners move in tight, they should run through #2 (counting outside in). The gunner will stab #2's rush and then release to the ball. The personal protector uses the same rules and calls he uses with regular spread punts. Punters should anticipate a 10-man rush whenever they kick from the end zone, so he should quicken his steps to get the kick off quickly. If the ball is inside the minus five-yard line, he will not be able to get his normal depth of 15 yards. He should get as much depth as possible, but should guard against touching the end line. The personal protector should also adjust by moving up. The punter must align with both feet in the field of play. The punter should step into the snap.

Distance, not hang time, is desired on this type of kick. To gain this added distance, he can use a lower drop and seek to drive the ball. The cover men should be aware of this goal and cover accordingly. The punter should be coached to anticipate a bad snap and what to do if there is an errant snap. As a basic rule, when a bad snap occurs late in the fourth quarter and a safety will beat the punting team, the punter should punt the ball at all costs. If a safety will tie the score, it might be better to give up two points rather than a touchdown on a blocked punt. If the kick team has a lead of three or more points, the punter should take a safety. Whenever a punter gives up a safety, he should run out of the end zone to avoid a fumble.

## Quarterback as a Punter

An innovation that some teams currently use, with great results, is to have the offense stay on the field on fourth down. This tactic is used on the plus side of the 50-yard line. A nebulous area exists on the plus-50 side of the field and is outside the place kicker's range, yet too close to the end zone for a punt. With the offense on the field, the defense cannot tell the offense's true intentions. As a result, the defense stays on the field and the punt return/block team stays on the sideline. The defense will usually be in "safe" mode, while the quarterback shifts to punt formation and calmly pooch kicks the ball. The defense will usually have no way to execute a coordinated punt return.

# Quick Kick

In an era of wide-open offenses, rules have tilted the field in favor of the offense; however, a place still exists for the quick kick. While many offensive geniuses disdain giving up a down to quick kick, some coaches still see the benefit of punting the ball unexpectedly. It is a way to punt the ball and not have to kick to an outstanding punt returner. Punting on third down takes the outstanding return man out of the game.

Very little return yardage will occur on a quick kick. Even if a safety hustles back to field the ball, no coordinated blocking scheme will be possible. A quick kick also keeps a good punt rush team off the field. An injury to the long snapper or the punter may necessitate a punt by another means. Most quick kicks are attempted on third down. A quick kick before third down *would* serve to shortchange the offense. However, wind conditions might demand a quick kick pre-third down. For example, a strong tailwind just before a change in the quarter might make an earlier down punt advisable.

Most quick kicks are executed with a running back who lines up deep in the backfield in a two-point stance. The I formation is tailor-made for a quick kick attempt. The player making the quick kick must have a strong leg and some kicking experience. Most quick kicks start out with a toss from the quarterback who reverses out from under the center. The back should first look the ball into his hands, and then step parallel to the line of scrimmage, or at a 45-degree angle away from the line of scrimmage with his right foot (right-footed kicker). He then takes the second step with his left foot. The third step will be the kick step. He wants to kick the ball near the rear third of the ball, which will cause the ball to travel end-over-end. This type of roll will serve to propel the ball along the ground toward the goal line. He should make sure he gets the ball over the head of the deepest defender; zone blocking to the right should supply the necessary protection to get the kick airborne. The use of a wing to the punter's kicking leg side should help secure the edge of the formation; however, a compact formation would hamper coverage. Coverage consists of sprinting downfield, keeping an inside shoulder position on the ball, coming to balance within five yards of the ball, and making a tackle if the ball is fielded.

# Fake Punts

### Pass/Run Rollout (Diagram 4-22)

This fake is a designated pass/run option. The center snaps the ball to the personal protector. The personal protector attacks the corner, and has the option of running or passing the ball. The left gunner motions across the formation and runs a flat route. As he stretches the flat area, he should look to turn upfield if he has a defender on his shoulder, or if he runs out of room on the sideline. The right gunner runs a curl route and slides to face up the personal protector, and should try to square up with the ball. The gunner should make sure he is past the first down sticks. The right tight end slams any defender who may line up in the C gap, and then releases to the curl area. If there is no defender, he should step down hard into the C gap drawing the 9 technique inside, which allows the off guard a better angle on the pin block. The offside guard pulls on the play and tries to pin the widest defender. If the widest defender is hard upfield, the guard should kick him out; if the personal protector gives him a "run" call, he should turn upfield and lead the ball carrier to the first down marker. The remaining members of the offensive line use turnback blocks. They block their backside gap, and can also be assigned to reach to the frontside. The punter can run a circle route to the left side and be available for a throwback.

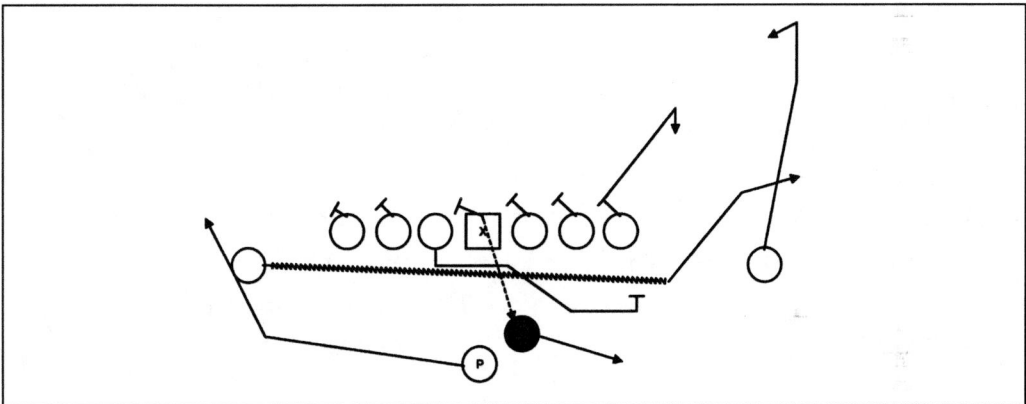

Diagram 4-22. Pass/run rollout

**Off-Tackle Run** (Diagram 4-23)

This fake is a true running play. The ball is snapped to the personal protector who takes the ball to the off-tackle area. The onside upback kicks out the first defender who shows outside the right tight end's down block. The tight end blocks any C-gap defender on or off the line of scrimmage. The offside upback follows the right upback and turns up inside his kick-out block. He should block the first off-colored jersey he sees. Everyone on the offensive line blocks his backside gap. They may also be coached to reach to the playside. The punter simulates a bad snap, jumping and acting as if the ball went over his head. The personal protector will run inside the upback's kick-out block, and may need to back up slightly for better timing of the play.

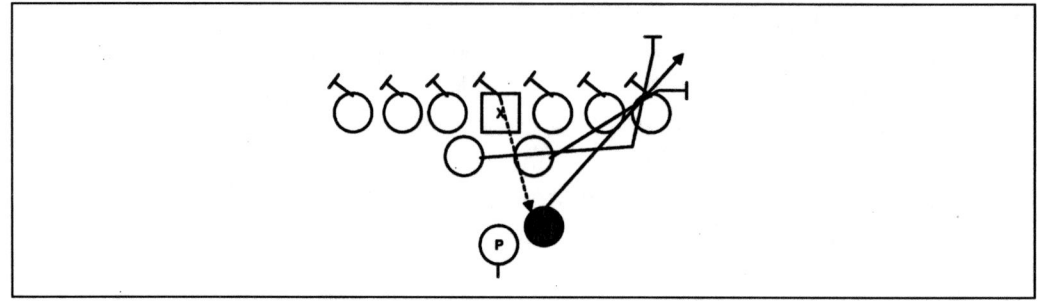

Diagram 4-23. Off-tackle run

# Punt Team Checklist

The following are situations that should be coached and understood for the punt team to be truly prepared. Each of the situations can arise during a game.

- Pooch punt
- Directional punt
- Backed up punt
- Punt out of end zone
- Out of bounds punt
- Take a safety punt
- Punt versus a "sell the farm" rush (11 men)
- Opponent's return/block philosophy
- Scramble and punt
- Bad snaps
- Punter drops the ball
- Blocked punts
- Fourth down punt
- Third down punt
- Quick kick
- Blocked ball crosses the line of scrimmage
- Blocked ball does not cross the line of scrimmage
- Coverage schemes
  - ✓ Normal
  - ✓ Lane changeups
- Center covered/uncovered
- Fair catch

- Muff of fair catch
- Downing the ball properly
- Ball punted from hashes
  - ✓ Right
  - ✓ Left
  - ✓ Middle
- Formation changeups
- Weather considerations
  - ✓ Wet field
  - ✓ Rain
  - ✓ Headwind
  - ✓ Tailwind
  - ✓ Crosswind
- Time considerations
  - ✓ Delayed punt (take a penalty)
  - ✓ Clock punt (run clock down to one or two seconds on play clock)
- "Peter" call by return team
- Incidental touching by the defense
- Fakes
- Quick tempo punts for slow or sluggish return teams
- Punt with normal offensive personnel (quick kick or the QB as the punter)

# Punt Rules and Regulations

- Any legal scrimmage kick should be made from behind the line of scrimmage.
- Any punt that touches a goal post is dead.
- NFL rules state that only the end men (eligible receivers) on the line of scrimmage are permitted to cross the line of scrimmage before the ball is kicked. College and high school rules do not contain such a provision.
- A blocked punt that does not cross the line of scrimmage can be recovered and advanced by either team.
- The kicking team may not advance its own kick, even though legal recovery is made beyond the line of scrimmage. They may gain possession only.
- A member of the receiving team may not run into or rough a kicker who kicks from behind his line unless contact (is):
    - ✓ Incidental to and after he had touched the ball in flight. NFHS rules state that if a punt blocker's teammate runs into the punter, it is not a foul.
    - ✓ Caused by the kicker's own motions, if it is incidental contact.
    - ✓ Occurs during a quick kick, a kick made after a run behind the line, or after the kicker recovers a loose ball, unless it becomes obvious a kick will be attempted.
    - ✓ Caused when a rusher is blocked into the kicker. NCAA rules state that he must be illegally blocked into the punter for it not to be a foul.
- If a member of the kicking team bats the ball out of the end zone it is ruled a touchback. NFHS rules declare any ball dead if it crosses the goal line.
- No inbounds member of the kicking team shall touch a punt that crosses the neutral zone before it touches an opponent. Illegal touching gives the receiving team the privilege of taking the ball at the spot of the violation. Illegal touching in the end zone is ignored.
- Any player may catch or recover the ball when the ball crosses the neutral zone and touches a player of the receiving team.
- A member of the receiving team is not deemed to have touched the ball if he is blocked into the ball.
- A member of the receiving team is deemed not to have touched the ball if the punt team batted the ball.
- If the ball is caught or recovered by a player of the receiving team, the ball is live. If the ball is caught or recovered by the punting team, it is declared dead at the spot.
- A ball simultaneously recovered by a member of each team is declared dead and is given to the receiving team.
- If a punt goes out of bounds between the goal lines or comes to rest inbounds, and no player attempts to possess it, the ball becomes dead and belongs to the receiving team at the spot.

- If the kick goes out of bounds behind the goal line, the ball becomes dead and belongs to the receiving team.
- A legal punt can be a punt or drop kick. High school rules allow the kick to be place kicked.
- A cover man who goes out of bounds on his own is ineligible to participate on that down. However, if the player is blocked out of bounds, he may participate if he attempts to return inbounds immediately (high school). NFL rules state that a player out of bounds cannot be the first person to touch the ball to down it.
- A return player attempting to catch the punt must be given an unimpeded opportunity to catch the ball.
- The cover team may not contact the potential receiver just before or simultaneously to his first touching the ball. The penalty is 15 yards from the spot of the contact. If this penalty occurs in the end zone, it is a touchback and the cover team is penalized from the succeeding spot.
- The ball is dead at the spot on a completed fair catch.
- When a team presents a punt formation, defensive pass interference is not to be called (unless a pass is thrown) for actions on the widest players eligible to go beyond the line. No NFL chuck rule exists; however, defensive holding may be called.

# Punt Axioms

- First touch rule: if the kicking team touches the ball, the receiving team can advance the ball without risk of losing possession. When downing the ball, the punt team should possess it. They should pick it up and hand it to the official. Hatch the ball.
- The punt team can advance a blocked punt, or a partially-blocked punt that does not cross the line of scrimmage.
- A partially-blocked punt that crosses the line of scrimmage is treated as a kick.
- Cover men should sprint in the assigned lane to the appropriate landmark. They should never follow the same colored jersey.
- A cover man should keep his shoulders square.
- Cover men should call out "fair catch" if it is signaled.
- If the return team makes a "Peter" call, the cover team should anticipate the ball hitting a returner. If this happens, they should fall on the ball since it cannot be advanced. Possession is the issue.
- The coverage team should keep the ball in front of them and never overrun the returner. They should come to balance five to seven yards from the return man.
- Timing goals to achieve:
  - ✓ Snap–0.75 seconds
  - ✓ Punter handling time–1.35 seconds
  - ✓ Total (snap to punt)–2.0/2.1 seconds
  - ✓ Hang time–4.3 seconds

# 5

# Punt Return/Block Team

Many coaches believe that a punt is the most important, and the most dangerous, play in football. Vast expanses of field position are lost or gained on each punt. Many coaches view a punt return as the first play of the offensive series; the yardage gained is no different than if it has been gained on a scrimmage snap. A blocked punt, or long return, changes both tempo and momentum, and many times a blocked punt will result in a score. One study of games over a 25-year period found that 90 percent of teams that had a punt blocked lost the game. Objectives for the punt return/block team include gaining possession of the ball, establishing field position, or breaking a big play with a long return or score.

## Key Elements of Punt Defense

### Returns

This element is an all out effort to return the ball. Sideline or middle returns can be used, and the type of return used can be based on the coverage used by the punt team, type of punter, and punt protection. Other variables such as field position, game situation, and weather considerations should be considered.

### Blocks

This element is an all out attempt to block the kick, or force a bad kick. This effort includes various numbers of rushers. A block attempt is based upon such variables as timing, protection, time left, field position, score, and so forth.

### Combination Return and Block

This combination can entail an all out block on one side of the formation while the opposite side sets up a return.

### Hold Up Returns

This type of return involves engaging the coverage team personnel throughout the entire play.

### Safe

This phase involves an all out effort to defend a potential punt fake. The defensive call has the objective of preventing a successful pass or run fake. The return team's focus is on covering all eligibles and deploying the rush to better play the fake.

# Personnel

Members of this special team usually belong to one of two general groups. The first, and largest, group is made up of blockers that block either an opponent or the ball. The second group, made up of only one or two people, handles the ball. The blockers should be physical enough to take on cover men on or near the line of scrimmage, fast enough to sprint down the field, and athletic enough to block in the open field. Quickness is the overriding quality needed. Not only do these individuals block for a return, but also they should be athletic enough to block the ball on a called pressure. A punt returner should possess good ball handling skills, be highly courageous in order to field a ball with opponents flying all around him, and be able to secure the ball and not turn it over.

# Philosophy

Teams approach punt defense differently. Some teams take a cautious and conservative approach, content to simply gain possession of the ball and return the ball, rather than take a chance to create a big play by applying pressure. Some teams, however, tend to be more offensive-minded when it comes to punt defense.

Aggressive coaches see punt defense as an opportunity to score a touchdown, or create a turnover. Teams with this mentality make use of prowling or moving the front to cause confusion with the protection scheme. Pressure can cause poor coverage and poor punts. When facing pressure, many punters will kick the ball quickly, which gives the coverage team less time to cover. Rushing the kick could also result in shanks or line drive kicks.

# Identification

When teaching communication and for game plan considerations, it is beneficial to number the members of both the punt team and punt defense team. Diagrams 5-1 through 5-5 show the various punt formations with eligible receivers denoted. Diagram 5-6 illustrates the numbering system for the punt defense team.

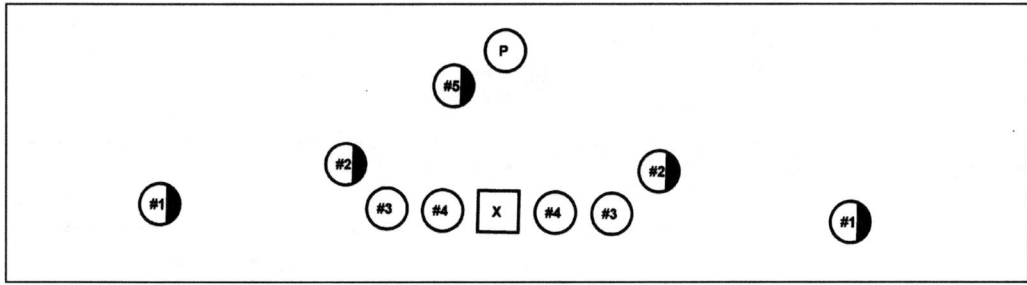

Diagram 5-1

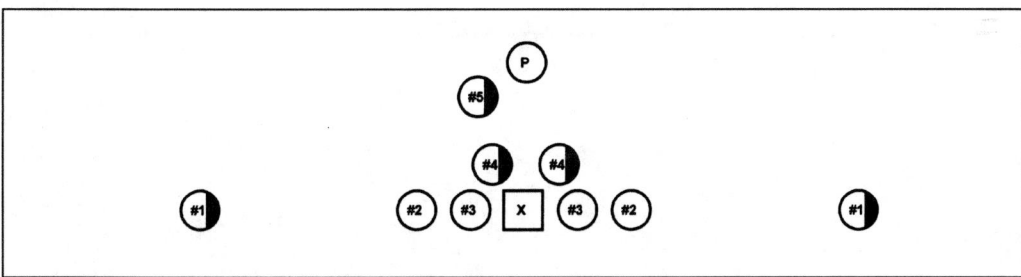

Diagram 5-2

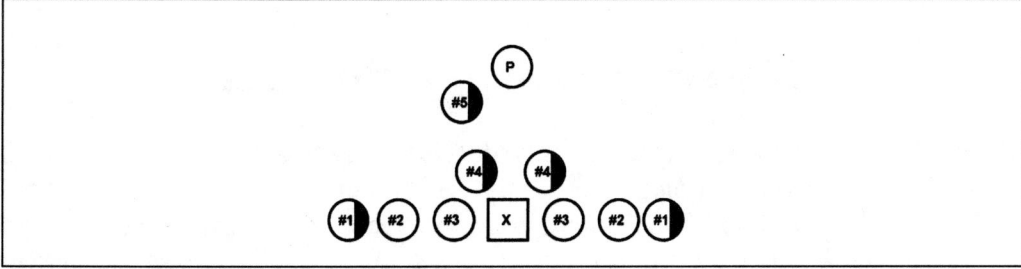

Diagram 5-3

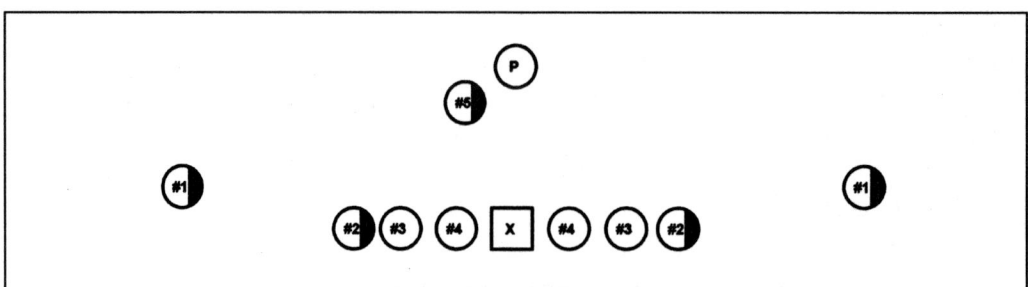

Diagram 5-4

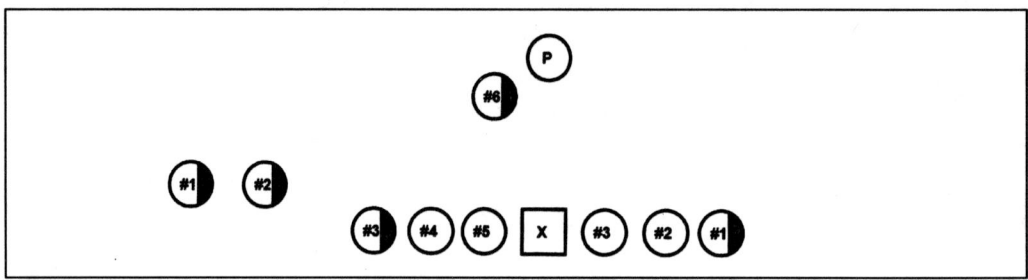

Diagram 5-5

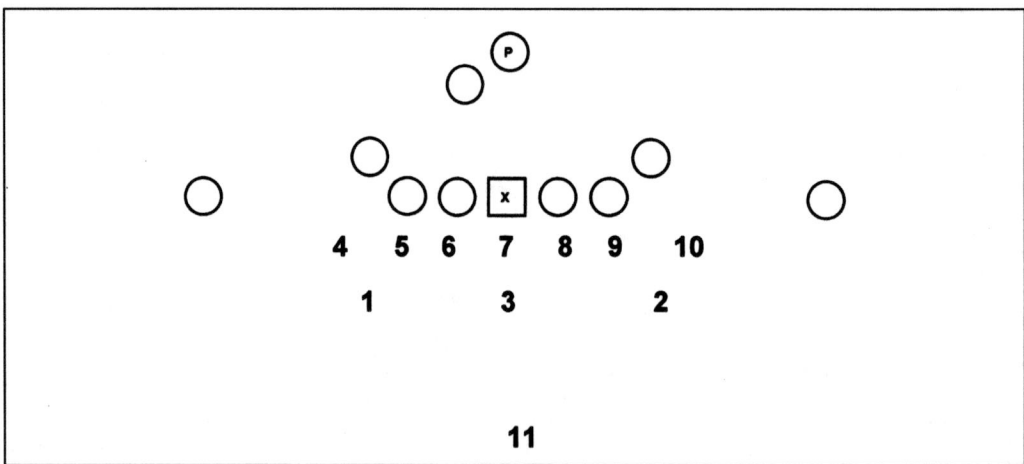

Diagram 5-6

# Blocking (Holdup) Techniques

This section deals with blocking techniques or schemes used on punt returns. Included will be information on the various ways to hold up and block gunners 1-on-1 or 2-on-1. Also included are ways to block and hold up interior cover men. More than one blocking scheme is needed to be effective against gunners, since these players are usually great athletes and have the advantage in which to maneuver.

## Whirlwind on a Gunner

A whirlwind block is a 2-on-1 block or holdup. Two men from the return team work in concert to nullify a gunner or anyone else designated on the cover team. When executing a double team, the following principles should apply:
- The defensive tandem should know the return call.
- Force the cover man to go a certain way.
- The cover man cannot be allowed to split the double team.
- Appropriate shoulder leverage must be used.
- Blocks should be above the waist and in front.
- Hands must be kept inside the framework of the body.

*Outside Release by the Gunner* (Diagram 5-7)

The outside man aligns with his inside eye on the gunner's outside eye. The inside man fits off the outside man's alignment. On an outside release by the gunner, the outside defender should use an aggressive bump and run technique, leveraging the gunner's inside shoulder with the outside half of his own body. From this position, the defender should keep a low shoulder position on the gunner. The inside defender should feather and ensure that the gunner does not dip under and escape inside. He should first seal off any inside escape, and then move downfield to work on the same level as the cover man.

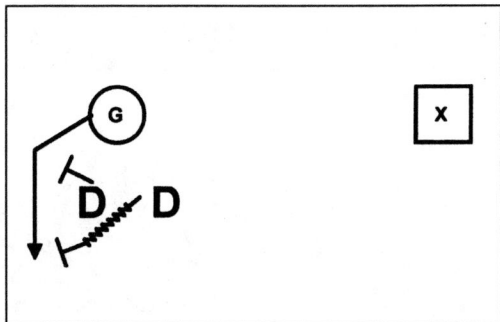

Diagram 5-7. Outside release by the gunner

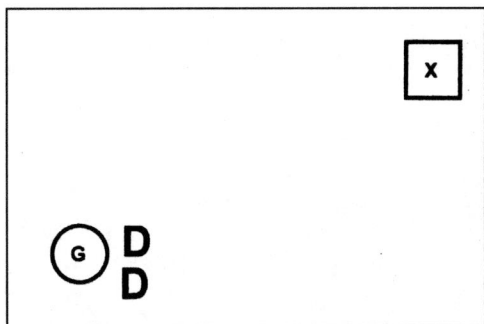

Diagram 5-8. Gunner downfielder

*Inside Release by the Gunner* (Diagram 5-9)

On an inside release by the gunner, the inside defender will use an aggressive bump and run technique, flattening the gunner as much as possible. The outside man will buzz over the top and keep outside leverage on the gunner. Once the gunner has given up the outside, he will be forced as far inside as possible, and will be driven inside and past the returner. When working downfield, the player with the best leverage will stay on the gunner, while his partner falls off to the alley and becomes the point man. A point man should sprint to meet the returner, time it up, and give the returner a point to cut off. The point man should block the most dangerous cover man, and should never get deeper than the ball.

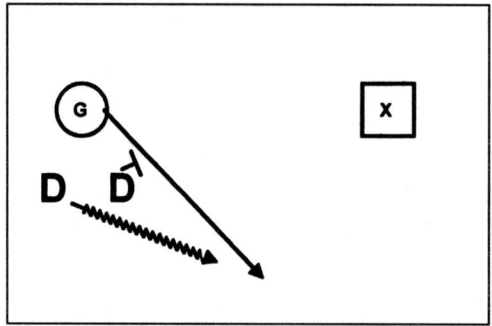

Diagram 5-9. Inside release by the gunner

## Whirlwind on an Interior Player (Diagram 5-10)

From film study and game plan, the holdup tandem will know which way the targeted man wants to release. The holdup men have an advantage on an inside man as opposed to a gunner because the inside man thinks they are part of a possible block. A good job of faking a block will facilitate the holdup. The holdup techniques described for a gunner are used in this situation also. In all probability, the slot will try to release outside.

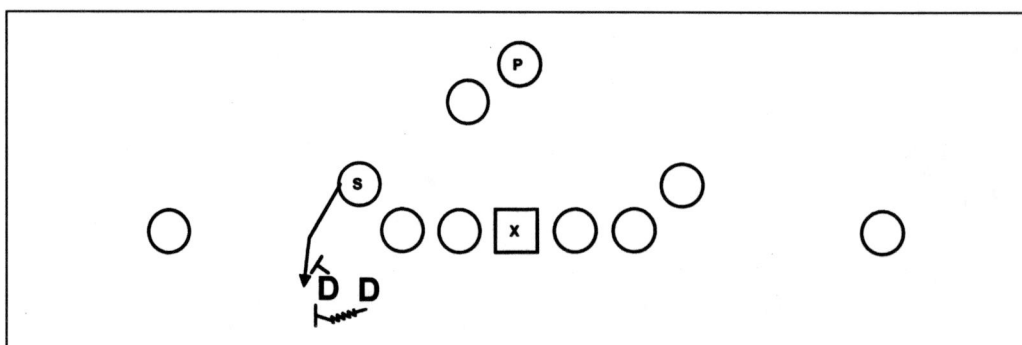

Diagram 5-10. Whirlwind on an interior player

## Vise on a Gunner

This blocking scheme, like the whirlwind technique, is also a 2-on-1 battle; however, it is somewhat different from the whirlwind. This holdup of the gunner has the inside defender using a mirror jab technique. The gunner is invited to go inside (Diagram 5-11).

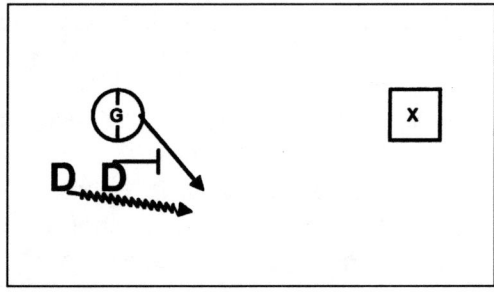

Diagram 5-11. Inside release

The inside defender aligns head up and overplays any inside release. He uses a quick, short, 45-degree step to the inside, while stabbing the gunner. The outside defender (who fits off the inside defender's alignment) will work from a trail technique to an overlap to a high shoulder angle, continuing to jam him inside, while the inside man stabs the gunner from a low shoulder position.

The initial alignment of both defenders serves to discourage an outside release. However, if the gunner chooses an outside release (Diagram 5-12), the inside man will punch with his outside hand, open up to the outside, and work the gunner to the outside man. The outside man will try to gain inside leverage, stab the gunner, and work him outside. From there, he will bump and run holding inside leverage. The inside man, in the meantime, feathers back, overlaps, and times it up so he can also jam the gunner inside-out as the three of them work downfield.

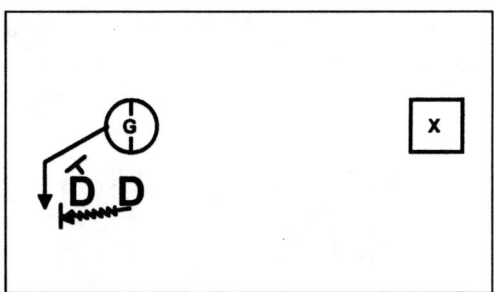

Diagram 5-12. Outside release

## Bump and Run on a Gunner

This technique is a 1-on-1 holdup or block on a gunner, which can be used on a punt block, or punt return. The main objective is to stay between the gunner and the ball, because the defender wants to force the gunner outside and make him run the long way to the ball. A defender using this technique should align as close to the gunner as possible, with his shoulders square to the line of scrimmage, and split the gunner's crotch with his outside foot. The defender aligns on the opponent's inside half with his hands held chest high and focused on the bottom of the gunner's numbers. Defenders using this technique should *never* bite on an outside fake because the defender wants him to go outside; however, he should *always* respect an inside fake.

When the gunner moves, the defender should step back with his inside foot, and then gather back to base. On an outside release, the blocker should open up at a 45-degree angle, which will keep him parallel (or just behind) in a trail technique. The defender wants a low shoulder attitude on the gunner, and should not allow the gunner to swat and duck inside and under him. On the snap, the holdup man should not overextend. If the cover man decides to go through the defender, the defender should strike him with the hard part of his hand and funnel him outside. From that position, the defender should run with him keeping inside leverage. At a point downfield, the gunner should decide whether to outrun the block, or slow and come underneath. The defender should squeeze into him and force him to try to outrun or take on the block.

## Stack on a Gunner

Another way to effectively nullify a good cover man is to work the 2-on-1 scheme from a stacked position. The closest man of the tandem can align inside or outside.

*Outside Stack* (Diagram 5-13)

The outside player in this tandem aligns with his inside foot on the gunner's outside foot. The defender plays from a squat position and forces the gunner inside, and fights to keep a low shoulder position on the cover man. The safety, who aligns 20 to 25 yards downfield, will attack out of the sky and squeeze the gunner's path. The squat player should *never* respect an inside fake but *always* respect an outside fake.

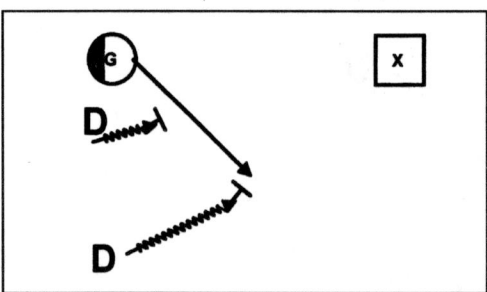

Diagram 5-13. Outside stack

*Inside Stack* (Diagram 5-14)

The inside player takes a hard inside shade by placing his outside foot on the gunner's inside foot. On movement he should work the gunner to the outside. He must *never* respect an outside fake but *always* respect an inside fake. The safety, who aligns 20 to 25 yards downfield, will attack out of the sky and widen the gunner's path.

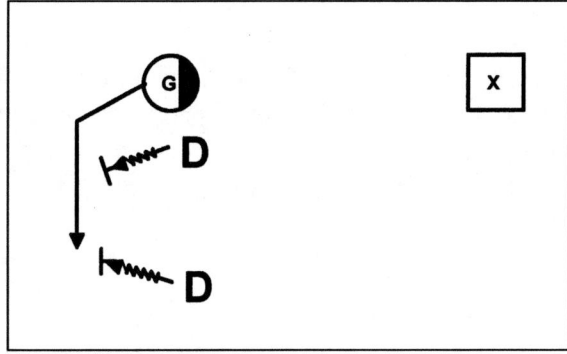

Diagram 5-14. Inside stack

## Pop Technique

Other members of the return team on the kicking team, with the exclusion of the gunners, use this holdup (or block) technique. A pop technique is a term that describes the actions used when attacking a kicking team player. The essence of this block is to attack the appropriate shoulder on a return. The return team members who use this holdup technique should know the directional call of the return, as well as how the targeted cover man releases. The fundamentals on this type of block are as follows:

- Hold the proper leverage.
- Hit the proper landmark.
- Block him above the waist and in front.
- Use hands to control the cover man.
- Keep the head up.
- Drop the tail and roll the hips.
- Hit upward and release the cover man away from the wall.

## Return Position

This technique is used after attacking the assigned cover man and releasing him away from the wall. The blocker should:

- Keep a yard vertical position in front of the assigned man.
- Keep a three- to five-yard position laterally from the man.
- Run with assignment at the proper angle.
- Time the block at a point 10 yards in front of the ball.
- Work hard to stay between the cover man and the ball.
- Block the assigned man immediately if he is losing him.
- Get his head in front when throwing the block. If this is not possible because of poor position, he should look for another man to either side or turn upfield.

## Sprint Technique

This technique is used when the assigned block is farther down the field. The blocker, after he uses a pop technique, releases his initial holdup assignment and sprints 25 to 30 yards downfield to execute his primary block. While sprinting back, he should keep proper leverage between the assigned man and the ball. At the point of contact, he should use a butt technique.

## Wall Technique

In a wall return, the defenders should sprint to the point of attack and gain width and depth. The first man in the wall should take the wall to the returner. The following defenders should keep a five-yard spacing between themselves and the next man toward the ball. Defenders should block toward the ball, but never block past the ball.

# Returns

## Force Man

On a return, at least one man should be assigned to force the punt. This man insures that the punter cannot hold the ball to allow for better coverage.

## Middle Return (Diagram 5-15)

#1/#4: Will whirlwind, vise, or stack on the gunner.

#3: Forces the punt. After he forces the kick, he peels back to block the first off-colored jersey.

#5: Attacks #3 inside out using a pop technique. He will leverage #3's inside shoulder and use a return technique on him.

#6: Attacks #4 inside out using a pop technique. He will leverage #4's inside shoulder and use a return technique on him.

#7: Attacks #4 inside out using a pop technique. He will leverage #4's inside shoulder and use a return technique on him.

#8: Attacks #3 inside out using a pop technique. He will leverage #3's inside shoulder and use a return technique on him.

#9: Attacks #2 inside out using a pop technique. He makes #2 release outside then head whips inside and picks up the personal protector.

#2/#10: They whirlwind, vise, or stack on the gunner.

#11: Fields the punt and gets north quickly.

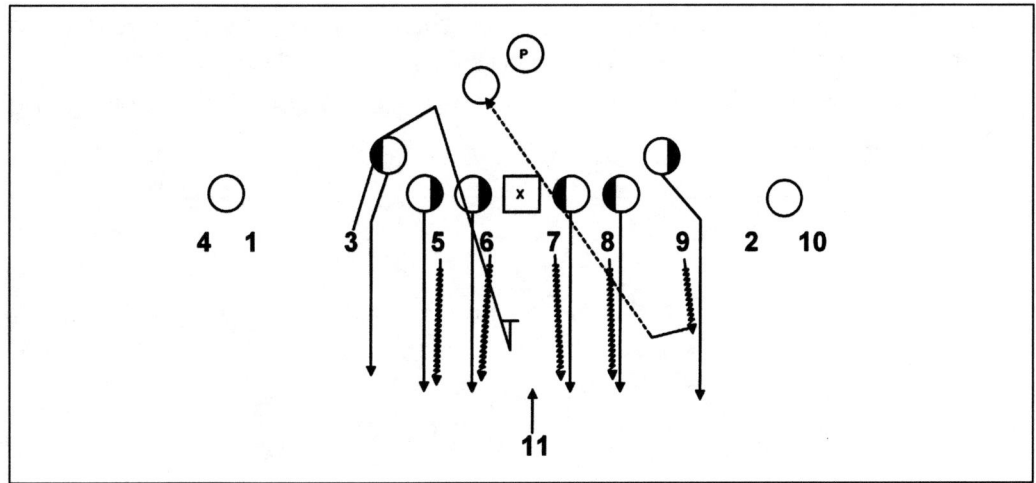

Diagram 5-15. Middle return

**Right Return** (Diagram 5-16)

Right return is a combination block and return. One side rushes the punter and then works their way to the wall if the ball is kicked. The side away from the rush forces their assigned men inside and away from the wall.

*#4*: Executes a bump and run technique on the gunner.

*#1*: Can align on his jump-off point, or he can creep. He tries to block the kick. If the ball is kicked, he continues and becomes the fourth man in the wall. He uses a wall technique.

*#5*: Aligns between the slot and the tackle. He tries to block the kick. If the ball is kicked, he continues and becomes the third man in the wall. He uses a wall technique.

*#6*: Aligns head up on the tackle. He tries to block the kick through B gap. If the ball is kicked, he continues and becomes the second man in the wall. He uses a wall technique.

*#7*: Shades the center to the block side. He tries to block the kick. He should go under the personal protector. If the ball is kicked, he continues and becomes the first man in the wall. He uses a wall technique.

*#8*: Aligns on the inside shoulder of the tackle. On the snap, he attacks the guard to his inside. He stabs and runs with the guard, and holds leverage on the guard by staying between the guard and the wall.

*#9*: Aligns head up on the slot. On the snap, he attacks the tackle to his inside. He stabs and runs with the tackle, and holds leverage on the tackle by staying between the tackle and the wall.

*#2*: Can align on his jump-off point, or he can creep. On the snap, he attacks the slot and holds leverage. He stabs the slot and runs him downfield staying between him and the wall.

*#3*: Stacks behind #7. On the snap, he will shuffle left to the slot and cover him man-to-man. After the ball is kicked, he attacks the gunner to the return side.

*#11*: After catching the ball, he will get north quickly to draw in the coverage. He then breaks to the wall.

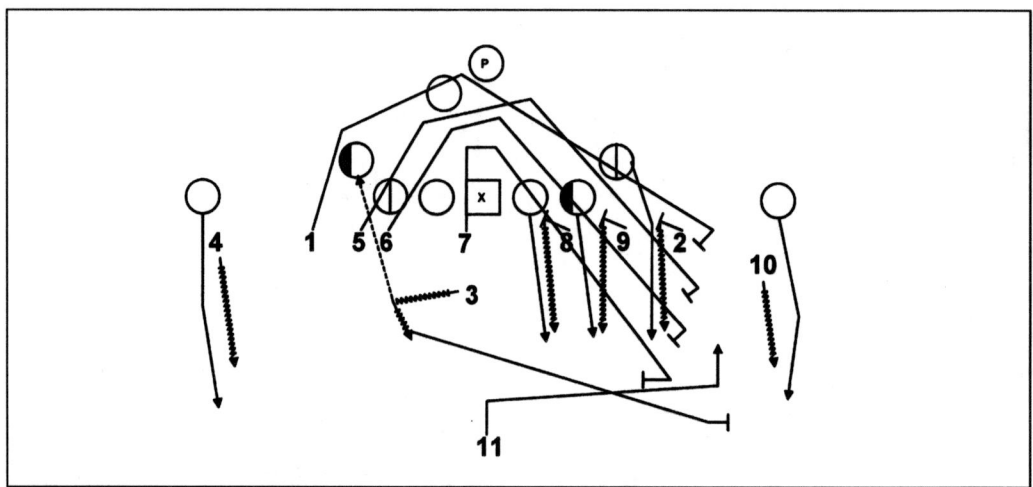

Diagram 5-16. Right return

## Throw Back Return (Diagram 5-17)

Every punt return package should have a trick or wrinkle. The throwback return takes advantage of a poorly disciplined coverage team, or functions as a surprise tactic.

*#4*: The recipient of the throwback, he aligns with an outside shade on the gunner, and forces the gunner inside by stabbing him inside 10-to-15 yards. At this point, he falls off outside and gets width and depth. He must be deeper than the ball, so a good rule to follow is to go to the depth of the catch. If the ball is kicked to the throwback area, the throwback phase will be aborted, and he should block for the returner.

*#5*: Blitz engages the slot. After he rides the slot for 10 to 15 yards, he releases him and peels off and sprints to #4. He should look to block for #4 at the point of the reception. He is the first man in the wall. He should use a wall technique.

*#1*: Pre-snap he should drop out to a depth of 20 to 25 yards. He should time it up and block the left gunner after #4 releases him. He should pin the gunner to the inside as the gunner recognizes the throwback and tries to recover.

*#6*: Aligns on the outside edge of the guard. He pops and pins the guard inside. He uses a return technique.

*#3*: Aligns over the ball. On the snap, he sprints to the returner, and protects the throw. He should lead the returner, and go to where the returner will be.

*#7*: Aligns head up on the guard. On the snap, he forces the kick. When the ball is kicked, he should sprint to the reception area. He is the second man in the wall. He should use a wall technique.

*#8*: Aligns inside shoulder of the tackle. He should leverage him by staying inside. He should use a return technique.

*#9*: Blitz engages the slot. He then peeks to see if the ball has been kicked, and becomes the number-three man in the wall. He should use a wall technique.

*#2/#10*: Use an inside stack technique on the gunner.

*#11*: After the catch, he starts upfield to his right, and should sell the return right run. After five to seven yards, he should stop, plant his outside foot, and throwback to #4. He must be sure the pass is backwards. If there is any off color in the throw lane, he should make sure the pass is *over* the man and not *through* him. If he is unsure about the safety of the throw, he should abort and keep the ball. If the kick is to his left, he should terminate the lateral and get what he can on a run. If the punt is short, he should simply fair catch the ball.

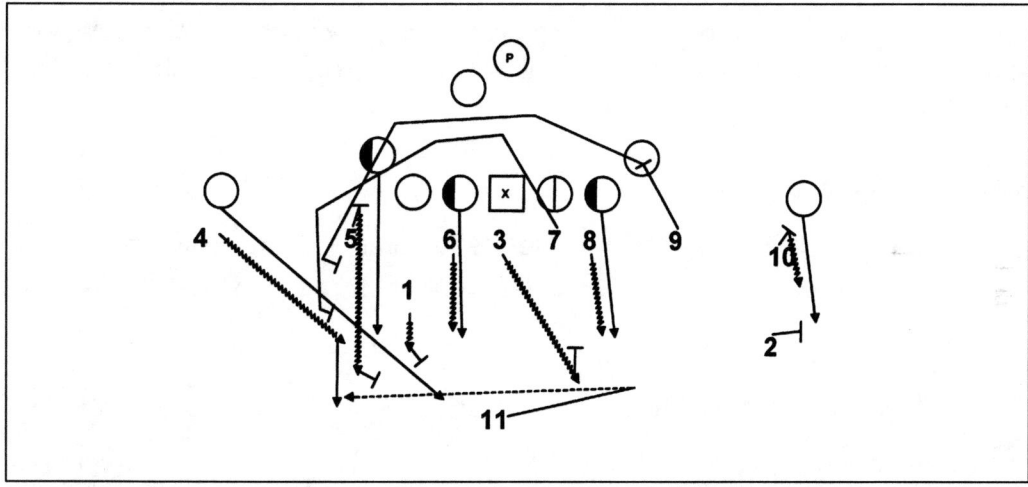

Diagram 5-17. Throw back return

# Pressures

### Punt Block Techniques

The following punt block techniques are used no matter the style or type of punt block. A correct stance is paramount to any punt block. The rusher should start in a sprinter's stance with his feet staggered and most of his weight on the down hand. The defender should place his hand just in front of the ball, and then get into his stance, crowding the ball as much as possible. The blocker should see the ball to facilitate a great takeoff.

One of the key ingredients to blocking a punt is a great takeoff. The rusher should be ready as soon as the center possesses the ball. Study and game plan pre-snap keys; additionally, study and take advantage of the center's mannerisms. If the center rocks or dips just prior to the snap, a defender can roll into and time-up his get off. On takeoff, the rushers should stay low and make themselves small by turning their shoulders  perpendicular to the line of scrimmage.

Lane rush integrity is crucial to a successful block. If a rusher deviates from his assigned lane, he could force other rushers out of their lanes. One offensive blocker can block multiple rushers if they clog up in a particular lane. If an offensive man takes on a rusher head up, the rusher should work to his assigned gap. If a rusher is blocked from the side, he should dip the nearest shoulder, rip through, and redirect toward his assignment. If the same color shows in a particular rusher's lane, he should overlap to the outside. At the launch point, the blocker should extend his arms and surge, instead of jumping or leaving his feet. If a rusher has to leave his feet, it should be a layout instead of a jump. The layout should be flat and parallel to the ground. At the contact point, the rusher should keep his eyes open and hands together with the thumbs touching. The blocker should look through the V of the hands with his eyes on the ball. A middle rusher should be very careful not to leave his feet, working to the side of the punter and placing his hands on the ball.

**Gap Eight Block** (Diagram 5-18)

#4: Takes the gunner man-to-man. He uses a bump and run technique.

#1: Blitz engages the slot. He draws the slot's block and then takes him man-to-man.

#5: Rushes the kick through the C gap.

#6: Aligns on the inside shoulder of the tackle. He rushes the kick through the B gap.

#7: Will get a right or left call from #3, giving #7 his assignment. He rushes the kick through the called gap.

#3: Gives #7 a right or left call. He goes opposite the call and rushes the kick.

#8: Aligns on the inside shoulder of the tackle. He rushes the kick through the B gap.

#9: Rushes the kick through the C gap.

#2: Blitz engages the slot. He draws the slot's block and then takes him man-to-man.

#10: Takes the gunner man-to-man. He uses a bump and run technique.

#11: Should fair catch a short kick. On a longer kick, he should get north and get what he can.

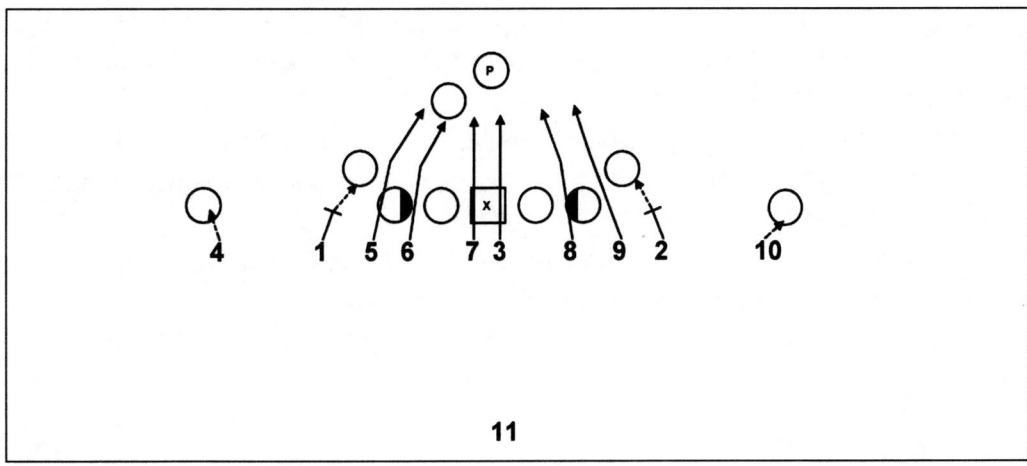

Diagram 5-18. Gap eight block

## Twist Block (Diagram 5-19)

From all appearances, this block is the same as the gap-eight block. However, on the snap, selected rushers twist or lane exchange.

*#4*: Takes the gunner man-to-man. He uses a bump and run technique.

*#1*: Blitz engages the slot. He draws the slot's block and takes him man-to-man.

*#5*: Aligns in C gap. On the snap he looks to go under the guard or tackle's block. He twists with #6.

*#6*: Aligns on the inside shoulder of the tackle. He rushes the B gap.

*#7*: Aligns on the right shoulder of the center. If the center blocks him, he rips and runs to the launch point; if the center blocks away from him, he attacks the inside shoulder of the personal protector.

*#3*: Aligns on the left shoulder of the center. If the center blocks away from him,

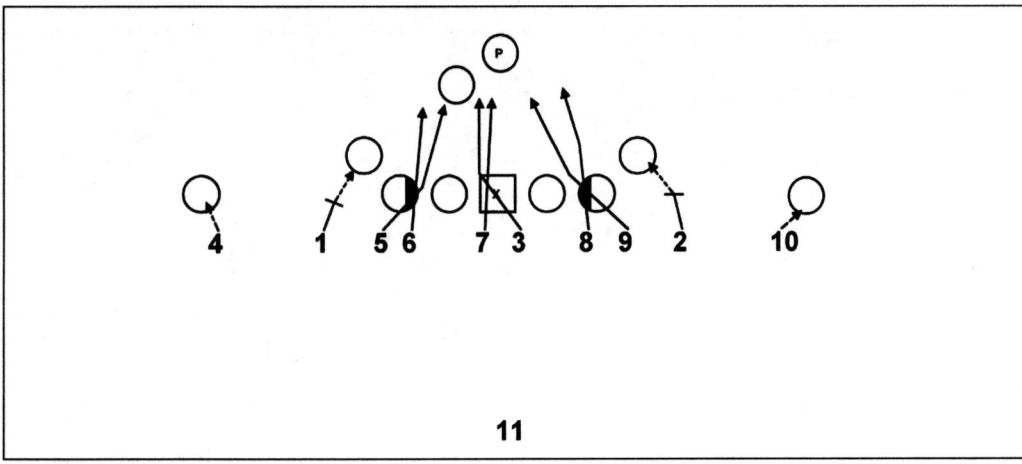

Diagram 5-19. Twist block

he tightens his angle and comes off the center's hip (#3 will go under the personal protector's block); if the center blocks toward him, he follows #7 and reads the personal protector's block on #7.

*#8*: Aligns on the inside shoulder of the tackle. He rushes the B gap.

*#9*: Aligns in the C gap. On the snap, he looks to go under the guard or tackle's block. He twists with #8.

*#2*: Blitz engages the slot. He draws the slot's block and takes him man-to-man.

*#10*: Takes the gunner man-to-man. He uses a bump and run technique.

*#11*: He should fair catch a short kick. On a longer kick, he should get north and get what he can.

### **Corner Loaded Block** (Diagram 5-20)

This particular block is a corner-loaded block with both edges attacked at the same time. A variation of this block can include a twist between #5 and #6 on the left side, and #8 and #9 on the right side.

*#4*: Takes the gunner man-to-man. He uses a bump and run technique.

*#1*: Rushes the D gap to the launch point. He may line up on the line, or he may creep from a wide alignment.

*#5*: Rushes the kick through the C gap.

*#6*: Aligns on the inside shoulder of the tackle. He rushes the kick through the B gap.

*#7*: #3 will give him a right or left call. From this alignment, he will bail outside and cover the slot to his side.

*#3*: He will give #7 a right or left call. #3 will then go opposite. From this alignment, he will bail outside and cover the slot to his side.

*#8*: Aligns on the inside shoulder of the tackle. He rushes the kick through the B gap.

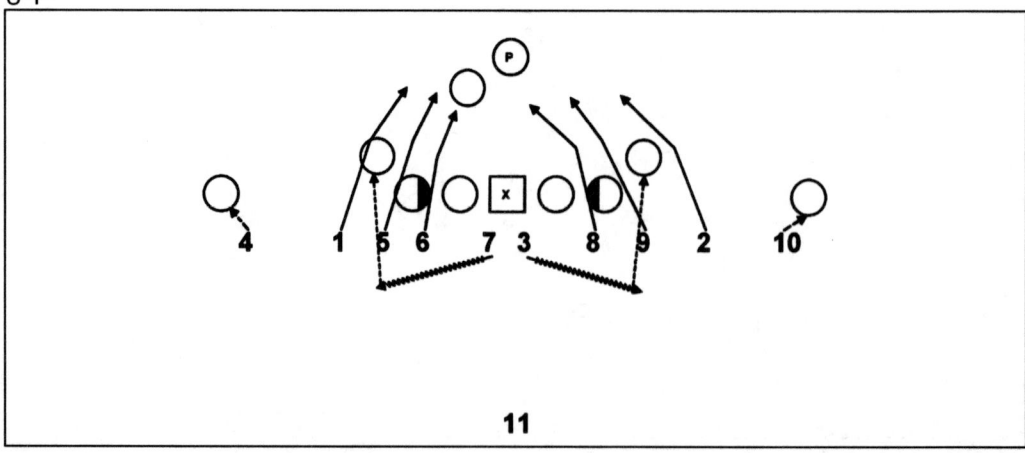

Diagram 5-20. Corner loaded block

*#9*: Rushes the kick through the C gap.

*#2*: Rushes the D gap to the launch point. He may line up on the line. or he may creep from a wide alignment.

*#10*: Takes the gunner man-to-man. He uses a bump and run technique.

*#11*: Should fair catch a short kick. On a longer kick, he should get north and get what he can.

## Overload Block (Diagram 5-21)

This block typifies the overloaded principle. This particular scheme overloads to the left, and is a planned block for a right-footed kicker.

*#4*: Takes the gunner man-to-man. He uses a bump and run technique.

*#1*: Rushes the D gap to the launch point. He may line up on the line or he may creep from a wide alignment.

*#5*: Rushes the kick through the C gap.

*#6*: Aligns on the inside shoulder of the tackle. He rushes the kick through the B gap.

*#7*: Gets a right or left call from #3. He rushes the kick through the called shoulder.

*#3*: Gives a right or left call to #7. He goes opposite the call and rushes the kick.

*#8*: Aligns on the inside shoulder of the tackle. He rushes the kick through the B gap.

*#9*: Aligns in the C gap. He gives the appearance that he is rushing the C gap; and then, just prior to the snap, he will bail across the ball and take the slot to that side man-to-man.

*#2*: Lines up outside the slot and blitz engages him. He takes the slot man-to-man. He may disguise his final alignment and creep from a wide alignment.

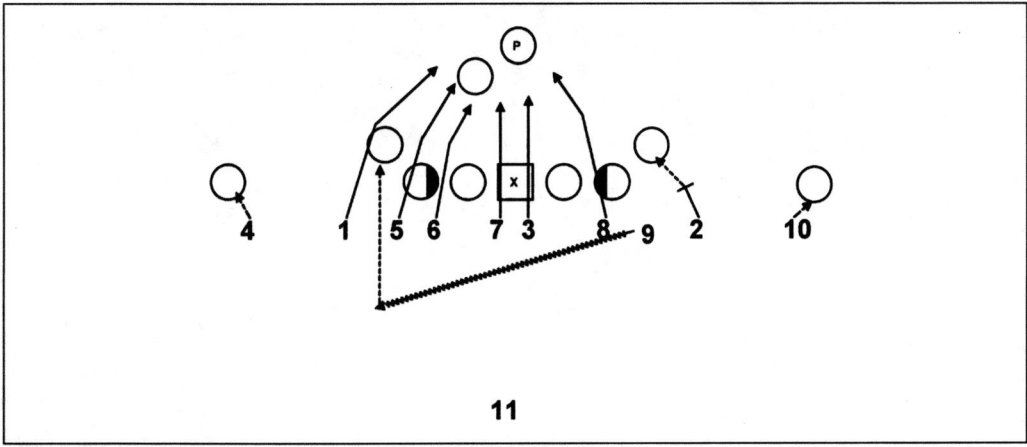

Diagram 5-21. Overload block

*#10*: Takes the gunner man-to-man. He uses a bump and run technique.

*#11*: Should fair catch a short kick. On a longer kick, he should get north to bait the coverage, and then return the ball to the overloaded side. The theory of returning left is that coverage should be softer on the overloaded side, because the offense will hold its blocks longer when they recognize the over-shifted rush.

**Sell the Farm** (Diagram 5-22)

Typically called near the end of a game when time is almost out, this type of block – an all out effort to block the kick – gives up coverage for a 10-man rush. Some teams will even bring 11 on this block. If the ball is successfully punted in this situation, for all intents and purposes the game is over. The chance for a fake punt is almost non-existent in this scenario. The ball must be blocked for the defensive team to have a legitimate chance to win the game.

*#4*: Rushes through the D gap. He must pre-align on the gunner and creep to his final jump off point.

*#5*: Rushes the kick through the C gap.

*#6*: Aligns on the outside shoulder of the guard. On the snap, he will clamp the guard and turn the guard's shoulders toward the sidelines. He is opening up a lane for a run-through by #1.

*#7*: #3 will give him a right or left call. He rushes the kick through the called gap. He should rush tight to avoid running into #1.

*#3*: Will give #7 a right or left call. He goes opposite the call and rushes the punt. He should rush tight to avoid running into #2.

*#8*: Aligns on the outside shoulder of the guard. On the snap, he will clamp the guard and turn the guard's shoulders toward the sidelines. He is opening up a lane for a run-through by #2.

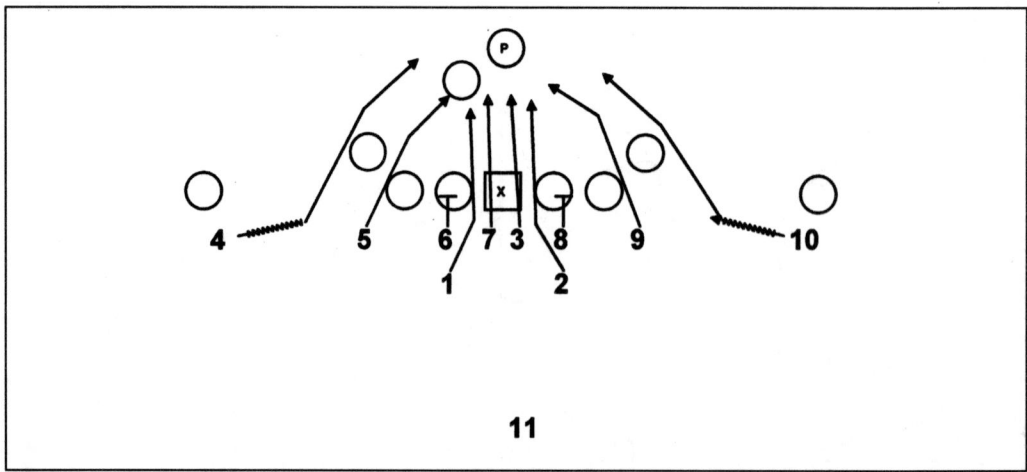

Diagram 5-22. Sell the farm

*#9*: Rushes the kick through the C gap.

*#10*: Rushes through the D gap. He should pre-align on the gunner and creep to his final jump-off point.

*#1*: Stacks behind #6. On the snap, he will run through the gap opened up by #6. #1 should rub tight off the guard, or he will become entangled with #7. He should read the personal protector's block. If the protector tries to block him, he stays to his outside; if the protector blocks #7 or steps away from #1, he should fit tight on his outside hip.

*#2*: Stacks behind #8. On the snap, he will run through the gap opened up by #8. #2 must rub tight off the guard, or he will become entangled with #3.

*#11*: Because of the situation, he should field the kick and get what he can.

# Safe Calls

No punt defense package is complete without schemes that are tailored to defeat fake attempts. Included in this package are three different types of safe calls. They include safe calls with inside force, outside force, and a built in five-man pressure. Game considerations such as time left, field position, and score determine which safe call to use.

### Safe with Inside Force (Diagram 5-23)

This call is a conservative call that involves nine men playing a possible fake and one man forcing the kick. It is used whenever there is a distinct possibility the punt team will fake the punt. #1, #2, #3, #4, and #10 cover eligible receivers, while #7 forces the kick.

*#4*: Takes the gunner man-to-man. He plays inside bump and run.

*#5*: Pins the outside shoulder of the tackle and gets his eyes into the backfield. He will use a holdup technique. If the ball is faked away from him, he looks for a throwback to either the personal protector or the kicker.

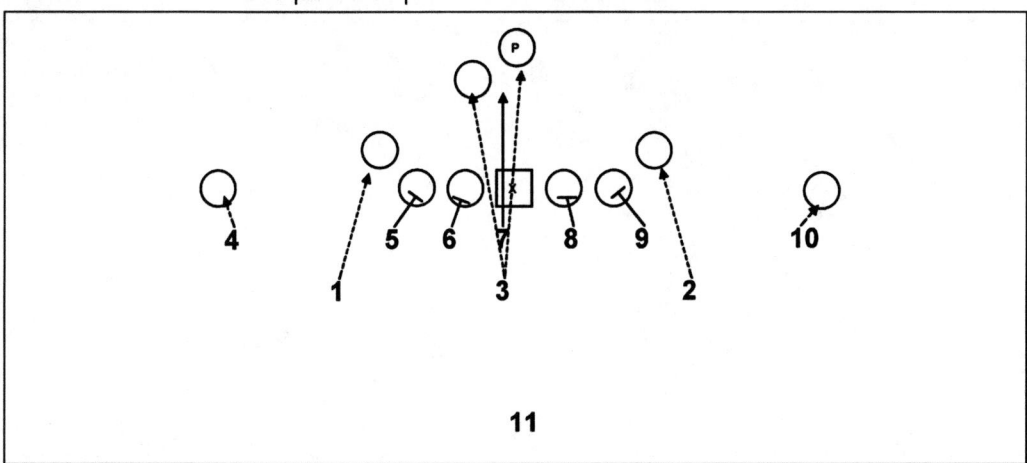

Diagram 5-23. Safe with inside force

**#6:** Pins the outside shoulder of the guard and gets his eyes into the backfield.

**#7:** Aligns on the center to the punter's foot side. He forces the kick.

**#8:** Pins the outside shoulder of the guard and gets his eyes into the backfield.

**#9:** Pins the outside shoulder of the tackle and gets his eyes into the backfield. He will use a holdup technique. If the ball is faked away from him, he looks for a throwback to the personal protector or the kicker.

**#10:** Takes the gunner man-to-man. He plays inside bump and run.

**#1:** Aligns five yards deep. He covers the slot man-to-man. If the ball is kicked, he should jump underneath the slot and stay between him and the ball.

**#3:** Aligns five yards deep. He is responsible for both the personal protector and punter. If either one shifts, he will take him; if the ball is kicked, he becomes the point man.

**#2:** Aligns five yards deep. He covers the slot man-to-man. If the ball is kicked, he should jump underneath the slot and stay between him and the ball.

**#11:** The returner should field the punt and get north immediately. He should try to get to the outside of the tackle and inside of the slot to either side. If there is no one in the punting position, he should move to within 15 yards of the ball and play the hole.

**Safe with Outside Force** (Diagram 5-24)

This safe scheme is very similar to the previous safe scheme, with numbers 1, 2, 3, 4, and 10 having the same assignment. Numbers 5 and 9 force the kick while #7 two gaps the center with his eyes fixed on the backfield. Numbers 6 and 8 attack the tackle's inside shoulder, while eyeballing the backfield. The returner should fair catch the ball if he feels pressure. If he returns the ball, he should get what he can without taking a big hit. If no one is in the punting position, he should move to within 15 yards of the ball and work down and play the hole.

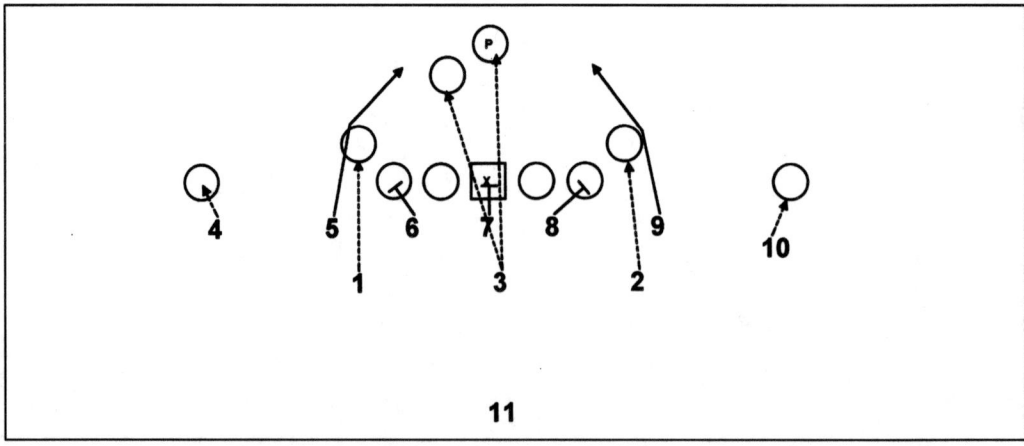

Diagram 5-24. Safe with outside force

**Safe with a Five-Man Pressure** (Diagram 5-25)

This call combines a safe concept with a five-man block scheme.

#4: Takes the gunner man-to-man. He plays inside bump and run.

#1: Rushes the punt through the D gap. He can line up outside the slot or he can creep.

#3: Rushes the kick through the C gap.

#5: Aligns in the B gap. Just prior to the snap, he bails and takes the slot man-to-man.

#6: Aligns head up on the guard. On the snap, he rips inside the guard and attempts to block the kick.

#7: Aligns head up on the guard. On the snap (or just prior to the snap), he bails and takes the personal protector and/or the punter.

#8: Aligns head up on the tackle. On the snap (or just prior to the snap), he bails and takes the slot man-to-man.

#9: Rushes the C gap.

#2: Rushes the punt through the D gap. He can line up outside the slot, or he can creep.

#10: Takes the gunner man-to-man. He plays inside bump and run.

#11: The returner should favor the left side on a return because coverage should be slower on that side because of an overload to that side.

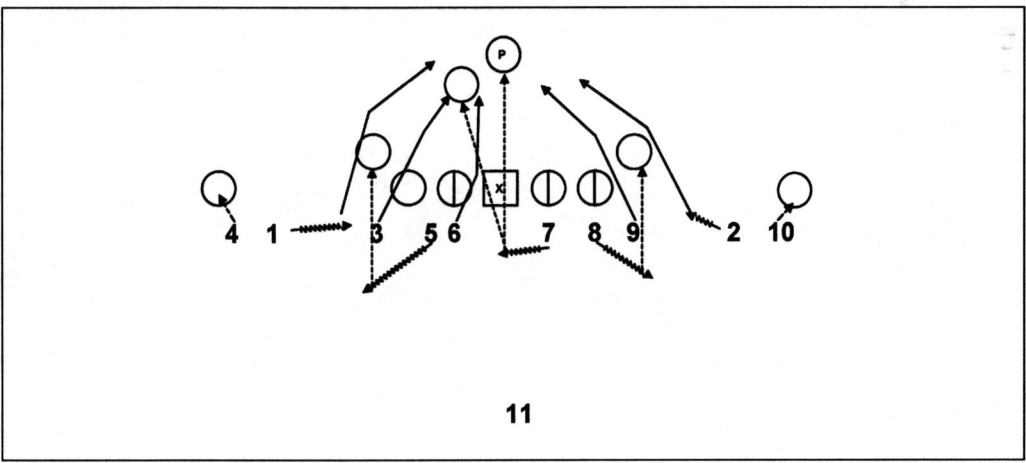

Diagram 5-25. Safe with a five-man pressure

# Emory and Henry Punt Formation

A recent phenomenon is the use of the Emory and Henry formation, popularized offensively in recent years by Steve Spurrier, as a punt formation. Steve Brewer, one of the originators of this punt concept, has written several articles and has spoken at numerous clinics on the use of this formation. The beauty of this formation, as a punt set, is that everyone except the center can be eligible.

This formation causes a lot of teams to give up on pressuring kicks, and instead they become passive and try to play pass defense. Valuable defensive practice time must be taken to thoroughly cover all the possibilities. Following is a good antidote to the Emory and Henry punt package. The thought process is to make a fourth down call in anticipation of the opponent using a basic punt formation. The call may be for a return, block, or safe. If the opponent comes out in the Emory and Henry formation, the defense automatically goes into the Emory and Henry defensive package. If the punt team shifts from the Emory and Henry into a regular punt formation, the defense checks into the original call.

The following are the basic formations of the Emory and Henry package and the defensive response. Most teams align off the ball and then shift up or back with a move call. The first priority in defending the formation is to identify the eligibles. Eligibles are identified in each of these formations.

**Pre-Shift Basic Defensive Alignment** (Diagram 5-26)

The first priority is to identify potential eligibles. Communication, at this stage is essential. When the offense moves into its final formation, the defense has about five seconds to identify and make its adjustments. The following are formations that can be employed and the defense's response.

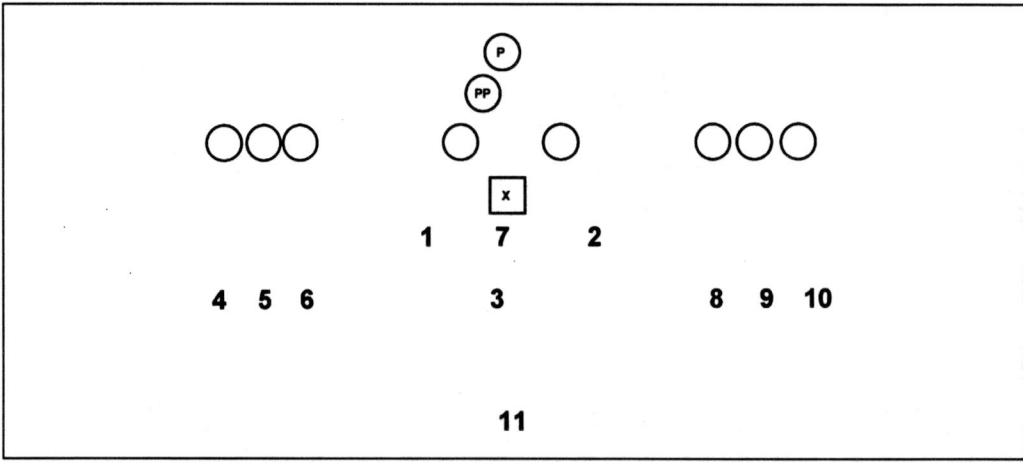

Diagram 5-26. Pre-shift basic defensive alignment

96

## Two Off in the Middle (Diagram 5-27)

*#4/#10*: Cover the widest receivers man-to-man.

*#5/#9*: *Shooters*. They line up as close to the line of scrimmage as possible. If the ball is snapped, they break across the line and attempt to intercept the ball. They should treat any throw as a lateral, possess the ball, and score.

*#6/#8*: *Adjusters*. They move inside and take the guards man-to-man.

*#1/#2*: *Rushers*. They rush just outside the widest man.

#7: Rushes the punter on his foot side.

#3: Takes the upback or the punter; whichever man does not get the snap.

*#11*: Fields the ball if it is kicked. If the ball is snapped to the upback, he should move to within 15 yards of the ball and play the hole.

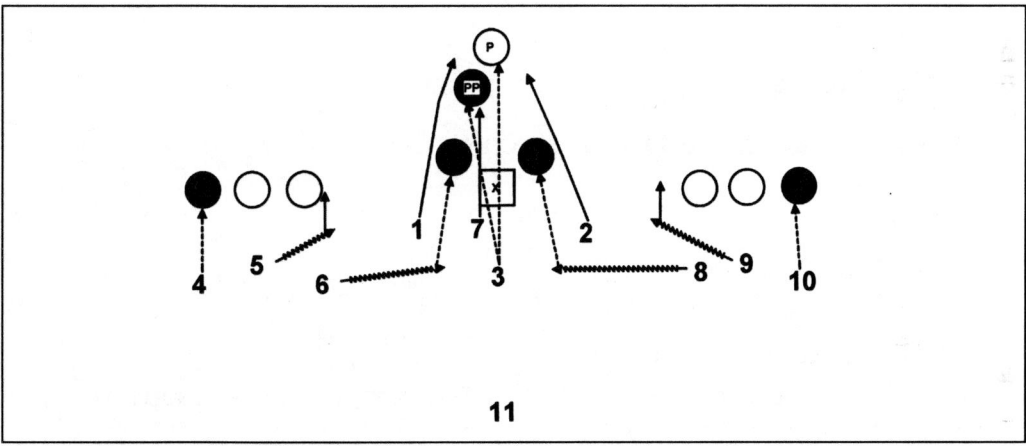

Diagram 5-27. Two off in the middle

## Two Off On the Left (Diagram 5-28)

*#4/#10*: Cover the widest receivers man-to-man.

#5: Covers #2 man-to-man.

#6: Covers #3 man-to-man

*#1/#7/#3/#2*: Rush the kick.

*#8*: *Adjuster*. He moves inside and takes the upback man-to-man.

*#9*: *Shooter*.

*#11*: Fields the ball if it is kicked. If the ball is snapped to the upback, he should move to within 15 yards of the ball and play the hole.

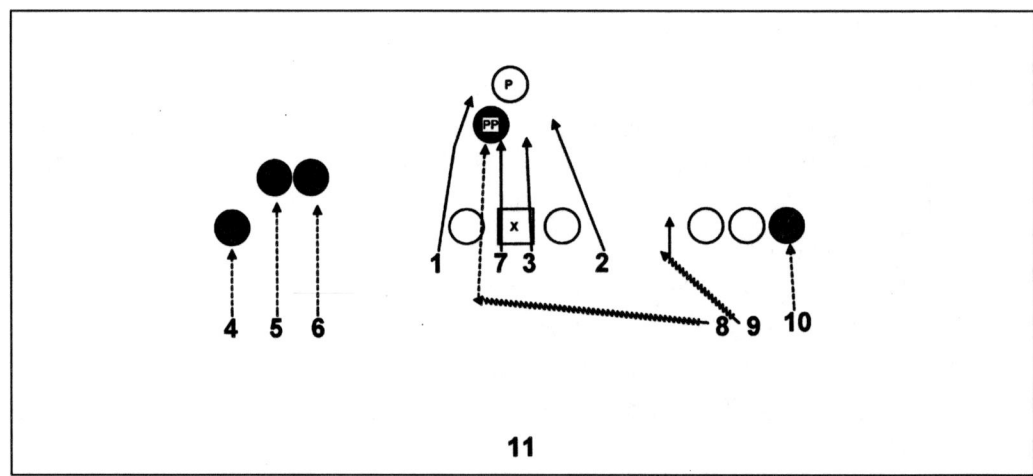

Diagram 5-28. Two off on the left

## Two Off on the Right (Diagram 5-29)

   #4/#10: Cover the widest receivers man-to-man.

   #5: Shooter.

   #6: Adjuster.

   #1/#7/#3/#2: Rush the kick.

   #8: Covers #3 man-to-man.

   #9: Covers #2 man-to-man.

   #11: Fields the ball if it is kicked. If the ball is snapped to the upback, he should move to within 15 yards of the ball and play the hole.

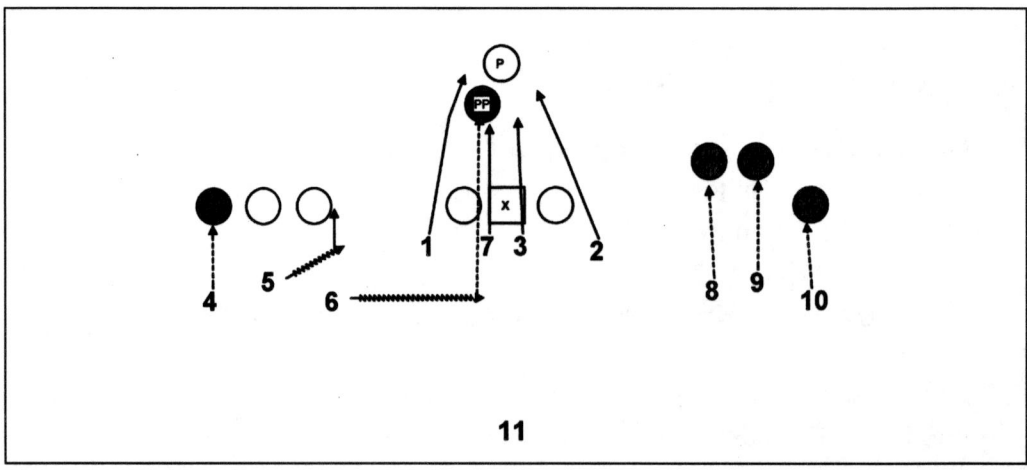

Diagram 5-29. Two off on the right

## One Off on Both Sides (Diagrams 5-30 through 5-32)

A team can align versus a one off on both sides in various ways; however, the reactions are the same for each.

*#4/#10*: Cover the widest receivers man-to-man.

*#5*: Shifts inside and takes #3 man-to-man.

*#6*: Versus one off to his side, he will insert into the rush. He will give a "company" call to #1, which tells #1 to go under the upback on his rush.

*#1/#7/#3/#2*: Rush the kick.

*#8: Adjuster.*

*#9*: Shifts inside and takes #3 man-to-man.

*#11*: Fields the ball if it is kicked. If the ball is snapped to the upback, he should move to within 15 yards of the ball and play the hole.

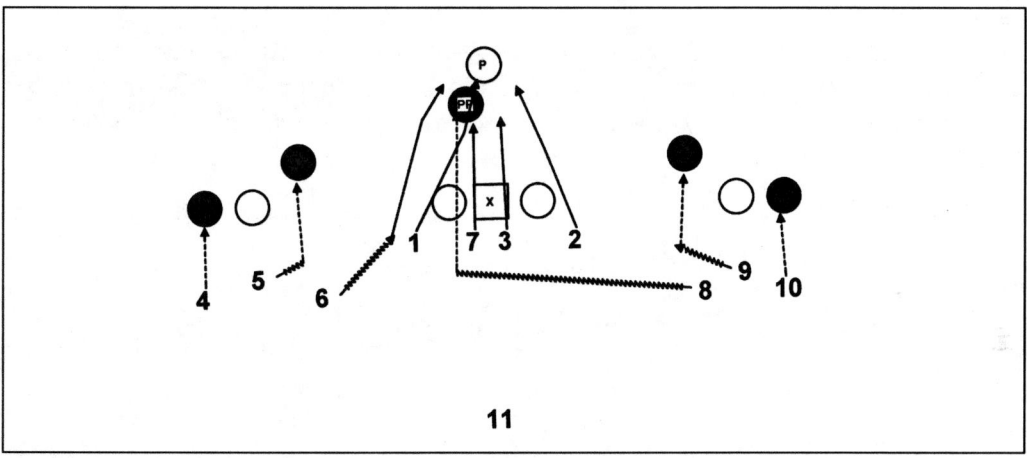

Diagram 5-30

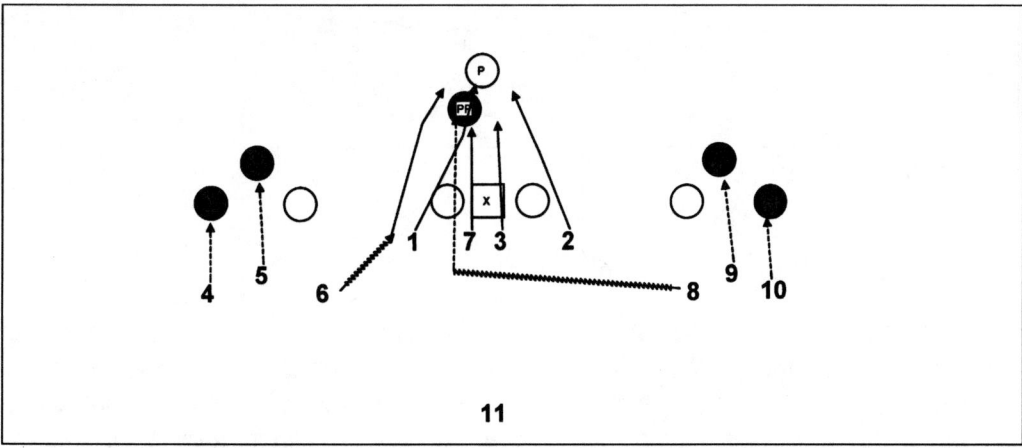

Diagram 5-31

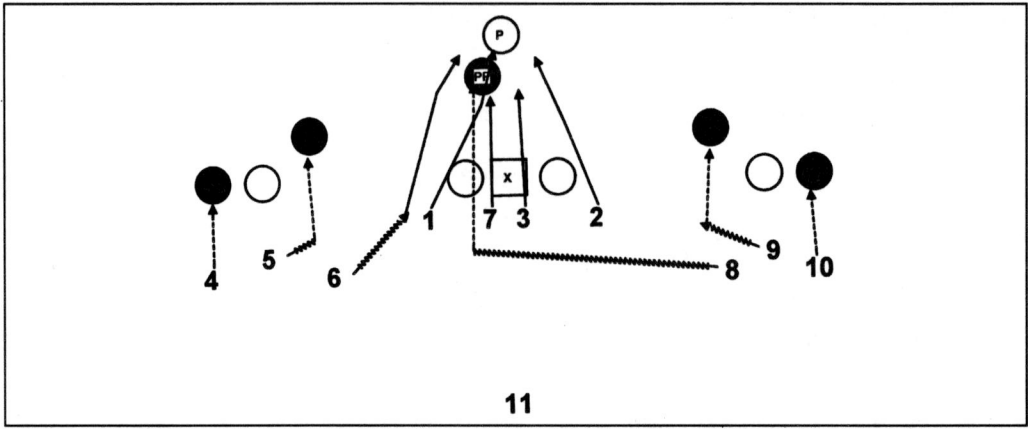

Diagram 5-32

## Motion (Diagram 5-33)

The defender assigned to the receiver who went in motion will handle motion. The basic rule is "once yours, always yours." If the ball is snapped to the upback, the returner will move toward the line of scrimmage to the side away from the motion and take the punter out the backdoor.

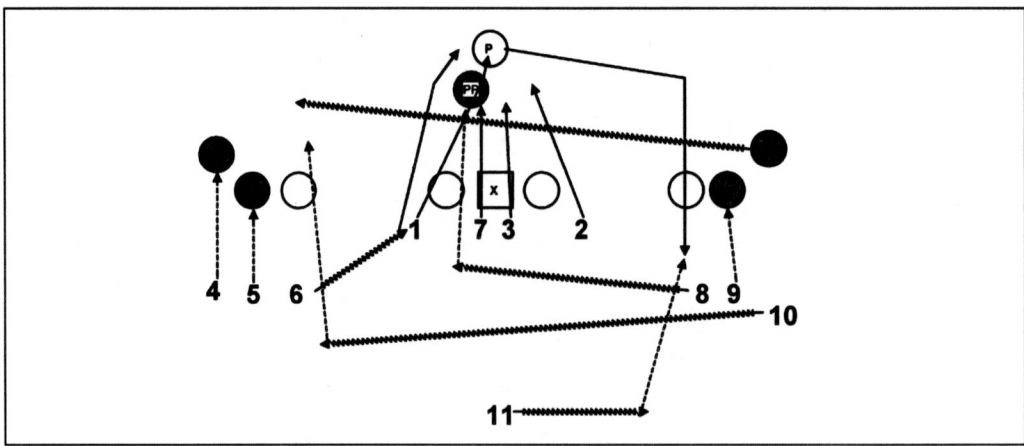

Diagram 5-33. Motion

# Return Man

The punt returner should understand that he has a great opportunity along with a great amount of responsibility. On one hand, he can break a play that would greatly benefit his team; on the other hand, he should be cognizant of the fact that a miscue by him can greatly harm his team. He should possess the mentality that he can score on any play, while recognizing when not to force the issue.

A punt returner faces a myriad of problems that the kickoff returner does not. One major difference is that the punt returner does not see the ball as easily from the launch point as the kickoff returner, his view blocked by both offensive and defensive players. He should pick up the flight of the ball as quickly as possible so he can discern its direction and depth. The punt returner, unlike the kickoff returner, does not have to field the kick. The kicking team cannot gain possession of the ball on a punt unless the ball touches a return team member. He may choose to field the ball, or he may choose to make a "Peter" call, which signals to his teammates that the ball will not be caught and will hit the ground; this important decision should be made by the punt returner. Another disadvantage a punt returner has to deal with is that a punt will usually spiral, making it difficult to judge.

In preparation for fielding a punt, the returner should be cognizant of the return call, score, time, field position, and weather conditions. He should especially be aware of wind conditions, checking field level flags or toss grass into the air to get a feel for wind direction. Additionally, he is in the best position to count the number of punt return members on the field, so he should be coached on what to do if either too many or not enough men are on the field. His alignment is dictated by game plan and wind conditions. He should know exactly how many yards he is from the line of scrimmage at all times. Returners should be coached to field all punted balls if possible. Statistics show that, on average, the return team loses 15 yards when a ball hits the ground. A returner must have a goal of gaining at least 10 yards (one first down) on every punt return. Many returners wait for the punt similar to a tennis player who bobs and weaves as he waits to receive a serve. When he picks up the flight of the ball, he should sprint full speed to the anticipated catch spot. If he gets to the catch spot early, it gives him time to adjust to the ball.

As the returner ascertains the correct line of the kick, he should focus on the front tip of the ball. If the ball begins to turn over, the returner knows the ball will usually carry to his right. A kicked ball that begins its descent with the nose still up will usually be shorter and will have a tendency to travel to the returner's left. A nose up punt will also drop much more quickly than a nose over punt. Once a returner decides where the ball will land, he should then cleanly field the ball.

Despite some major differences, many aspects of catching a punt are similar to a kickoff. The returner should form a pocket (extended upward toward the ball) by placing his hands together with the little fingers touching and palms up. He should keep his elbows in and use his forearms and chest to expand the pocket. The returner's feet should square up to the line of scrimmage if possible, and his feet should be under his body. The ball should first be contacted near the shoulder area, and the ball drawn into the returner's chest. On contact, the return man should bend slightly at the knees and waist to cushion the ball. He should look the ball all the way to the tuck. The ball should be put away before he eyeballs the coverage. Most fumbles or muffs occur when the return man takes his eyes off the ball too quickly, allows the ball to contact his pads, attempts to field a ball he should have not, or when he disdains a fair catch.

The punt returner should be coached to fall on a muff or dropped ball unless there is absolutely no pressure. If the ball does hit the ground, it is permissible to play it on one good bounce; if a ball bounces more than once, or the ball takes a tricky bounce, he should yell "Peter" and get away. He should, however, be alert for first touch. Experienced returners may be allowed to return a rolling punt if they can pick the ball up while facing the cover team. A mortar shot that carries over the returner's head and hits the ground, can be fielded if the returner will first circle the ball so he can face the coverage team as he decides whether to field the kick or not.

If a punt is away from the called return, the returner should be disciplined enough to take it straight upfield and get what he can. A good returner should make the first man miss. On sideline returns, the returner should draw the coverage toward the middle of the field by running straight ahead three or four steps before breaking to the wall. If a block is called, he should get north; if an overloaded block is called, he should run to the side of the overload. As a basic rule, a returner should not field a punt inside his own 10-yard line.

# Fair Catch

To be entitled to a fair catch, the returner must raise one arm full length above his head and wave it from side to side. This signal enables the receiver to catch the ball without interference from the cover team. The cover team may not interfere with the ball, the returner's path to the ball, or hit the returner after he catches the ball. A player who signals for a fair catch is not required to actually catch the ball; however, a player who signals for a fair catch may not block a member of the coverage team. If a punt hits the ground, or a member of either team, the fair catch situation is off and all rules for a kicked ball apply. If the returner advances the ball after a fair catch, his team is penalized for delay of the game. Many returners will fake a fair catch on a punt inside the 10-yard line. A better strategy might be to sprint up the middle or either sideline in the direction of the kick, and fake a running catch.

A fair catch should be used on short kicks with good coverage or great hang time. A fair catch might be advantageous when an eight-man block has been called. If the weather is rainy, it might be better to allow the ball to hit the ground because the ball will not roll far on the wet turf.

# Punt Return/Block Checklist

## Returns

- Directional kicks
- Short kicks
- Kicks away from return call
- Fair catch
- "Peter"
- First touch rule
- Various coverage schemes
- Various containment schemes
- Punt from end zone
- Return change-ups
- Multiple fronts
- Safe
- Fakes
- Offensive play
- Quick kick
- Tight punt

## Blocks

- Reaction to blocked punt (behind line of scrimmage)
- Reaction to blocked punt (crosses line of scrimmage)
- Fourth down block
- Third down block
- Safe versus shifts/motion
- Returns after rush

## Receivers

- Into the sun
- Into the wind
- With wind
- With a crosswind
- Wet ball
- In a crowd
- Pooch kick
- Fair catch
- Catch on the run (short kick)
- Rolling punt
- Rocket punt
- Sideline kick

# Punt Return Rules and Regulations

- The return team may not block below the waist or make contact with the back of an opponent. It is legal to block a man out of bounds, or a man who has returned from out of bounds, but it is illegal to block a man while he is out of bounds.
- The cover team must possess the ball to down it, or touch it after it comes to rest. If the cover team only touches the ball while it is still moving, the ball can be picked up and advanced by the return team (first touch rule). The ball is live until an official blows the ball dead. The return team can advance the ball and have the outcome of the play or have the ball at the spot of the illegal touch.
- If the return man carries the ball into the end zone, he may not down it. He must bring it out of the end zone, or it is a safety; however, if the returner's momentum carries the ball into the end zone, he does not have to bring it out. It will go to the spot of the catch if the ball is declared dead in the end zone in the return team's possession.

- A returner has the right to catch the ball whether he signals for a fair catch or not.
- The ball cannot be advanced after a valid fair catch signal (NFHS-NCAA). NFL rules allow the ball to be advanced if the ball touches the ground or the ball strikes a kick team member.
- The cover team may not advance a muff; however, if the returner has gained possession and then fumbles the ball, the kick team may advance it.
- A blocked punt that does not cross the line of scrimmage is a free ball and can be advanced by either team.

# Punt Return Principles

- Do not allow assigned man to make the tackle.
- Attack assigned man pad under pad with the proper leverage.
- Do not allow assigned man to release toward the wall.
- Block with head in front.
- Keep hands within the framework of your body.
- Block above the waist.
- Stay on your feet.
- Block assigned man at least 10 yards from the returner.
- Block toward the returner if in a wall.
- Block the area between self and teammate toward the ball.
- Stay on assigned man if he falls or is knocked down. Do not look for other work.
- Apply quick pressure, and then gather if assigned to force the kick. Quick pressure might force a bad kick. Quick force also does not allow the punter to hold the ball longer so coverage can develop.
- Recognize formation or personnel changes, since they offer tip-offs on fakes.
- Avoid fielding a punt inside the 10-yard line.
- Make sure the ball is kicked.
- Do not block behind the ball, but do protect the returner near the end of the run.
- Know that a punt return is considered a change of possession play. If time is a consideration, the returner does not have to get out of bounds to stop the clock. A time out will be called at the end of the play.
- Do not be offside. Be ready for a shift.
- Do not give away return or block by stance.
- Catch the ball. Do not allow it to hit the ground.
- A blocked punt that crosses the line of scrimmage is treated as if it has not been touched. It is a "Peter" situation. The return team should not touch the ball.

- A fourth down punt that does not cross the line of scrimmage should be a scoop and score situation. A quick kick or a third down punt should be recovered to gain possession.

# Punt Block Axioms

- Align as close to the ball as possible.
- Keep down hand out in front of the head.
- Key the ball. Get a great jump on the snap.
- Stay low on the charge. Become small by turning the shoulders toward the ball. Run behind pads.
- Understand the block point will be well out in front of the spot where the kicker originally aligned. The actual block area will be a yard in front of the punter's foot.
- Take the ball off the punter's foot.
- Run through the block point. Do not leave feet if possible. Avoid roughing or running into the kicker. Run straight lines.
- Keep the eyes open and do not turn the head at the point of contact.
- Yell "Bingo" if the ball is blocked.
- Call "Peter" if the ball is blocked and crosses the line of scrimmage.
- Scoop and score if the blocked punt does not cross the line on fourth down.
- Fall on a blocked punt that does not cross the line on a quick kick or a third down punt.
- Block the punter on a blocked kick.
- Stay square and slide outside if blocked solidly on the charge. At this point, check for a fake.
- Execute the fall back return, usually a middle return, if the ball is not blocked and the ball is kicked.

# 6

# Extra-Point/Field-Goal Team

One of the most seemingly mundane and overlooked plays in football, particularly to the average football fan, is the point after a touchdown try. Most fans do not grasp the importance of the upcoming kick, failing to understand that the extra point try can strategically affect offensive, defensive, and special teams calls for the rest of the game. Failure to convert a point after touchdown kick can spell doom for the offending team. Many games have been lost by a single point, or lost as the result of succeeding calls after a missed extra-point attempt.

A successful point or field-goal attempt is not as easy as it looks. A high degree of timing goes into the execution of this kick. The kick must be executed in slightly over one second to have a chance to be successful, with flawless timing between the snapper, holder, and kicker. With the ball placed on the two-yard line, an NFL point after touchdown equates to a 19-yard field goal. College and high school rules place the ball on the three-yard line. This makes the kick a 20-yard attempt. Coaches have three choices on an extra point try: kick the ball for one point, run or pass the ball for two points, or drop kick the ball for one point. Drop kicks have gone the way of the dinosaur because of the evolution of the football to a more tapered ball.

A team's ability to successfully kick field goals positively affects their offensive game plan and negatively impacts the defense. A defense's mindset can be drastically affected by a superior field-goal kicker. Not only is an opponent's defensive game plan affected by an effective kicker, but the kicking team's offensive play calling is influenced by field position considerations. With a capable kicker, the offense is often playing on a shortened field.

# Personnel

The extra-point/field-goal team can be divided into three distinct personnel groupings: four blockers, eligible receivers, and a middle trio. The first group of four blockers includes the guards and tackles. The requirements for this position are size, size, and more size; in other words, large girth is desirable. These players should be able to take up a lot of space, and should be strong enough to block their inside gap and not allow penetration. They should possess upper body strength to avoid having their shoulders turned by a member of the block team, which would allow a kick blocker to run through the gap. The second group, consisting of the eligible receivers (the tight ends and wings should have receiving skills as well as blocking skills), should be effective blockers and also be able to catch a pass on a called fake or a "fire" call.

The third group is made up of the middle trio. The snapper, holder, and kicker do the skill work required. The center should not only be proficient at snapping the ball, but should possess enough bulk so he is not knocked back, thus creating a soft spot in the middle. The holder is one of the most underrated positions on the football field, seldom noticed until he mishandles a snap. In many cases, a quarterback is used at this position. This rule is not ironclad, but whoever is chosen should have a lot of experience and practice at handling a football. The holder should also possess a high level of intelligence and confidence. He is the quarterback of the kick team, controlling the tempo and alignment phase of the kick. He then turns over the tempo to the center, who snaps the ball when he is ready. The holder should be able to run, or throw the ball if a fake is called or a bad snap occurs. The kicker finishes the play, informing the holder where he wants the ball placed and nods when he is ready to kick. Right or wrong, he gets the lion's share of the credit on a successful attempt and the blame if the kick goes awry.

# Huddle

Teams can use a variety of ways to huddle for an extra point kick: huddle off the ball, on the ball, or water bucket style. The coach should decide if he wants to leave open the possibility that he can catch the defense napping, gain a numbers advantage and score two points, or simply line up and execute the kick. Some teams use an off-the-line huddle, or simply mill around on a field-goal attempt. No eligibles exist on the off-the-line huddle, thus no fakes are possible (Diagram 6-1). However, when on the line, a fake is possible (Diagram 6-2).

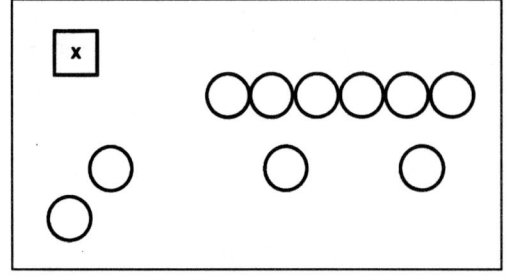

Diagram 6-1

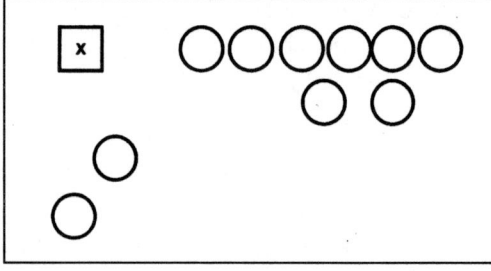

Diagram 6-2

# Formations

A wide variety of kick formations can be used on an extra-point or field-goal attempt, the most commonly used being the universal kick formation (see Diagram 6-3). Following are the strengths and weaknesses for several place kick formations.

**Universal Formation** (Diagram 6-3)

*Strengths*:
- Four quick receivers exist.
- Picks and rubs are possible on fakes.
- It is a balanced formation.
- The kicker or holder can easily be the #3 receiver to either side.

*Weaknesses*:
- Since it is the most commonly used formation, everyone is familiar with this formation.
- The defense can carry over basic blocks from game to game. The defense needs less preparation time when faced with the same formation from week to week.

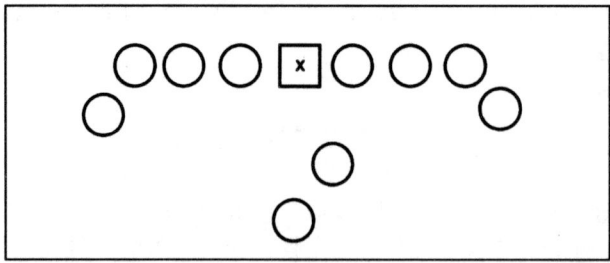

Diagram 6-3. Universal formation

**One Wing on the Line of Scrimmage** (Diagram 6-4)

*Strengths*:
- The defense must adjust to the unbalanced line or be outflanked.

- It is an easy "move to" formation. The wing simply moves up on the ball. This movement could cause the block team to jump offside.
- The defensive block scheme must adjust to the four men on one side of the line of scrimmage or be outflanked.
- The unbalanced side widens the corner.

*Weaknesses*:
- Only three quick receivers exist.
- The block team can insert the defender who had the tight end man-to-man into the rush, since the tight end is covered up and ineligible.

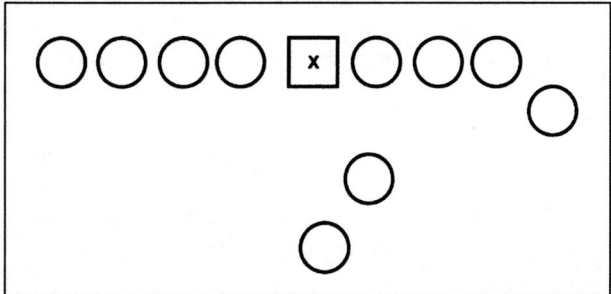

Diagram 6-4. One wing on the line of scrimmage

**Tackle Over Unbalanced** (Diagram 6-5)

*Strengths*:
- Four quick receivers exist.
- Picks and rubs are possible on fakes.
- The defense must adjust to the five-man side or be outflanked.
- The holder or kicker can easily become the #3 receiver to either side.

*Weaknesses*:
- A short corner exists away from the overload.
- The release by the two eligibles away from the overload makes the corner only one man wide.

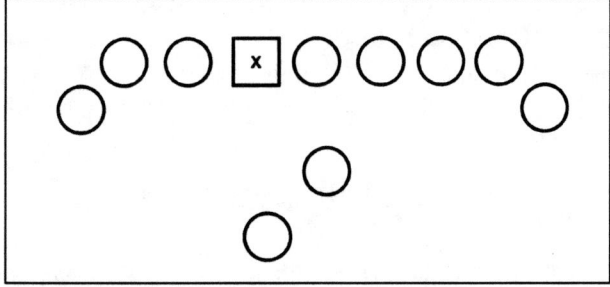

Diagram 6-5. Tackle over unbalanced

**Unbalanced with Wings on Same Side** (Diagram 6-6)

*Strengths*:
- The unusual nature of the formation requires radical adjustments.
- Four quick receivers exist.
- Trips routes are possible to the two-wing side.
- The holder or kicker can become #4 to the wing side.

*Weakness*:
- Only one eligible receiver exists to the unbalanced side.

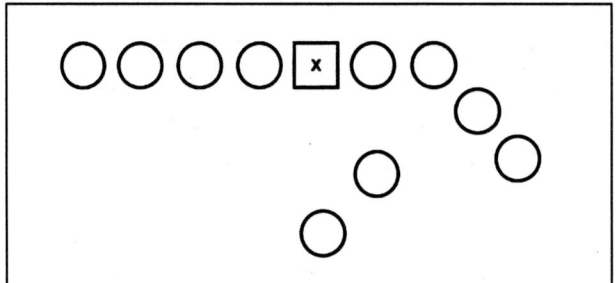

Diagram 6-6. Unbalanced with wings on same side

# Alignment

The center will align first. The other linemen get their alignment off the center. Linemen want to get off the ball vertically as much as legally possible. Their helmet should intersect the bottom of the center's numbers. They should be able to see the ball out of the corner of their eye. The wings want to place their inside foot behind the groin of the ends, and face out at a 45-degree angle. They want to be an arm's length away from the end. Horizontally, linemen want to place their inside foot slightly behind the next lineman inside.

# Stance

Guards, tackles, and ends should be in a three-point stance with the inside foot back and inside hand down. Their feet should be shoulder width apart. The wings align in a two-point stance with their hands on the thigh boards. The knees should have good bend, and the outside foot should be slightly in front of the inside foot.

# Steps/Protection

The center will set solid on the line of scrimmage after the snap. He should hold his ground, snap his head and arms up quickly and get big. He should not allow the defense to pull him forward or knock him back, nor should he allow his shoulders to be turned for a run through player. Interior linemen should key the ball for movement, and step with their inside foot to interlock with the next man inside. They should anchor the outside foot and not move it. Each man should bench-press his inside gap. The hands should be extended with the elbows locked. Wingmen should step with their inside foot and be ready to hinge both gaps, forcing pressure to the outside and not allowing it to go through them. Wings should never allow penetration to the inside, and at least put an extended arm on the outside rusher. Each blocker needs to keep a base: sink his tail, keep his head up, get big with hands and shoulders, and stay square to the line of scrimmage. These stances and steps are used for both extra-point and field-goal situations.

# Coverage

When the blockers hear the ball kicked they should shift into a cover mode. A field-goal attempt should be treated as a punt. The line and wings should fan out and sprint to the ball. As they sprint, they should locate the ball. The center should go directly to the ball. Other members of the coverage should keep the ball on their inside shoulder. As they converge on the ball, they should come to balance. The holder becomes the right safety, while the kicker works to the left and becomes the left safety. If the coverage hears a double thud, they should yell, "ball, ball." The ends will peel to the hash mark on their side and find the ball; the wings peel to the numbers on their side and locate the ball. The holder will work to his right, while the kicker follows his momentum and peels to his left (right footed kicker). The remaining members of the team should pivot and locate the ball (see Diagram 6-7).

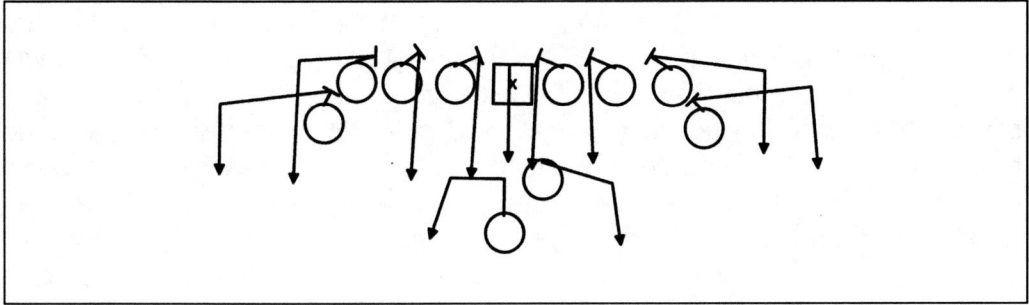

Diagram 6-7

# Middle Players

A saying in baseball states that to be successful, a team must be strong up the middle. The same can be said about the extra-point/field-goal team. For a kick to be successful, the center, holder, and kicker must perform with a high degree of proficiency.

The center initiates the sequence of events. Without a good snap, the kick can be doomed from the start. The center is free to snap the ball anytime after the "set" or "ready" call. He should vary the timing of the snap after the "set" call. However, he should be aware of the play clock, and not allow the defense the luxury of timing up the snap. He should not allow himself to create a rhythm that the defense can use to its advantage, avoiding the development of habits such as head or hip rhythm that would allow the rush team to get a jump on the snap. The center should aim the snap at the holder's outstretched hand. Snapping techniques are covered in detail in Chapter 9.

The most important pre-requisite for the holding job is good hands; hence, this position should be filled by a player who handles the ball a lot. Usually, the holder is a receiver or backup quarterback. Not only does the holder have to execute a difficult motor skill, but also he should possess a high degree of intelligence. The holder (the only player who should call time out) should know and understand the time out rules. He should not use a time out on an extra point, instead taking a delay of the game penalty in this situation. On a field-goal attempt inside the 15-yard line, he should also take a delay of the game. However, as a basic rule, if the ball is outside the 15-yard line, he should call time out. As the quarterback of the kicking team, he should check the offensive line, count the number of players, check with the kicker to see if he is ready, make a "set" or "ready" call, catch the ball when it is snapped, turn the laces away from the kicker, and become a safety when covering the kick.

He also should know what to do with the ball if an errant snap occurs. As a basic rule, the holder lines up seven yards from the center. His body is even with, and to the right of, the kicking spot (for a right-footed kicker). He should place his left knee on the ground and keep his right knee up. He should lean slightly forward and place his left hand on the spot. At this point, the holder will ask the kicker if he is ready. When he gets an affirmative answer, he will extend his right arm and hand with his palm toward the ground and his fingers pointed toward the center. His right hand should be even with the middle of his numbers. When the holder removes his hand from the spot and brings it up to his right hand, the thumbs should touch. When the ball is snapped, the holder should completely concentrate on the ball. When he catches the ball, he places it on the spot. The ball should be held straight up, two inches to the right and tilted slightly back from the line of scrimmage. This tilted position will facilitate good foot contact by a soccer style kicker's foot. The ball should be placed straight up for a straight on kicker. The left hand spins the ball so the laces face toward the goal post. The ball is held with the index finger of the right hand. The ball should be tilted slightly toward the holder. The holder and the kicker should not look up until the ball is kicked. After the ball is airborne, the holder becomes the right safety (right-footed kicker).

The kicking position is possibly the most pressure packed position in the sports world. The intricacies of placekicking are detailed in Chapter 8. Basically, the kicker's first physical act is to set the placement spot seven yards behind the ball. The spot changes, however, if the protection scheme calls for a tackle or end to cross over. If the ball is on a hash, or within a yard of the hash, an adjustment should be made. In this case, the placement should be one yard inside the hash, or behind the guard. The kicker, after identifying the spot for the holder, will then measure his steps and assume his stance. He informs the holder when he is physically and psychologically ready to make the kick. In the interval between his ready reply and the snap, the kicker should concentrate, relax, and visualize the perfect kick.

# Fakes

Sound scouting techniques should be used when designing extra-point or field-goal fakes. Film study should be used to answer some basic questions concerning that week's opponent.

- How does the opponent react to a score?
- How quickly do they get their block team on the field?
- Do they use the same rush each week?
- Do they cover all the eligibles?
- Who takes #3 (holder-kicker)?

Creation of a fake involves choosing the style and type of the fake. A special teams coach can choose to pass or run for two points. An option play can be very effective when a run is desired. Fakes can be designed to be a run/pass option, especially when the holder is a gifted athlete. When the decision has been made on how to attack the defense, and the mode of the fake has been defined, the coach should next decide the type of formation to use. The use of a basic formation would serve to offer an element of surprise. The use of swinging gate or water bucket fakes can take advantage of personnel mismatches or a numbers advantage. A third way to execute a fake field goal or extra point is to shift or use motion.

## Run Fake

The run fake is designed to attack a defense that pressures up the middle and off the edge. This particular fake takes advantage of soft B and C gaps. The holder should decide which side looks the most inviting. He then makes a directional call; a simple "rip" and "liz" call would be sufficient. The linemen from the onside tackle to the backside end block down and bench press their inside gap. The onside end and wing block out on the first man to their outside. The center snaps the ball to the holder, who places the ball on the spot. At the last second, he flips the ball to the wing, who is folding behind the linemen. After the holder flips the ball, he should block anyone chasing the wing. Since his first and most important job is to sell the kick, the kicker should go through the kicking action and then also block any chasers. A coach might decide to execute this particular fake by pulling the backside guard. The guard would look to block out on any defender penetrating in the C gap. If no penetrator exists, he should be coached to turn up and lead through the hole. With this pull scheme, the center should turn back and fill the backside A gap. The onside guard and the tackle should block down hard and not allow any penetration (see Diagrams 6-8 and 6-9).

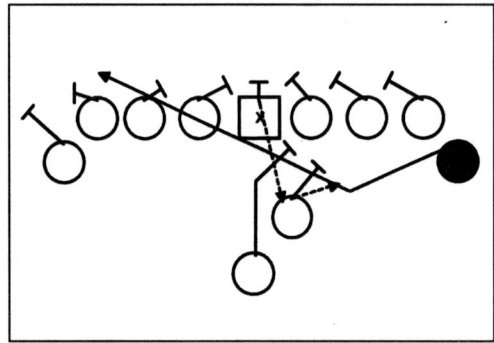

Diagram 6-8

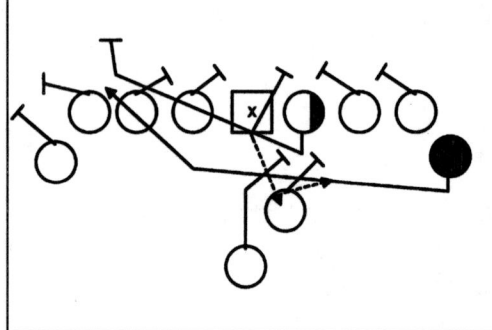

Diagram 6-9

### Short Trap Fake

The short trap fake is similar to the run fake play just diagrammed, also using a trap technique. This fake is best suited for rushes that load up on the outside or place the inside rushers in the gaps, and involves a direct snap to the holder who follows the off guard's trap block into the B gap. The onside guard and the center block away from the point of attack; the backside tackle, end, and wing zone block toward the play. The playside tackle, end, and wing turn out and block the first man to their outside. The backside guard pulls and traps the defender penetrating the B gap. The kicker steps up and blocks any chasers (see Diagram 6-10).

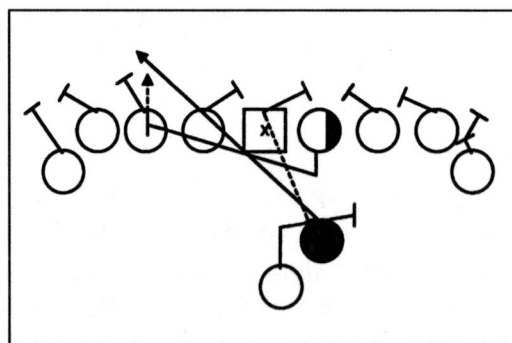

Diagram 6-10. Short trap

### Pass/Run Option

The next fake is a designed pass/run option play, and a more slowly developing play than the previously diagrammed fakes. This fake involves a direct snap to the holder, who shuffles the ball to a wingback. The wingback then has an option to pass the ball to the end or a wingback. Frontside linemen block down. The center blocks the backside A gap. The backside guard pulls and leads the wing to the corner; he is coached to pass block unless he gets a "go" call from the wing. With a "go" call, he leads the wing downfield. Once the holder shuffles the ball to the wing, he then turns and blocks any defender running through the B gap. The kicker's first job is to sell the kick, and then he also turns to block anyone chasing the wing. On the snap, the wing runs through the feet of the kicker's initial alignment. The wing has the option of throwing the ball to either the wing or the end. These individuals must be sure that they run their route far enough to get the needed score or first down. The wing should eyeball the end first, and then look for the wing. If either player is open, he should throw a catch-able ball. If both receivers are covered, he will give a "go" call to the guard and run the ball (see Diagram 6-11).

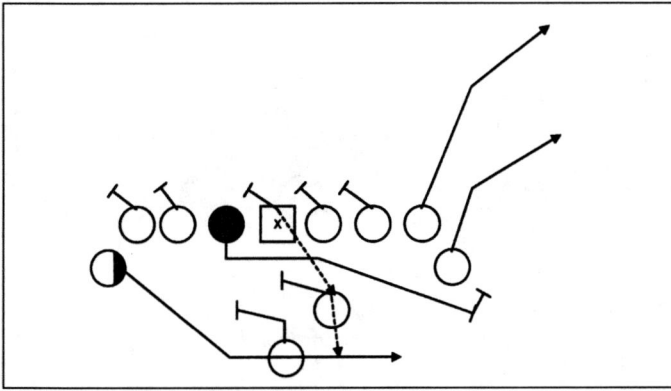

Diagram 6-11. Pass/run option

## Duke Fake

A most unique fake occurred in 1992 when Duke faked a field goal against North Carolina. This fake involved Duke running a player onto the field late, and the kicker waving him off the field as if he were the twelfth man. As the player retraced his steps, the ball was snapped to the holder who threw it to the player who was giving the appearance he was leaving the field (see Diagram 6-12).

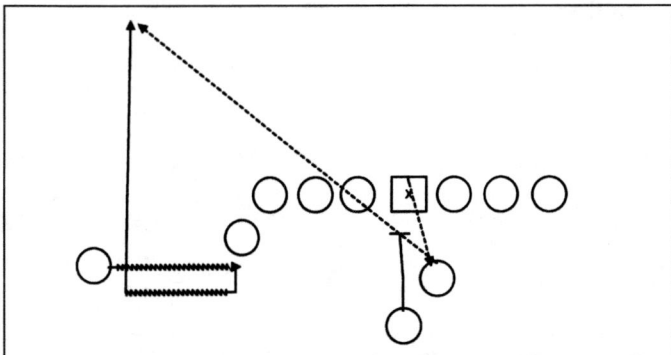

Diagram 6-12. Duke fake

## Swinging Gate

Swinging gate fakes can also have a pass/run option component. If the defense is not fundamentally sound with its adjustment, and is outnumbered to the overload, the holder will simply call for the ball, and throw the ball to the overload (see Diagram 6-13). If the offense has a 3-on-2 advantage in the middle, the ball can be snapped to the kicker who follows the center and holder into the end zone (see Diagram 6-14). If the wideout is not covered, the ball can simply be thrown to the uncovered man. The uncovered rule can lead to an easy two-point conversion (see Diagram 6-15). No matter what the defensive response, a swinging gate pass play with all eligible receivers out can be effective (see Diagram 6-16). Shifts can be very effective when attempting to fake a kick. Trips routes are available when employing a shift type fake. Motion can be added after the shift (see Diagrams 6-17 and 6-18).

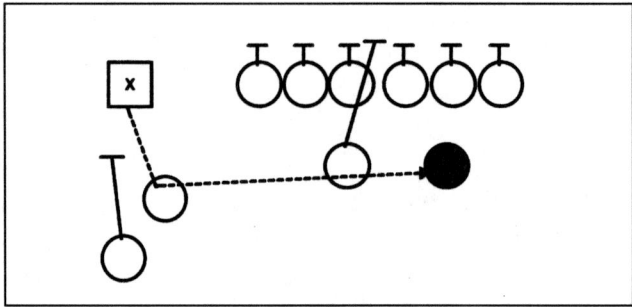

Diagram 6-13

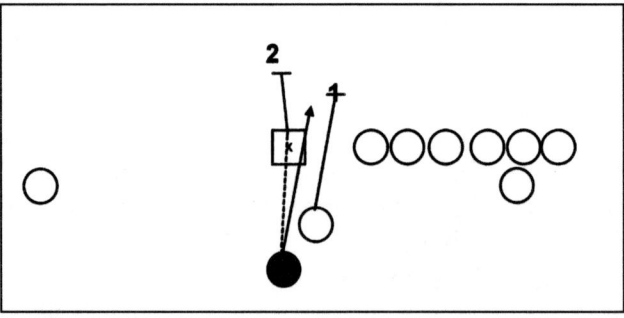

Diagram 6-14

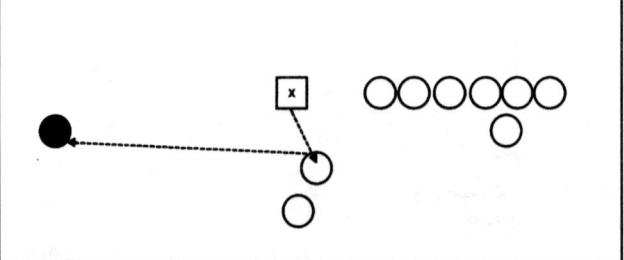

Diagram 6-15

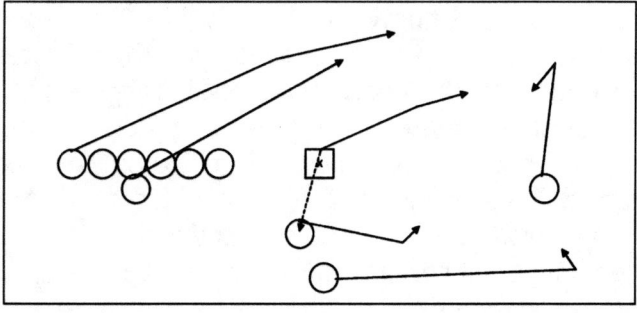

Diagram 6-16

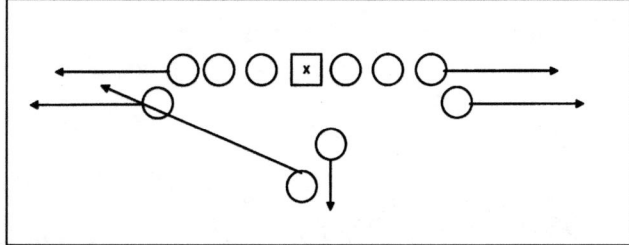

Diagram 6-17

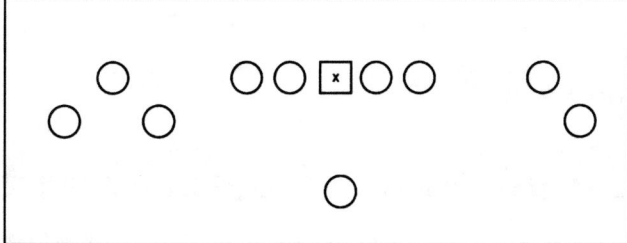

Diagram 6-18

Extra-point and field-goal fakes are limited only by the coach's imagination and the quality of work involved in scouting the opponent. Specialized fakes are tailored for a specific opponent and will vary from week to week. These should be game planned weekly. In addition to this planned fake, a well-prepared special teams coach should also have a basic fake, which will be practiced every week and can be used when needed against an opponent, regardless of what formation in which they line up.

## Fire Play

A plan should be practiced on how to react if the holder or snapper aborts a field-goal try or an extra-point try, due to a miscue. Even with a bad snap, or a muff by the holder, it is still possible for the kicking team to score a touchdown in a field-goal situation, or two points in a try after touchdown situation. The conventional approach to this situation is to have the holder roll out to the side of his dominant hand. For example, if the holder were right handed, he would roll to the right. The holder should signal his teammates with a "fire" call if he is going to roll out. Eligible receivers have a pre-determined route to run when they hear a "fire" call. If a fire call is used on a field-goal attempt, the receivers should make certain they run a route that would at least get a first down. If the fire is run on an aborted extra-point attempt, the receivers must score. Linemen also play a valuable role in a fire play, blocking in the pre-determined direction. They should work to the desired side and work backward from the line of scrimmage. If linemen are not coached to work slightly backward, they may drift over the line of scrimmage and incur a penalty for an illegal receiver downfield. The kicker should become a blocker and protect the holder's backside (see Diagram 6-19).

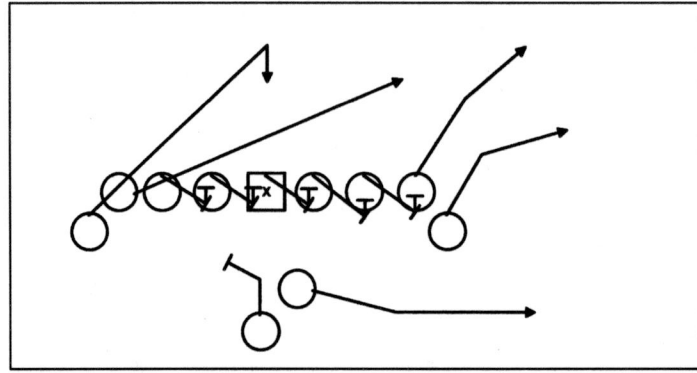

Diagram 6-19

## Extra-Point/Field-Goal Checklist

- Middle kick
- Hash kick
- Swinging gate
- Bad snap
- Fakes
- Fast field goal
- Fast extra point
- Unbalanced

- No time out – field goal (10 men)
- No time out – extra point (10 men)
- Coverage
- Fire call
- Partially blocked kick that crosses line of scrimmage
- Blocked kick that does not cross line of scrimmage

## Try Down/Extra Point Rules and Regulations

- A try is an opportunity for the scoring team to score one or two points, while the game clock is stopped.
- The ball will be put into play by the team that scored the six-point touchdown.
- The try is a scrimmage down when the ball is signaled as ready for play.

- The snap will be midway between the hash marks or from any other point on or between the hash marks. The scoring team can request the ball be placed anywhere between the hashes as long as the request is made before the ready for play signal. However, the ball may be relocated after a charged time out (NFL-NCAA), or for a replay after an accepted penalty against the defense (NFL-NCAA-NFHS). High school and college rules place the ball at the three-yard line. In the NFL, the ball is spotted on the two-yard line.
- The try is considered over if the attempt fails, or if the defense gains possession. However, college rules allow the defense to score. NFL and high school rules do not allow the defense to score points.
- NFL and college rules do not allow a member of the offense to recover a teammate's fumble. The only man allowed to recover this type of fumble is the player who fumbled the ball. Only the fumbling player can recover and advance a fumble during a try.
- Fouls after a try are enforced on the succeeding kickoff.

# Extra-Point/Field-Goal Rules and Regulations

- A field goal shall be scored for the kicking team if a drop kick or place kick passes over the crossbar between the uprights of the receiving team's goal before it touches a player of the kicking team or the ground.
- An unsuccessful field-goal attempt that is ruled dead in the end zone is put in play at the previous spot. If the previous spot was between the kicking team's +20 and the goal line, the ball will be put in play at the 20-yard line. High school rules state that the kick is dead and the ball will be placed at the 20-yard line regardless of the spot of the kick.
- A missed field-goal attempt that touches a goal post is dead.
- Offsetting penalties will result in a replay from the previous spot.
- Roughing or running into the kicker or holder is a live ball foul.
- All snaps to the holder are a "direct snap," or "backward pass," and if mishandled are treated as a fumble and may be advanced.
- It is illegal for a defensive player to jump or stand on any player, to be picked up by a teammate, or to use a hand or hands on a teammate to gain additional height in an attempt to block the kick. These actions are considered unsportsmanlike conduct, and a 15-yard penalty will be assessed.
- The defensive team may advance an unsuccessful field-goal attempt, whether or not the ball crosses the line of scrimmage.
- Either team can advance a ball that is blocked, and does not cross the line of scrimmage.
- If the ball is blocked, and does cross the line of scrimmage, the ball is dead when it comes to rest and no one attempts to recover, or when the kicking team downs it.

| Two-Point Conversion Chart | | | | | |
|---|---|---|---|---|---|
| Points Ahead | Go for 1 | Go for 2 | Points Behind | Go for 1 | Go for 2 |
| 0 | X | | 0 | X | |
| 1 | | X | 1 | Decision | |
| 2 | X | | 2 | | X |
| 3 | X | | 3 | X | |
| 4 | | X | 4 | Decision | |
| 5 | | X | 5 | | X |
| 6 | X | | 6 | X | |
| 7 | X | | 7 | X | |
| 8 | X | | 8 | X | |
| 9 | X | | 9 | | X |
| 10 | X | | 10 | | X |
| 11 | | X | 11 | X | |
| 12 | | X | 12 | X | |
| 13 | X | | 13 | X | |
| 14 | X | | 14 | X | |
| 15 | X | | 15 | X | |
| 16 | X | | 16 | | X |
| 17 | | X | 17 | | X |
| 18 | X | | 18 | | X |
| 19 | | X | 19 | | X |
| 20 | X | | 20 | X | |
| 21 | X | | 21 | | X |
| 22 | | X | 22 | X | |
| 23 | X | | 23 | X | |
| 24 | X | | 24 | | X |
| 25 | | X | 25 | | X |
| 26 | X | | 26 | | X |
| 27 | X | | 27 | X | |

Diagram 6-20

# 7

# Extra-Point/Field-Goal Defense Team

How many games have been won or lost by a single point? One point can make all the difference in the world. A failed extra point can affect strategy for the rest of the game. In a 2002 wild card game between the 49ers and the Packers, John Madden made the following statement when the 49ers blocked an extra point attempt in the first quarter of that game: "That point sits there the whole game."

A blocked extra point is the only way a team can take away a point from its opponent. Many observers think a touchdown is worth seven points. If the extra point fails, only six points is put on the scoreboard. NFL statistics show that only one out of 20 extra-point kicks fail. Teams that want to increase the failure rate must design ways to pressure the try. Three ways exist to block an extra point or field goal: from the middle, the sides, or over the top.

Penetration up the middle is the most effective way to block the kick, but it is very difficult to get penetration because of tight line splits and the blocking scheme. Blocks from the sides require speed, timing, and correct angles. Jumpers in the middle have more success on the college and NFL levels because kickers are not allowed to use a tee; whereas, high school kickers are able to get quick elevation on their kicks because they *can* use a tee. Each unit has inherent advantages on an extra-point or field-goal try. The rush team outnumbers the kick team by an 11 to nine ratio, since the holder must hold the ball and the kicker kicks the ball. Time is the major advantage of the kick team. If the kick is launched quickly and with good trajectory it is unlikely to be blocked;

however, the attempt to block a kick can have a profound influence on the game if the block attempt is successful. A block team does not necessarily have to actually block the kick to be successful. A good push and penetration on a previous attempt could cause the kicker to misfire on a later attempt. The effect of constantly pressuring the kicker could pay dividends later. The reward makes the effort worthwhile.

An astute observer can learn a lot about a team's mental state and desire by observing its block team. All out effort to block a kick indicates a high degree of intensity and desire. A token rush many times indicates a deficiency in desire and intensity. The universal kick formation described in Chapter 6 will be used in diagramming pressures in this chapter (see Diagram 7-1).

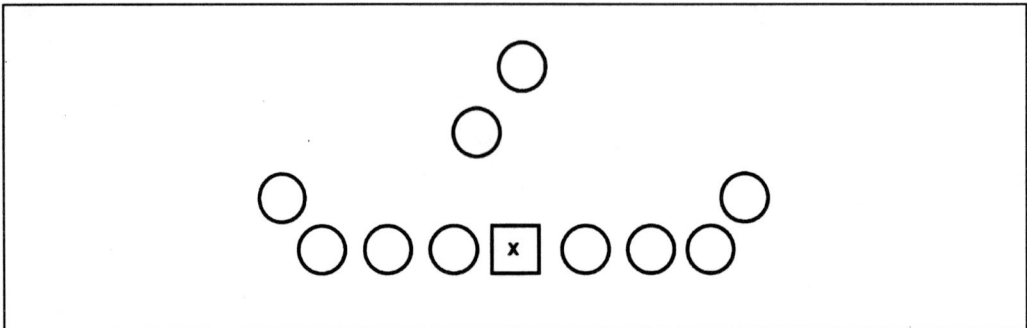

Diagram 7-1. Universal formation

# Personnel

Kick rush personnel can be divided into two major groups. The largest group is made up of rushers. This group usually includes six to seven men whose job is to block the kick. The other group normally includes three or four men whose more passive, but equally vital, job is that they are assigned man-to-man coverage on the eligible receivers. Sometimes, wholesale changes have to be made when the defense gives up a score, or when the opponent is attempting a field goal. Regular defensive personnel may not contain the 11 best-qualified people for a kick rush, since some of the regular defensive members may be too large and slow footed to contribute to a kick rush.

Fast, agile people should be strategically placed on the rush team. Usually the biggest and strongest rushers are placed in the middle area, matched with the hulks that kick teams use in the interior line. The fastest and most agile rushers usually rush off the edge, both inside and outside the wings. These edge rushers should have good get-off skills. They should line up close to the ball and explode out of their stance on ball movement. One of the major attributes of an effective extra point rusher is mental toughness. His team has just given up a score. A mentally tough player will focus on the next play and hustle onto the field, line up, and try his best to block the extra point try. An extra point block rush is an excellent way to gauge the mental toughness and competitiveness of a football team.

# Defensive Position Designations

LC – Left Corner
RC – Right Corner
LS – Left Safety
RS – Right Safety
LOB – Left Outside Backer
ROB – Right Outside Backer

LE – Left End
RE – Right End
LT – Left Tackle
RT – Right Tackle
M – Monster

# Blocks

## Block Left (Diagram 7-2)

*LC*: His first assignment is to check alignment inside. He makes a "stay onside" call to his side of the formation. On the snap, he rushes hard through the outside half of the wing. He will align at an angle to the inside with the outside foot back, and should line up wide enough to get a good angle to the kicking spot. The first step is with the outside foot across the line of scrimmage. The second step is with the inside foot; the third step (again with the outside foot) becomes a re-direction step. The fourth step, with the inside foot, is followed by a layout with the arms extended.

*LS*: On the snap, he rushes hard through the wing/end gap. He should align at an angle to the inside shoulder of the wing. The first step is with the outside foot across the line of scrimmage. On the second step, he should jump over and step through the gap between the end and wing. He makes himself small by ripping through with his outside shoulder and turning his numbers to the ball.

*LOB*: He will blitz engage the tight end and try to draw his block. He will take the end man-to-man if he releases.

*LE*: He power rushes through the outside shoulder of the guard, and tries to knock the guard back. After he gets movement, he will climb and throw his inside hand up.

*LT*: He power rushes through the inside shoulder of the guard and tries to knock the guard back. After he gets movement, he will climb and throw his inside hand up.

*RT*: He power rushes through the inside shoulder of the guard and tries to knock the guard back. After he gets movement, he will climb and throw his inside hand up.

*RE*: He power rushes through the outside shoulder of the guard and tries to knock the guard back. After he gets movement, he will climb and throw his inside hand up.

*ROB*: He will blitz engage the tight end and try to draw his block. He will take the end man-to-man if he releases.

*RS*: He rushes hard through the wing/end gap and reads the block of the wing. If the wing blocks down with his head across, the RS will take him man-to-man (corral technique).

*RC*: His first assignment is to check alignment inside. He makes a "stay onside" call, and rushes hard through the outside half of the wing. He will read the block of the wing. If the wing blocks down, the corner will continue on his rush and try to block the kick. If the wing steps out or does not move, the corner will blitz engage him and take the wing man-to-man if he releases (corral technique).

*M*: He aligns near the ball and, just prior to the snap, pulls out and covers the wing to the block side.

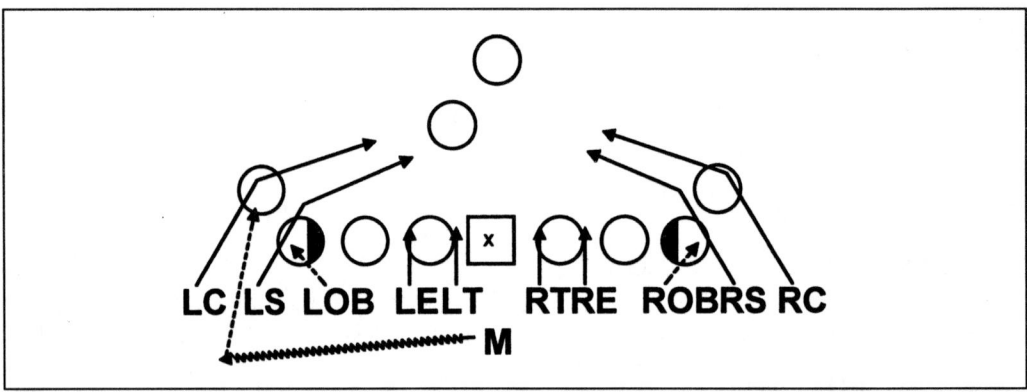

Diagram 7-2. Block left

## Corral Technique

This technique is a read scheme between the corner and safety away from the called block. Each man will read the block of the wing. The safety will take the wing man-to-man if the wing blocks down. If the wing blocks out or does not move, the corner will take him man-to-man. The other man in the scheme continues on to block the kick (see Diagrams 7-3 and 7-4).

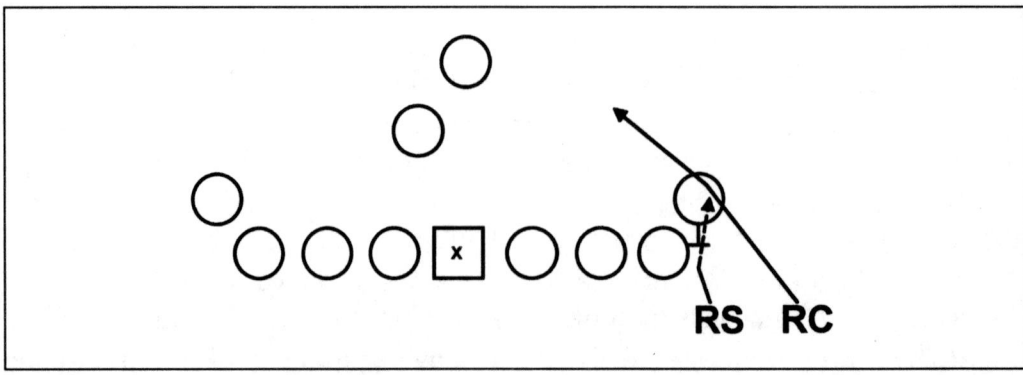

Diagram 7-3

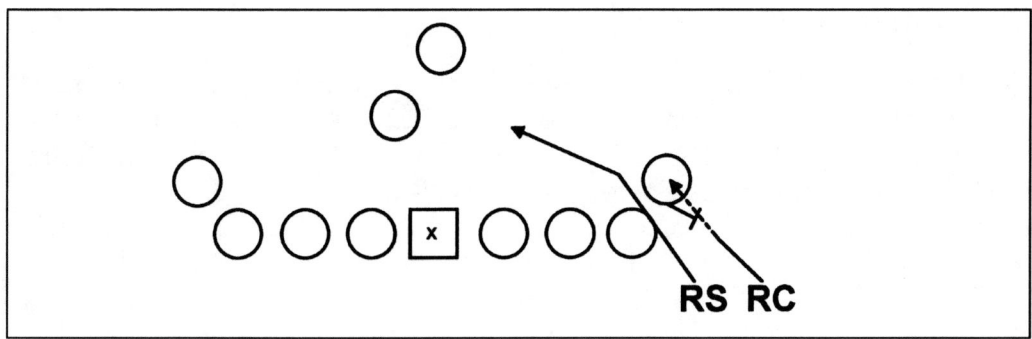

Diagram 7-4

## Block Right (Diagram 7-5)

*LC*: Checks alignment inside and reminds his side to stay on side (corral technique).

*LS*: Corral.

*LOB*: Same as block left.

*LE*: Same as block left.

*LT*: Same as block left.

*RT*: Same as block left.

*RE*: Same as block left.

*ROB*: Same as block left.

*RS*: Rushes hard through the wing/end gap. He makes himself small by ripping through with his outside shoulder and turning his numbers to the ball.

*RC*: His first assignment is to check alignment inside. He makes a "stay onside" call to his side of the formation. On the snap, he rushes hard through the outside half of the wing.

*M*: Aligns near the ball and, just prior to the snap, pulls out and covers the wing to the block side.

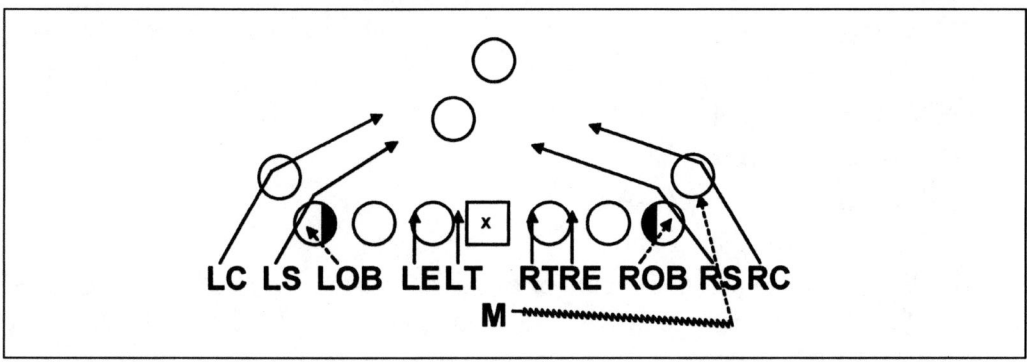

Diagram 7-5. Block right

**Block Left Switch** (Diagram 7-6)

This block is used whenever the tight end can be beaten inside by the outside linebacker, or the tight end blocks the safety. The OLB rushes the C gap, while the left safety blitz engages the tight end. Everyone else executes their normal block left rules. On block right switch, the assignments simply flip flop.

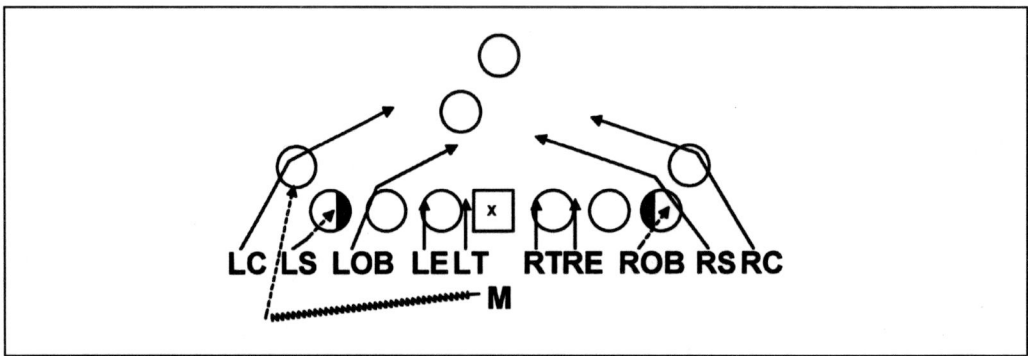

Diagram 7-6. Block left switch

**Combo Left** (Diagram 7-7)

This block sends the monster through the C gap to the directional call. The OLB and end will use a pull technique to the call side. On a combo right block, the assignments simply flip flop.

　　*LC*: Same as block left.

　　*LS*: Blitz engages the wing. Takes him man-to-man.

　　*LOB*: Blitz engages the tight end. The LOB attacks the end by grabbing his outside shoulder with his outside hand, while grabbing the end's inside shoulder with his inside hand. The LOB tries to turn the end's shoulders away from the ball, opening up the C gap for the run through by the monster.

　　*LE*: The end aligns in a wide three- or four-I alignment on the offensive tackle. His technique is similar to the one used by the OLB on the end.

　　*LT*: Same as block left.

　　*RT*: Same as block left.

　　*RE*: Same as block left.

　　*ROB*: Same as block left.

　　*RS*: Same as block left (corral).

　　*RC*: Same as block left (corral).

　　*M*: Aligns near the ball and just prior to the snap he will pull out, but instead of covering the wing, he will time up the snap and run through the C gap. He should hit the gap with a slight outside-in angle.

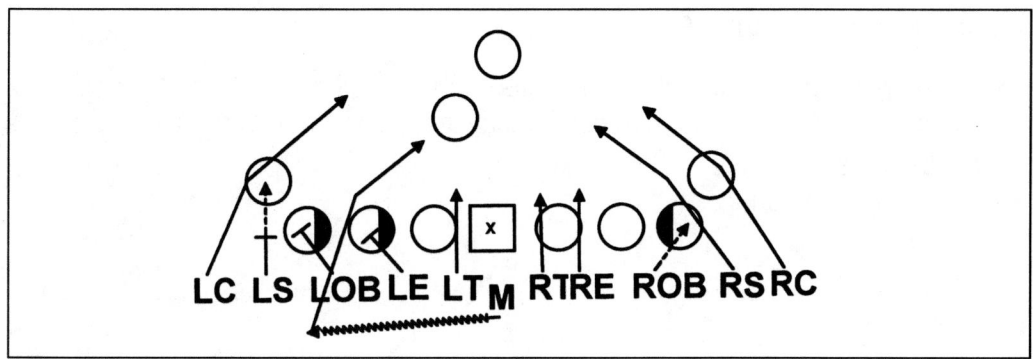

Diagram 7-7. Combo left

## Middle Blast (Diagram 7-8)

*LC*: Checks alignments inside. He should give a "stay onside" call. On the snap, he should work to the wing and explode upfield for contain.

*LS*: Blitz engages the wing, taking him man-to-man.

*LOB*: Blitz engages the tight end, taking him man-to-man.

*LE*: Same as block left.

*LT*: Same as block left.

*RT*: He widens out on the guard to a zero alignment. On the snap, he concentrates on getting a good push and movement on the guard. He should get his inside hand up.

*RE*: Same as block left.

*ROB*: Blitz engages the tight end, taking him man-to-man.

*RS*: Blitz engages the wing, taking him man-to-man.

*RC*: Checks alignments inside. On the snap, he works to the wing and explodes upfield for contain.

*M*: He will work to the call (game plan). On the snap, he will rush the A gap or over the center. He can also delay, or lag behind the tackle to the call side.

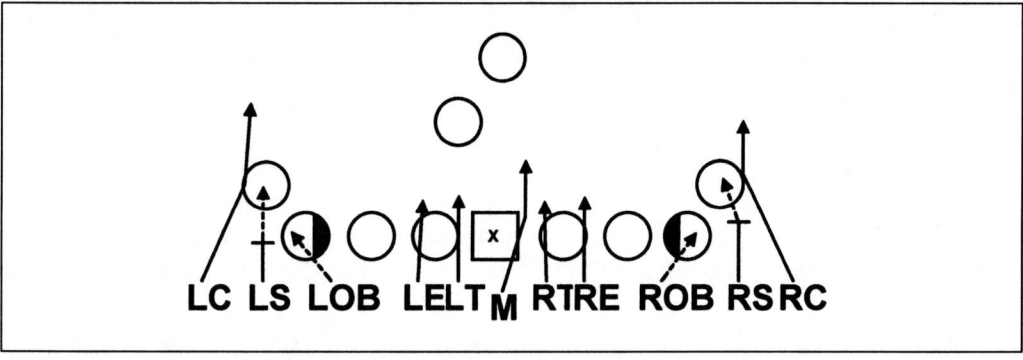

Diagram 7-8. Middle blast

**Overload Left** (Diagram 7-9)

This scheme seeks to outnumber the protection unit to the called side by placing six rushers to one side of the ball. On overload right the assignments simply flip flop.

*LC*: Same as block left.

*LS*: Same as block left.

*LOB*: Rushes the C gap.

*LE*: Widens to a four-I alignment, and rushes hard through this landmark. He gets his inside hand up.

*LT*: Power rushes through the outside shoulder of the guard, and tries to knock the guard back. After he gets movement, he climbs and throws his inside hand up.

*RT*: He moves across the ball to the call side, aligns on the inside shoulder of the guard, and power rushes through the inside shoulder of the guard, trying to knock the guard back. After he gets movement, he climbs and throws his inside hand up.

*RE*: Shifts down to the A gap. On the snap, he gets movement and gets his inside hand up.

*ROB*: Blitz engages the tight end, and covers him man-to-man.

*RS*: Blitz engages the wing. He has contain. He takes the wing man-to-man.

*RC*: Moves late to the overload side, taking the tight end man-to-man.

*M*: Aligns near the ball and moves late to the block side, taking the wing man-to-man.

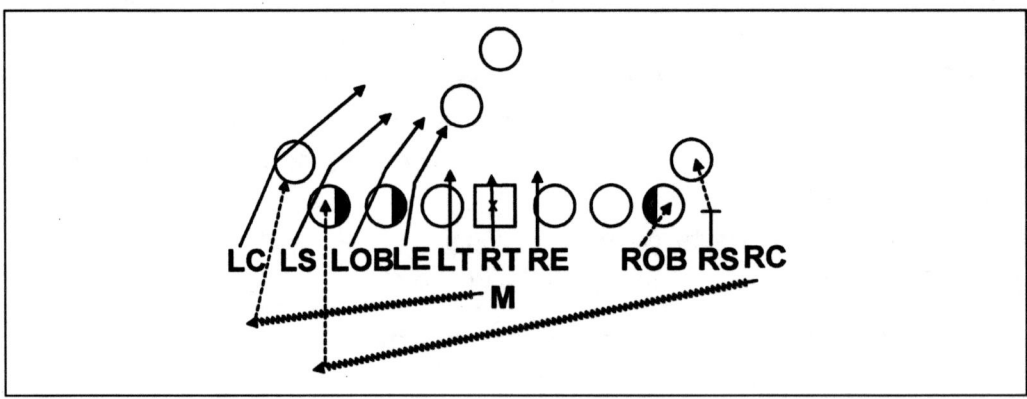

Diagram 7-9. Overload left

**Sell the Farm** (Diagram 7-10)

This scheme is an 11-man rush that is usually employed at the end of a game in a win-or-lose situation. It is used when there is a minimal chance of a fake. Eligibles are uncovered because all 11 men rush.

*LC*: Checks alignments inside. He makes a "stay onside" call. He rushes hard through the outside half of the wing.

*LS*: Rushes hard through the wing/end gap. He makes himself small by ripping through with his outside shoulder and turning his number to the ball.

*LOB*: Rushes hard through the C gap.

*LE*: Power rushes through the outside shoulder of the guard, and tries to knock the guard back. After he gets movement, he climbs and throws his inside hand up.

*LT*: Power rushes through the inside shoulder of the guard, and tries to knock the guard back. After he gets movement, he climbs and throws his inside hand up.

*RT*: Widens out on the guard to a zero alignment. On the snap, he should get a good push on the guard and get his inside hand up.

*RE*: Power rushes through the outside shoulder of the guard, and tries to knock the guard back. After he gets movement, he climbs and throws his inside hand up.

*ROB*: Rushes hard through the C gap.

*RS*: Rushes hard through the wing/end gap. He makes himself small by ripping through with his outside shoulder and turning his numbers to the ball.

*RC*: Checks alignments inside. He makes a "stay onside" call. He rushes hard through the outside half of the wing    .

*M*: On the snap, he will rush through the A gap, or over the center to the call side. He can also delay, or lag behind the tackle to the call side.

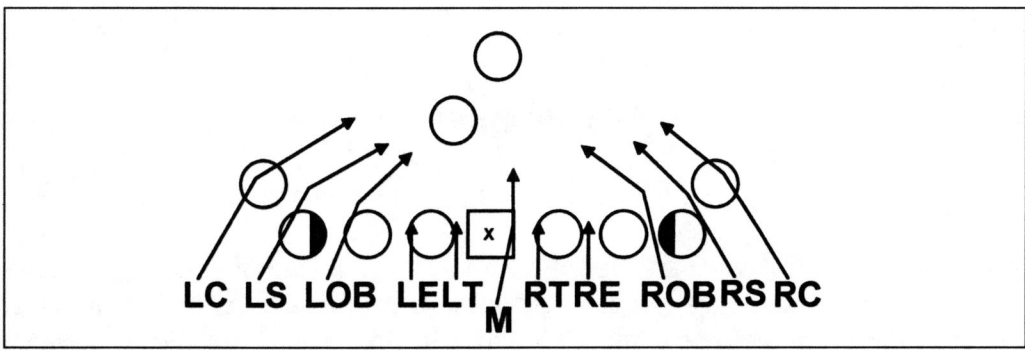

Diagram 7-10. Sell the farm

# Safe

This call is used when the defense is not sure the field-goal team will actually kick the ball. This scheme allows the rush team to pressure the kick and cover all eligibles. The "safe" call is a six-man pressure with potential pass receivers covered (Diagram 7-11).

*LC/RC*: Check alignments to the inside. On the snap, each will explode upfield and slam the wing with his inside hand and contain to the depth of the holder. They take pitch on an option play. On flow away, the corner checks for someone coming out the backdoor (holder-kicker). He checks for throwbacks, screens, or reverses.

*LS/RS*: Blitz engage the wings, taking them man-to-man.

*LOB/ROB*: Back off the ball five yards. They are responsible for the end to their side, and must not be picked by the wing.

*LE/RE*: Align in the C gap. They rush hard through the C gap. They are assigned to block the kick. If the wing and end shift out, the ends have contain rush.

*LT/RT*: Align in the B gap. They rush the B gap. Their assignment is to block the kick.

*M*: Must give a "tango" call, which alerts the defense watch for a shift or some tactic designed to draw the defense offside. He is responsible for either the holder or kicker shifting out of the backfield. He is assigned the holder on an option play.

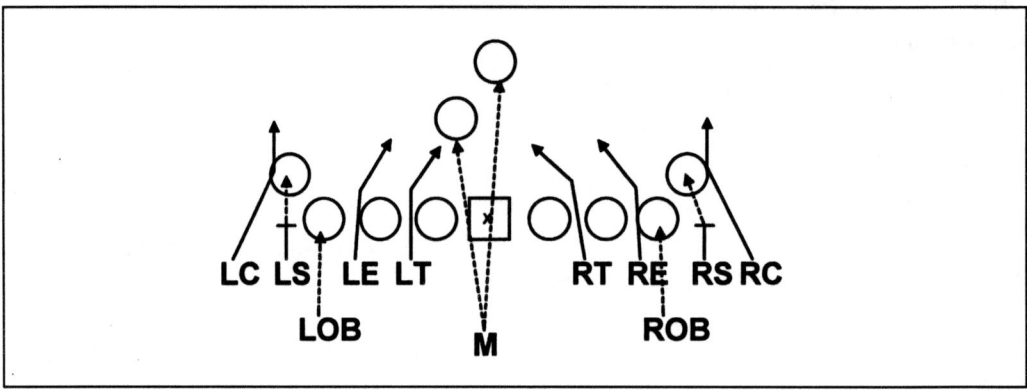

Diagram 7-11. Safe

# Water Bucket

Many coaches disdain simplicity when they line up for a try after a touchdown. Some coaches spice up their pre-snap formations in the hope they can convert an easy two-point play. Not only can the offense score two points, but the use of unusual formations causes defensive teams to use valuable practice time to prepare for all of the possibilities. Coaches use a variety of terms when referring to this interval between a touchdown and the try: swinging gate, Emory Henry, or water bucket.

Following are some commonly used water bucket formations. These formations are designed to get a numbers advantage, or an uncovered receiver, in the hopes of scoring two points instead of a single point. Included are the defensive reactions and responsibilities to the various sets.

### Water Bucket Right (Diagram 7-12)

*LC*: Takes the holder man-to-man versus pass. Versus an option play away, he takes the center.

*LS*: Takes the kicker man-to-man versus pass. Versus an option, he forces the holder to pitch.

*LOB*: Aligns in a loose 9 technique. He keys the ball. If the ball is snapped, he is a "shooter." A shooter crosses the LOS and attempts to pick off a pass from the holder or kicker. College rules allow an interception to be returned for two points. NFL and high school rules declare the ball dead when it is possessed by the defense. Versus an option toward him, the shooter will sprint outside into the pitch.

*LE/RE*: Take an outside shoulder alignment on the #2 man (counting outside in). They penetrate when the ball is snapped. If there is no OLB to his side, the end becomes the shooter.

*LT/RT*: Take an outside shoulder alignment on the #3 man (counting outside in). They penetrate when the ball is snapped.

*ROB*: Aligns in a loose 9 technique. He takes the end man-to-man. He has force if the end blocks.

*RS*: Takes the inside back man-to-man.

*RC*: Takes the outside back man-to-man.

*M*: Aligns head up on the center. He should check the center's number for eligibility. If the center is ineligible, he gains depth and looks for crossers on passes. Versus an option, he overlaps to the pitch

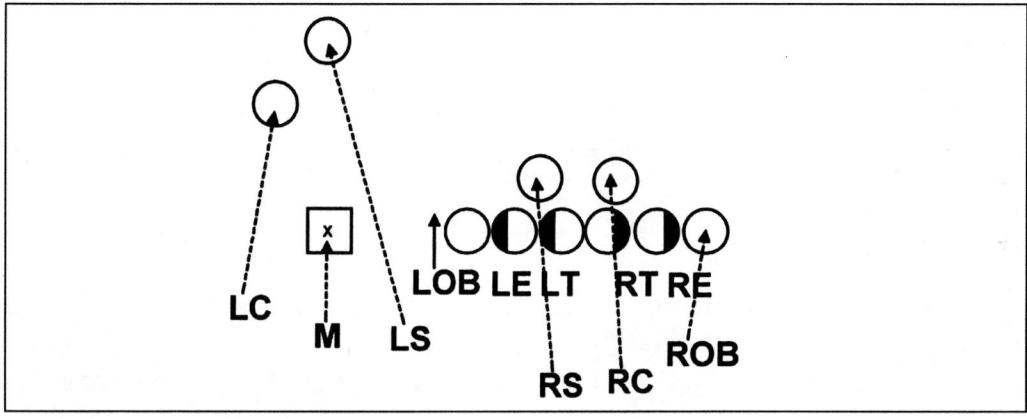

Diagram 7-12. Water bucket right

## Option to the Overload (Diagram 7-13)

To gain proper pitch relationship, the option will probably be run in the direction opposite the holder's alignment. The LS will force the holder to pitch the ball. The monster and the LC will overlap to the pitch. The LOB is in position to run to the pitch also. The LC assumes coverage on the snapper if he is eligible.

## Option Away From the Overload (Diagram 7-14)

The LC forces the pitch while the monster overlaps. The LS takes the center if he has an eligible number.

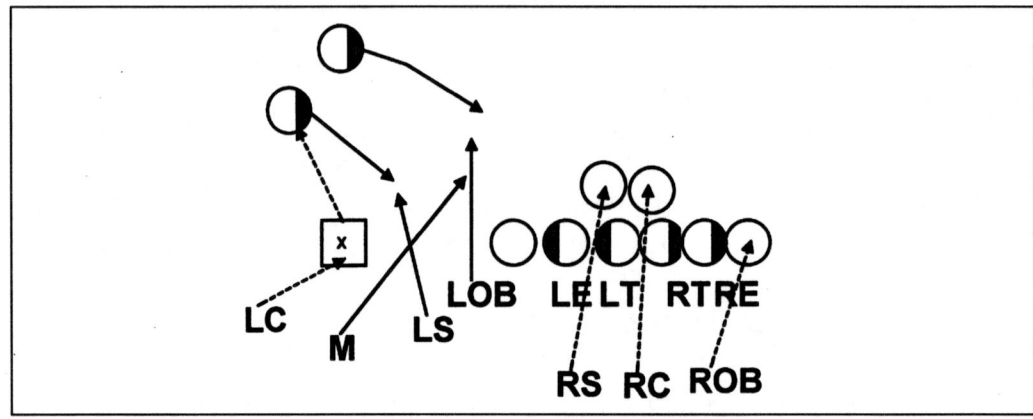

Diagram 7-13. Option to the overload

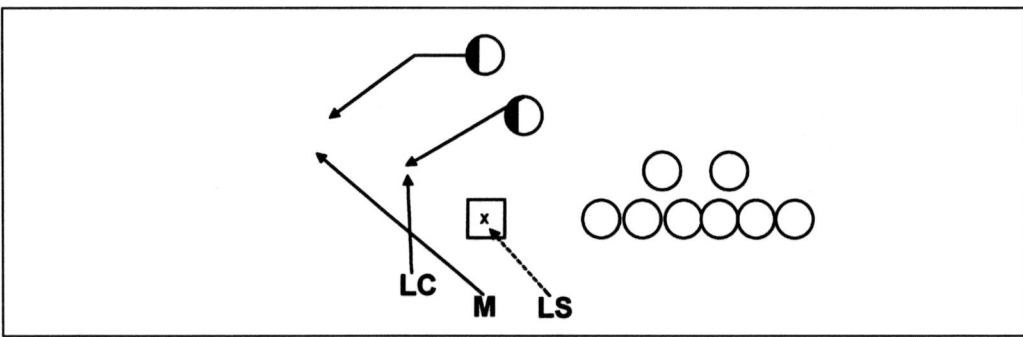

Diagram 7-14. Option away from the overload

## Water Bucket Left (Diagram 7-15)

*LC*: Takes the holder man-to-man versus pass. Versus an option play, he forces the pitch.

*LS*: Takes the kicker man-to-man versus pass. Versus an option, he overlaps to the pitch.

*LOB*: Aligns in a loose 9 technique. He has the end man-to-man. If the end blocks, he has force.

*LE/RE*: Take an outside shoulder alignment on the #2 man (counting outside in). If there is no OLB to his side, the end becomes the shooter.

*LT/RT*: Take an outside shoulder alignment on the #3 man (counting outside in). Their job is to penetrate if the ball is snapped.

*ROB*: Aligns in a loose 9 technique. He keys the ball. If the ball is snapped, he is a "shooter." A shooter crosses the LOS and attempts to pick off the pass. College rules allow a run back for two points. NFL and high school rules declare the ball is dead.

*RS*: Takes the inside back man-to-man.

*RC*: Takes the outside back man-to-man.

*M*: Aligns head up on the center. He must check the center's number for eligibility. If the center is ineligible, the monster gains depth and looks for crossers on passes. Versus an option, he overlaps to the pitch.

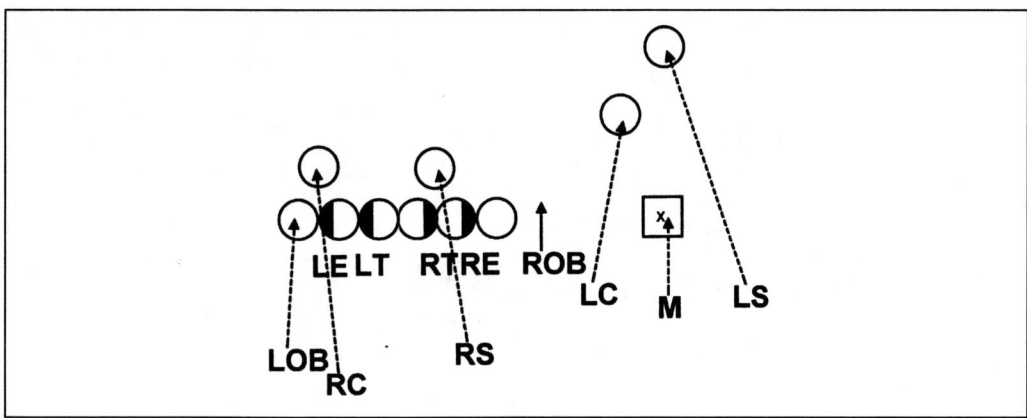

Diagram 7-15. Water bucket left

## Double Width Right Water Bucket (Diagram 7-16)

*LC/LS*: Normal

*LOB/ROB*: Normal

*LT/RT*: Normal

*LE/RE*: Normal

*RS*: Takes the back to the overload.

*RC*: He is the adjuster versus double width formations. He takes the wide back man-to-man.

*Monster*: Normal

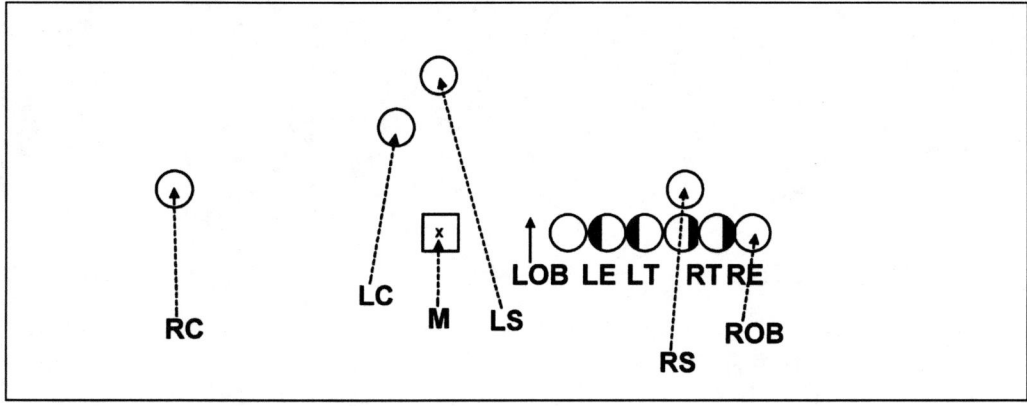

Diagram 7-16. Double width right water bucket

## Double Width Left Water Bucket (Diagram 7-17)

The responsibilities for a double width water bucket left are the same as for a double width water bucket right call.

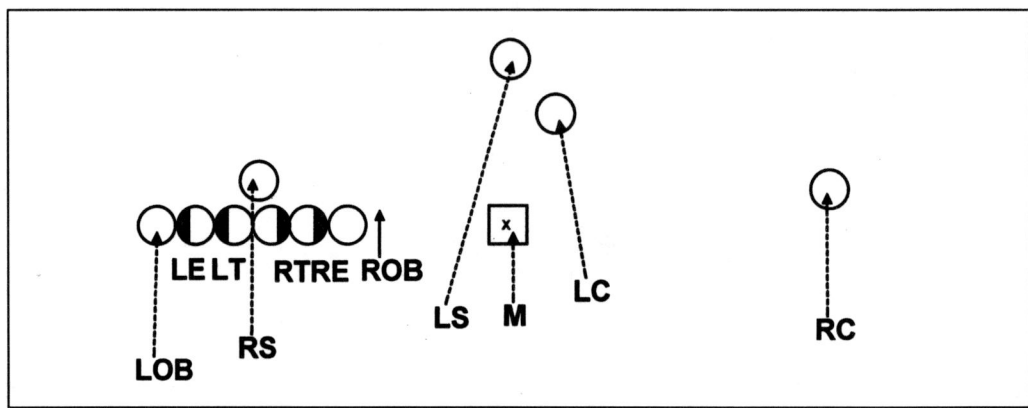

Diagram 7-17. Double width left water bucket

## Double Width Twins Left and Right (Diagrams 7-18 and 7-19)

If the offense presents a double width formation with two receivers away from the overload, the right corner will give a "help" call, bringing the OLB (whose alignment is nearest the ball) to the right corner. The OLB will take #2 man-to-man. The OLB will give a "gone" call to the end, instructing the end nearest the ball to become the shooter. The end in turn will give a "gone" call to the tackle, who will slide one man to the "gone" call.

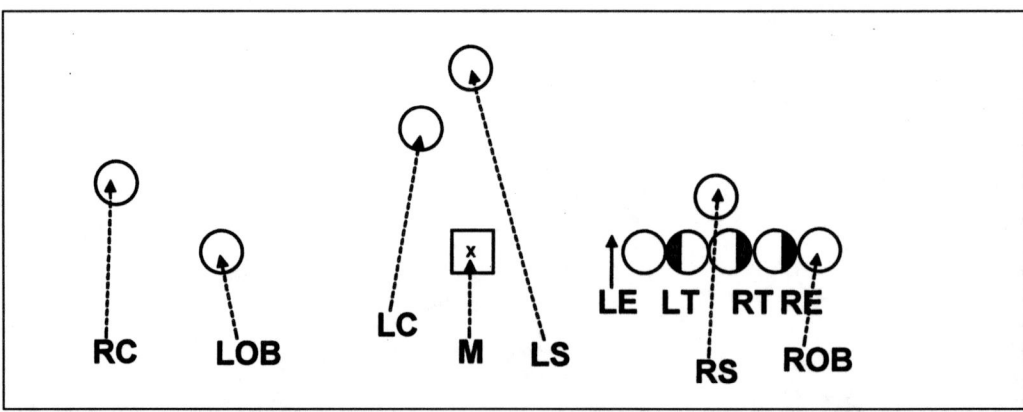

Diagram 7-18. Double width twins left

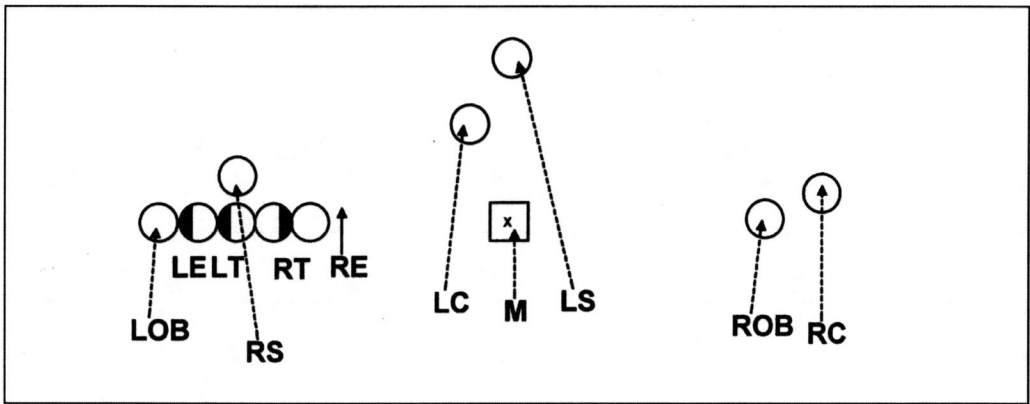

Diagram 7-19. Double width twins right

## Emory and Henry Water Bucket (Diagram 7-20)

Some teams choose to use the Emory and Henry formation. When the defense adjusts to the water bucket, the offense makes a "move" call and shifts into their normal kick formation. The defense will re-check to the called block.

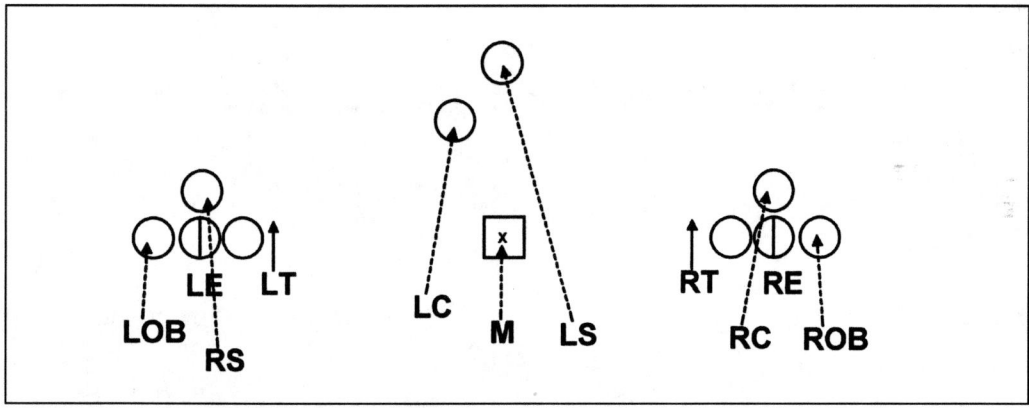

Diagram 7-20. Emory and Henry water bucket

# Shifts

A well-prepared defense must be ready to react to a "break" or "scatter" from a kick formation. The defense will check out of the block and defend the new formation (see Diagrams 7-21 and 7-22).

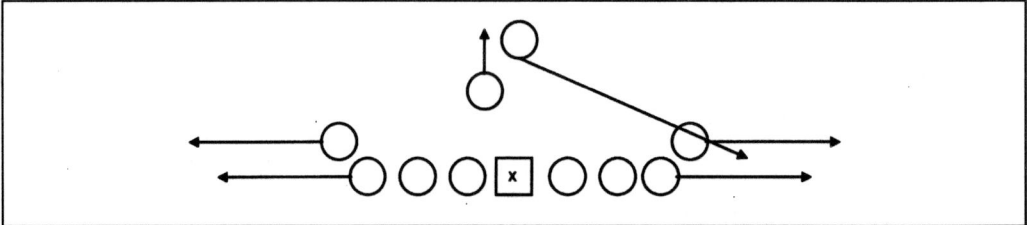

Diagram 7-21

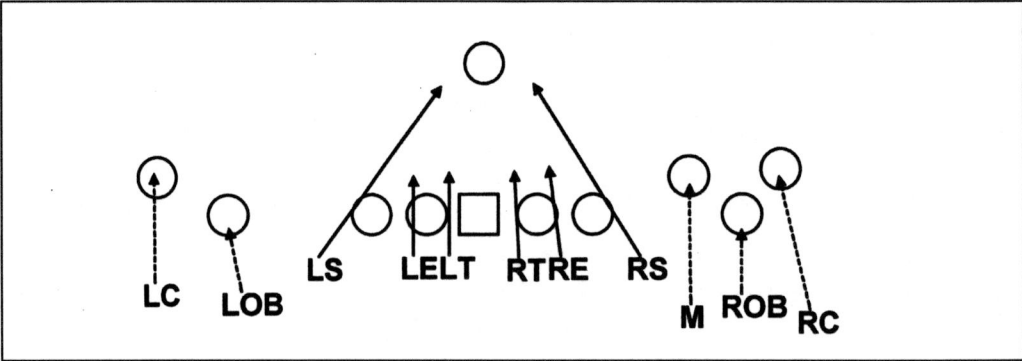

Diagram 7-22

## Extra-Point/Field-Goal Defense Checklist

- Middle kicks
- Hash kicks
- Swinging gate
- Fakes
- Fire call
- Bad snap
- Two-point play
- Fast field goal
- Sell the farm
- Spy responsibilities
- Offensive shifts and movements

## Extra-Point/Field-Goal Block Principles

- Players should know their responsibilities. Who has pass responsibility? Who has run responsibility? Who has contain responsibility? Always be alert for fakes. Rushers rush and cover men cover.
- Scoop and score on a blocked kick that does not cross the line of scrimmage on fourth down. Fall on the ball if it is third down.
- Give a "Peter" call if a partially blocked kick crosses the line of scrimmage. A missed field goal is a live ball. Treat it like a punt.

- Avoid penalties. A penalty can give the offense a second attempt at a score, a first down, or put them in a better position to go for it on a fourth-down play. A penalty on an extra point can place the offense closer to the goal line and give them a better opportunity to go for two points.
- Make sure the correct number of players is on the field. One man should have the responsibility to count the defenders and call time out if there are more than 11. He should be coached when to call time out if the defense is short on personnel. In some situations, it might be better to go short-handed than lose a time out.
- Do not rough the kicker or holder.
- Defenders should be coached to key the ball. Be alert for shifts, motion, and Dallas shifts, which are tactics to draw the rush team offside.
- When blocking kicks, rushers should run through the spot. Edge rushers should lie out and not jump.
- When blocking the kick, blockers should not turn their heads away. They should keep their eyes open and their thumbs touching.
- Everyone assigned to rush should rush as if he will be the man to block the kick. He should give maximum effort on each kick.
- Know the kicking team personnel. Know their regular holder, kicker, and eligible receivers. Changes in personnel might indicate a fake. "Safe" check is possible.
- Penetrate! Penetrate! Penetrate!

# 8

# Kicking Techniques

This chapter takes an in-depth look at the motor skills involved in kicking a football. Included will be the intricacies of placekicking, punting, and kickoff techniques. Alignments, approaches, the kick, and follow-through are detailed. This chapter will also deal with how to kick in adverse weather conditions. The how-to of kicking with the wind or against the wind is explored. Tips are also offered on how to correct a hook, how to kick in deep grass, and the type of shoe to use, just to name a few. Information is also included on how to kick the old-fashioned, straight-ahead way, in addition to the popular soccer style. Comparisons between these two major kick styles will be examined.

## Kickoffs

Kickoff specialists can be developed. On the high school level, the coach should try everyone on the team as a potential kickoff man in the pre-season. The coach should look for someone with a naturally strong leg and who also gets good height on his kicks. The coach should take the best two or three candidates, teach them some basics, and supply them with the equipment and time to develop their skill. The coach can drill them on their approach, keeping their eyes on the ball during the approach, correct foot impact, and a good follow-through. A tee may be used on all levels of play; the kicker has the choice of using a conventional or soccer-style tee. Both straight-on and soccer-style kickoffs will be explored.

## Soccer-Style Technique

*Alignment*: The ball should be placed on the tee at a slightly backward angle, with the laces facing away from the kicker. Many kickers align themselves by taking nine backward steps away from the tee and five steps to the side. When the kicker has finished his steps, he should place his kicking foot six inches in front of his plant foot. The kicker should have some flexion in his knees, and his shoulders should be in front of his hips with the arms loose and hanging to his side.

*Approach*: The kicker should start his approach by taking a short relaxed step toward the ball with his kicking foot. Each step should be progressively quicker as he attacks the ball. The kicker's plant foot should be two to four inches behind the ball, and six inches to the side of the tee. His plant toe should be pointed toward the direction of the kick.

*Kick and Follow-Through*: As the kicker contacts the ball, he should keep his head down and focused on the ball. His shoulders should be in front of his hips at the point of contact. The kicking leg should move in a high arc, with the kicking toe pointed down and the knee preceding the foot. The inside part of the instep should strike the ball one inch below the center of the ball. With the correct approach and body balance, he will feel himself being lifted off the ground, and should land two or three feet in front of the tee.

## Straight-on Technique

The ball should be placed the same as for a soccer-style kickoff. The ball should be tilted back toward the kicker with the laces downfield. Straight-on kickers should use a conventional tee as opposed to a soccer-style tee.

*Alignment*: Most straight-on kickers align 10 yards deep on a straight line with the tee. His stance should find the kicking foot in front of his plant foot. His shoulders should be slightly in front of his feet, with his head down and eyes focused on the ball. His arms should hang loosely at his side.

*Approach*: The kicker's movement to the ball should start with his kicking foot. His first five yards should gain momentum as his steps gradually become quicker. The second five yards should find the kicker increasing his momentum as he attacks the ball. These last five yards should be covered with three steps. The plant foot should contact the ground four to six inches to the side and eight inches behind the tee.

*Kick and Follow-Through*: At the point of contact, the kicker should keep his shoulders forward and his head down. The ankle of the kicking foot should be locked. The toes should not be pointed up or down, but in a flat or neutral position. Contact with the ball should be an inch below the center of the ball. The follow-through should be smooth and extended with the head focused on the tee.

## Directional Kicks

A recent phenomenon on the kicking scene is directional kicking. A coach may decide to kick in a desired direction for many reasons: kicking to an inferior returner instead of kicking to a more dangerous teammate, kicking to overloaded coverage, or in an attempt to pin the returner to the sideline. Two basic approaches exist when directional kicking. The easiest method is to place the ball on the hash, allowing the kicker to kick the ball using his basic motion. The other method is to place the ball in the middle of the field and have the kicker point his plant toe in the direction he wants the kick to go.

## Weather Considerations

As with other aspects of the kicking game, weather conditions, especially wind, can affect a kickoff.

### Tailwind

With the wind at the kicker's back, he should strike the ball a little lower. This would serve to lift the ball with the wind, and as a result get better distance and hang time.

### Headwind

With wind blowing into the kicker's face, he should hit the ball more in the middle in an attempt to drive the ball low into the wind.

### Crosswind

When a kicker must deal with a strong crosswind, the best tactic may be to directional kick using the wind as an aid. For example, if the wind were blowing left to right, it would be advantageous to directional kick to the right. If the crosswind were blowing right to left, a directional kick to the left would result in additional hang time and distance. However, other variables enter into the decision on whether to directional kick. For example, it might not be beneficial to kick to a particularly dangerous returner in an attempt to execute a wind-aided kick.

# Placekicking

A placekicker probably has the most pressure-packed job in football, or any sport for that matter. He is usually called on to perform only a handful of times during the course of a game, but each time points are on the line. When a lineman misses a block, only a handful of people know; when a kick goes awry, *everyone* knows it. Any mistake made by a placekicker is magnified. He is expected to perform flawlessly each time he is called on to kick. Mental toughness and leg strength are the two most important attributes a kicker should have.

The effectiveness of a placekicker depends upon many different factors. To execute a successful kick, the kicker must depend upon a solid supporting cast: the snapper, holder, and the protection. A miscue by any of these three can dramatically affect the kick. Regardless of how effective the other participants are, the kicker gets the blame when a kick fails. A good example of how the component parts must work in concert to be successful happened in Super Bowl XXV, when Scott Norwood missed a late field-goal attempt. Even though Norwood was the scapegoat, many people feel the holder had a negative effect because the laces on the ball ended up facing Norwood instead of the goal post.

Most kickers can be grouped into one of two distinct styles: *straight* on kickers, and soccer style kickers (who approach the ball from the side). Currently, the overwhelming majority of kickers, on all levels of play, are soccer types. In former years, when kickers played other positions (and kicked as a sideline), they preferred the straight-on technique. Each style has advantages and disadvantages. Many stages or phases of kicking exist that kickers should understand and master. Following is a breakdown for each phase or stage for both soccer-style and straight-on kicking.

## Soccer-Style Technique

*Alignment*: The kicker should place his non-kicking foot or plant foot to the side of the tee (high school), or the launch point (NFL, college), which is usually seven yards from the center. With his kicking foot is placed directly behind the spot, he takes three normal steps backward starting with the kicking foot. After three steps, he should end up with his kicking foot in a direct line with the ball. At this point, he takes two sideways steps at a 90-degree angle, turns, and faces the launch point. The kicker places his plant foot slightly ahead of the kick foot, his feet slightly less than shoulder width apart. His body weight should be distributed equally on the balls of the feet, with a slight bend in the knees. The kicker should bend at the waist so his shoulders are in front of the hips, and his arms should hang loosely by his side. Eyes should be on the kicking spot. From this pre-snap position, he shifts his weight forward and signals to the holder that he is ready. The kicker should peripherally see the ball in order to time-up the kick.

*Approach*: On cue, the kicker steps with the kicking foot in a smooth relaxed manner. The second step, with the plant foot, is a longer step and should come down even with, and six inches from, the ball. The plant foot placement is crucial to the success of the kick. If the plant foot is placed too close to the ball, the ball will have a tendency to be pushed to the right (right footed kicker). If the plant foot is too far from the ball, the kick will usually hook. A plant too far behind the ball will also result in a hook. If the plant foot goes past the ball, the result is usually a low line drive. Hips that are too open in contact usually cause a ball that slices to the right. The big toe of the plant foot should be pointed toward the goal post. This open step will allow the hips to open up. A closed toe tends to lock the hips, which will not allow for a good follow-through.

*Kick and Follow-Through*: The kicking leg starts forward once the plant foot hits the ground, and should follow on a high arc with the leg almost fully extended. With a slight knee bend, the kicking toe should be pointed down and the ankle locked. The open toe of the plant foot allows the hips to lead and supply the power for the kick. Contact with the ball is on the top inside part of the kicking foot. The shoe-laced portion of the foot, not the toe, should strike the ball because it is the area of a big hard bone. The ball should not make contact with the toes. Contact with the ball should occur one inch below the center of the ball; meanwhile, the kicker's hips should be fully opened and pointed to the goal post. A good follow-through brings the body straight down the target line, the shoulders remaining square with the target throughout the follow-through. It is crucial that the kicker not look up at the point of contact. He should keep his head down and focused on the launch point.

## Straight-On Technique

*Alignment*: The straight-on kicker gains his alignment the same way the soccer-style kicker does. He begins by putting his plant foot to the side of the block or launch point, his kicking foot placed directly behind the spot. From there, he takes three natural steps backward. He takes the first step with his kicking foot. After the third step, he shifts his feet so the instep of the kick foot is even with the toe of the plant foot. His feet should be six to eight inches apart, focusing most of his weight on the non-kicking foot. His weight should be forward, accomplished when the kicker bends forward at the waist and moves his shoulders in front of his feet. His arms should hang down and forward.

*Approach*: The approach is a two-step motion. The first step, with the kicking foot, serves to start the kicker's body forward. This first step is a natural relaxed step. The second step, with the non-kicking (or plant) foot, is more explosive than the previous step. The second step lands eight inches behind and to the left (right footed kicker) of the kicking spot. Throughout these steps the kicker's shoulders should remain forward.

*Kick and Follow-Through*: As the plant foot hits the ground, the kicker should bring his kick leg forward in a big arc. Straight-on kickers should lock the ankle so the sole of the foot is even with the ground. If the kick toe were pointed up, it would cause the heel to strike the ground just before contact with the ball. If the kicker points his toe down, the toe of the kicking foot would strike the ground just prior to contact. The kicker's momentum carries the kicker straight ahead over the spot. The kicker's arms will bend to spread naturally during the kick, providing balance.

*Comparison of the Two Styles*

Soccer and straight-on kicking styles have both advantages and disadvantages . Currently, most kickers choose the soccer approach. Given the popularity of youth league soccer, most youngsters learn this style of kicking. Most professional and collegiate kickers prefer the soccer style, which affects young kickers who seek to emulate them. Upper level kickers, who usually do not play another position, spend all their practice time kicking the football. These kickers prefer the soccer approach. The major advantage soccer kickers have over straight-on advocates is better range. Another advantage, that has been previously mentioned, is that since most youngsters learn to kick this way because of participation in soccer programs, soccer style is as natural to them as straight-on kicking was to a bygone generation. Straight-on kickers have two major advantages over soccer-style kickers: first, it is easier to line up the kick, especially when the ball is near a hash; and second, straight-on kickers have better balance and superior traction on a wet field. Straight-on kicking is also easier to teach and perfect, which is significant if the kicker plays another position. One major disadvantage of the straight-on style, however, is that the kicker should use a square-toed shoe to be consistent. This shoe can be costly to buy, and the kicker would have to put it on and take it off in a limited amount of time if he plays another position.

## Kicking in Deep Grass

Deep grass can affect the lift and distance of a kick. To offset this disadvantage, the kicker can discreetly pat the ground at the launch point to flatten the grass in front of the spot and hopefully nullify drag on the ball.

## Playing a Hook

A major drawback with soccer-style kicking is that nearly all soccer kickers have a natural hook on their ball. Right-footed kickers tend to pull the ball to the left, while left-footed kicks usually work from left right. Compensating techniques include aiming slightly right of the middle of the uprights (right footed kicker). Another tactic is for the holder to tilt the ball slightly. For a right-footed kicker, the holder leans the ball slightly to the right. This tilt serves to minimize the hook. Care must be taken, however, if there is a left to right wind, since this type of wind will nullify the hook. Any adjustment would, in effect, push the ball too far to the right. With this type of wind, the ball should be placed straight up and down.

## Kicking Into a Headwind

If the kicker is faced with wind blowing into his face he can have the holder lean the ball forward slightly. This tactic will lower the trajectory of the ball, and will help the ball slice through the wind. Care must be taken, however, because if the trajectory is too low the kick is in danger of being blocked.

## Kicking Without a Tee

High school kickers who wish to play on the next level should learn to kick without the benefit of a kicking tee. This transition can be a tough, since kickers may notice a loss of distance and height at first. A compensating technique for the absence of a tee would be to move half a foot back from the normal starting point. To do this, the kicker should go through his regular alignment routine, and then back up six inches. The kicker may have to experiment with this new starting point to get it exactly right. This new spot will serve to cause the toe of the plant foot to strike the ground even with the ball at impact. As a basic rule, the ankle of the plant foot ends up even with the ball when kicked. This simple adjustment will cause more lift on the ball to compensate for the loss of the tee.

## Shoes

A recent innovation that is gaining many converts is the wearing of shoes that are very snug. Many kickers have opted to wear a shoe on the kicking foot that is several sizes too small. Some kickers soak the shoe in water and wear it around to get the leather stretched and molded to the shape of the foot. Kickers believe that the tight fit allows them to get a better feel for the ball; punters and placekickers both use this technique. Placekickers believe it is beneficial to have less shoe beyond the tip of the toe. Less shoe forward on the foot allows the kicker to make contact on the sweet part of the ball without taking too much grass on the swing.

# Punting

## Stance

The punter should assume a stance that is relaxed and comfortable. His feet should be no wider than shoulder width apart. A two-step punter should place his kicking foot forward with a toe to instep relationship. Weight should be distributed on the instep of both feet, allowing the punter to move nimbly to either side to field an errant snap. He should bend at the knees with his upper body tilted forward, which serves to abet the forward motion. The punter should anticipate a bad snap each time he lines up, and should adjust his stance in anticipation of a bad snap. If he gets a low snap, he should drop his body and attempt to block the ball with his hands, arms, legs, or chest. However, he should not allow his knee to touch the ground.

## Steps

The two most common approaches to punting can be broken down into two- or three-step approaches. Advantages exist with either method. An advantage of the two-step approach includes quicker punt time, which naturally makes it harder to block. The three-step approach provides better balance, and supplies more momentum into the ball. This book will focus on techniques for a two-step punt. A punter must understand that no matter the preferred style, the needed power comes from correct balance and body position. Quick jerky movements with unnecessary body movements serve to adversely affect the kick; compact and mechanically correct movements enhance the effectiveness of the kick. The punter's first step should be with the forward or kicking foot. The forward step serves to build momentum and provide a split second edge over the rush. The punter should step into the snap by moving his body to keep it in front of the ball, and look the ball all the way into his hands. The first step is a short, controlled step, slightly open, allowing the punter's hips to open. and should land on the ball of the foot. The second step is with the back foot, and should be a normal stride. The toe of the back foot should follow the same angle as the toe of the kicking foot. The trail foot should also contact the ground on the ball of the foot. The upper body should stay in the pre-snap position throughout the movement. Hips should be kept over the feet. As the trail foot hits the ground, the kick foot should be swung forward with the ankle locked and the kicking toe pointed downward.

## Hands

To receive the ball, the punter should extend his hands waist high with the palms up and the little fingers touching. As the punter steps into the ball, a slight bend of the elbows will allow the hands to give slightly and soften the blow of the ball striking the hands. The ball should be caught just inside the hip of the kicking leg. Care must be taken on a low snap that the knees do not touch the ground. The punter should bend at the waist and knees on a low snap. Care must be taken, however, that the ball is not brought into the body. The hands should remain extended, as the extension of the ball will facilitate getting the kick off quickly. The ball should be presented with the laces at 12 o'clock. The grip on the ball should be with light pressure, which facilitates a smooth and consistent drop. The ball should be extended with the ball on a direct line with the outer edge of the punting leg.

## Dropping the Ball

Some punters present the ball with both hands, while some choose to drop the ball with one hand. Some coaches prefer the two-hand method because it offers better ball security. Most punters secure the ball by gripping the back tip of the ball with the dominant hand. For example, a right-footed punter would hold the back tip between the right thumb and forefinger. The off hand rests lightly on the inside lower panel of the ball. The ball's front point should be slightly tilted downward and inward. Care must be taken that the ball is rotated so the laces face straight up. As the punter takes his second step, he should remove his off hand and allow it to fall away and then swing back above and outside the hip. A one-hand drop will enable the punter to hold on to the ball a little longer, and allows the ball to be extended farther, which permits better control and a better transfer of power. The ball should be dropped slightly to the outside of the punting leg, from a height between the bottom of the jersey numbers and the waist. As the kicker drops the ball, his kicking leg should swing through and contact the kicking foot.

## Ball Contact

The punter should use a smooth controlled swing of the kicking leg. He should lock out his kicking ankle and point the toe downward, seeing the ball strike the top of his foot. The follow-through includes the leg swinging straight downfield and upward toward the same side shoulder. At the moment of contact, the support leg will lock and generate power from the ground up. Close observation of the ball after it has been kicked can tell the punter what he did correctly, and tip him off on what he did wrong. If the back tip of the ball hits the ground first, it tells the punter that the front of the ball struck the kicking foot first. If a punt goes end-over-end, it would signify that the back of the ball struck the foot first.

## Weather Considerations

Weather considerations impact various phases of a football game, especially special teams play. Wind and rain can wreak havoc with a kicked ball.

### Headwind

The most important component of kicking into the wind is the drop. The ball should be dropped just slightly below waist level with the contact point just below knee level. A ball kicked in this way will have a lower trajectory. The front tip of the ball will have a tendency to turn over quickly, allowing the ball to slice through the wind. This type of punt, however, has several drawbacks. A low line-drive kick will have a short hang time, and is easier to block.

### Tailwind

If the wind is coming from behind and to his right, the punter should use his normal steps with a higher drop. The ball should be dropped from the bottom of the numbers, causing the ball to travel in a higher trajectory, and getting the ball up into the wind. A wind-aided punt will obviously increase hang time and distance. With the wind coming from the left and behind the punter, he should use the same form and technique he uses when he directional kicks to the right. This angle will serve to place the ball in the air stream, and should result in an increase in distance. Again, the ball should be dropped from the bottom of the numbers.

*Crosswind*

The punter should treat this as a directional kick. He should discern which way the wind is blowing and kick it to that side of the field. Care must be taken, however, that the angle is not too great and have the ball go out of bounds short.

*Wet Weather*

When punting on a wet field or in rainy conditions, the punter should first understand that the number one priority is to catch the ball. The punter should always be ready for a bad snap anytime he punts, especially in adverse conditions. The punter should also focus on his steps, concentrating on landing on the balls of his feet and striving to keep his feet under his hips. He may have to shorten his steps to insure good footing. The punter should slide to square up with an off target snap; fronting the ball will serve to block the ball if it slips through his hands. Obviously, punters and snappers should practice with a wet ball on occasion. Snapping and punting practice during bad weather is always a good idea. Punting practice should be automatically inserted into rainy day practices. A wet ball drill should regularly be incorporated into the practice schedule.

## Common Problems for the Punter

- Stance too wide
- Crossover step makes the kick leg cross the body
- Drop
  ✓ Too far inside
  ✓ Too far outside
  ✓ Nose down
  ✓ Nose up
  ✓ Nose turned too far inside
  ✓ Not enough extension
  ✓ Too high
  ✓ Too low
- Leg swing
  ✓ Knee bent
  ✓ Across the body
  ✓ Punch instead of kick
  ✓ Toe up
  ✓ Head up

# 9

# Snapping

The goal for every snapper is anonymity. Snappers who do their job remain nameless. The only time snappers are noticed is when they launch an errant snap. Face time on television, or having their name called, usually signals failure. Snappers play a very integral part in the kicking game. They initiate three of the most important downs in football. Two of those three plays, an extra-point attempt and a field-goal effort, lead directly to points. The other play, a punt, involves gaining or losing large chunks of field position. A snapper's worst enemy is time. Coaches want a snapper who can get the ball to the holder on a placement kick, and allow the kick to get airborne in slightly more than one second. Snaps for punts should be in the .07 to .08 second range. However, accuracy and location are just as important.

A common problem for snappers, especially on the lower levels where most snappers play other positions, is the injury factor. Snappers who do more than snap are susceptible to injury. A small hurt or injury can adversely affect the snapper's ability to perform. Thus, an effective backup snapper is imperative, and the snapper should be encouraged to let the coach know if he is hurt and he feels his ability to snap has been affected.

# Grip

The first step in training a snapper is perfecting the grip. The prospective snapper begins by grasping the ball with his dominant hand, like a quarterback. It should be placed just forward of the center of the ball. The forefinger and middle finger are touch fingers. The ring finger and pinkie should contact the laces. The thumb should be kept on the underside of the ball about the same distance from the back tip of the ball as the middle finger. The dominant hand supplies the power in the snap. The off (or guide) hand should be placed on the opposite side of the ball, with the fingers pointed toward the line of scrimmage. The thumb of the guide hand should be stretched down toward the bottom of the ball. This positioning influences the tightness of the spiral. A ball with a tight spiral gets to the target quickly and is easier to catch. The finger pads of the off hand should be the only part of that hand gripping the ball. Care should be taken to avoid palming the ball. The forefinger should be placed on the seam. The guide hand can be slightly adjusted forward or backward for more comfort.

# Stance

The center's stance should be slightly wider than shoulder width. The toes on his right foot should be even with the instep of the left foot (right handed snapper). The toes should point straight ahead. His weight should be on the balls of the feet, with the feet planted firmly to prevent slipping. From this stance, he should bend his knees and reach out to grip the ball. To avoid a high snap, he should force the butt down by flexing the knees and ankles instead of widening the base, or inward flexing the knees and ankles. The center's stance should allow him to be far enough off the ball to keep it at arm's length. Little or no weight is exerted on the ball. His shoulders should remain square, and his back level, when he bends over the ball. Hip position is critical. A center who positions his hips high in his stance will cause the snap to sail high; whereas, low hips can cause the snap to be low. The center should experiment with his stance to attain a balanced position. Legs create needed power. In this respect, the center is like a pitcher in baseball; the sudden extension of the legs supply the power needed for good velocity.

# Addressing the Ball

The ball should be at arm's length from the center after he settles into his stance. Arms should be 90 to 95 percent extended. Adjustment in arm bend and knee bend to facilitate comfort is permissible. The center will pre-position the ball so the laces are rotated toward the right and facing down toward the ground. Once the ball has been positioned, the center will then reach out and grip the ball as has been described. After correct hand placement has been accomplished, he will tilt his dominant hand so it is under the ball. The dominant hand passes the ball, while the off hand guides it.

# Snap

On an extra-point or field-goal snap (short snap), the target is the holder's hands. When snapping for a punt (long snap), the target is usually the punter's kick leg, thigh, and hip. After the center gets the ready signal from the holder (or upback), he is free to snap the ball when he is ready. He should vary this interval so the defense cannot time up the block. The center looks through his legs to focus on the target. The target on a short snap is usually seven yards deep, while a long snap travels 14 to 15 yards. When snapping the ball, the center should pull both arms through his legs with equal effort. The dominant hand, which is under the ball, will graze the grass as the ball moves toward the target. The guide hand stays on top of the ball as the arms extend toward the target; meanwhile, the dominant hand is basically throwing the ball to the target. This hand supplies the spin and velocity. The dominant wrist should roll so the forefinger goes over the top and points toward the target. As the arms extend backwards, the fingers and hand should be flexed toward the forearm to get full extension. The guide hand's purpose is to steer the ball in a straight line during and after the snap. The snapper should end with his arms fully extended toward the target, with his fingers pointing toward the punter. The palms should be facing up and out. The center should get a feeling of his entire body moving toward the target. He should try to drive the shoulders between the legs to get good follow-through and body weight behind the ball.

Snapping for a punt is almost the same as an extra-point or field-goal snap. However, some adjustments have to be made for the differences. The major variation is the distance the ball must travel. A field-goal or extra-point snap usually covers seven yards. Most punters set up 15 yards deep. This doubles the distance the ball must travel. Another dissimilarity is the height of the snap. The target for a punt is higher than a place kick. To compensate for the differences in the two types of snaps, a snapper should drastically angle the front tip of the ball for a punt. Velocity of the snap is another major difference. The impetus of a punt snap should cause the center to slide back more than on an extra-point or field-goal try.

## Evaluating the Snap

If the ball is missing the target horizontally, the problem might be the snapper's feet. If the feet are staggered, it should be no more than a toe to instep relationship. Both feet should move back toward the target as a result of the momentum of the body and the arms during the snap. The center's hands on the follow-through should finish on the same plane. If the dominant hand finishes on a higher plane than the guide hand, the ball will drift to the side of the dominant hand. For example, if the dominant hand is the right hand, the ball will miss to the right of the target. If the dominant hand ends up lower than the guide hand, the ball will tail toward the side of the guide hand.

A snap that floats high might signal that the center's butt and hips were too high. Another cause could be the center's hands did not stay low on the backward movement. The ball may have been released too high between the legs. Hand adjustment should include making the forearms hit lower on the inside part of the thighs. Lower body adjustments include keeping the butt and back flat and parallel to the ground. The snapper should visualize that a table is setting above his back and he cannot let his back or butt touch the table. A low snap is usually caused by a low release point. A simple adjustment is to make the forearms hit higher on the thighs on the follow-through. Another major cause for a low snap is letting go of the ball too soon; holding on for a split second longer will remedy this.

## Telegraphing the Snap

If the rush team is getting a great takeoff, the reason may be the center's mannerisms. Many snappers give away the timing of the snap by hitching. Hitching involves moving the hips a split second before moving the hands. Astute scouting techniques will allow the rush team to gain a head start on the snap. The result could be a blocked kick. The snapper should practice activating the hips and hands at the same time.

# 10

# Scouting Special Teams

Just as sound scouting techniques are required to study an opponent's offense and defense, a thorough study of an opponent's special teams can give your team an edge. Film study, as well as close observation during pre-game warm-ups, can offer useful intelligence on the opponent. Unlike most offensive or defensive observations, special teams study can extend right up to the opening kickoff. The following are scouting sheets that can be used during film study. Pre-game scouting sheets are also included where appropriate.

# Kickoff – Film Study

## Alignment

Stacks?
Choir?
Diagram: (Main Alignment)

## Launch Points

Right Hash       _____
Left Hash       _____
Middle       _____

## Kicker

Type:
Soccer       _____
Straight on       _____

Hang Time       _____
Depth of Kick       _____

## Coverage

Stay in lanes       _____
Lane exchanges       _____
First player to ball _____
Contain       _____
Safeties       _____

Onside Kick (Alignment):

Safety Kick (Alignment):

# Kickoff Return – Film Study

Basic Alignment/Numbers:

Diagram:

## Types of Returns

Wall          _____
Wedge       _____
Middle        _____
Cross Blocks   _____

Does the center take cover team to the wall?      _____

Do linemen leave early?_____      Which ones?    _____

## Holes or Soft Spots

Diagram of Soft Spots:

Most dangerous return man      _____
Return man with the worst hands    _____
Reverse possibility        _____

## Hands Team

Diagram:

# Punt Return – Film Study

## Fronts

How many normally in the box? _____
Diagrams:


Pressure Philosophy _____
Return Philosophy _____
Personnel Change for Philosophy _____

## Returns

Wall Returns _____
Middle Returns _____
Holdup Returns _____
How many safeties _____
Who do we want to catch the ball _____
Reverse Possibility _____
Do we directional kick _____


Return Diagrams:

# Punt Block – Film Study

## Types of Blocks Used

Diagrams:



Most Dangerous Rusher _____
Do they fair catch on called blocks? _____
Do they tip off return or block? _____
Where can we fake by alignment or personnel? _____

# Punt – Film Study

**Base Formation**
Diagram:

**Backed Up Formation**
Diagram:

**Quick Kick – Formation – Who – When**
Diagram:

**Personnel**

| | | | | |
|---|---|---|---|---|
| Center | # | _____ | Grade | _____ |
| Right Guard | # | _____ | Grade | _____ |
| Left Guard | # | _____ | Grade | _____ |
| Right Tackle | # | _____ | Grade | _____ |
| Left Tackle | # | _____ | Grade | _____ |
| Right End | # | _____ | Grade | _____ |
| Left End | # | _____ | Grade | _____ |
| Right Back | # | _____ | Grade | _____ |
| Left Back | # | _____ | Grade | _____ |
| Personal Protector | # | _____ | Grade | _____ |
| Punter | # | _____ | Grade | _____ |

**Punter**

| | |
|---|---|
| Depth | _____ |
| How many steps | _____ |
| Right Footed | _____ |
| Left Footed | _____ |

**Block Scheme**

| | |
|---|---|
| Line Splits | _____ |
| Man | _____ |
| Zone | _____ |
| Combo | _____ |
| First Man Downfield | _____ |

Safeties           _____

Contain           _____


Snapper Mannerisms:

| Times: | #1 | #2 | #3 | #4 | #5 | #6 |
|---|---|---|---|---|---|---|
| Snap | _____ | _____ | _____ | _____ | _____ | _____ |
| Punter | _____ | _____ | _____ | _____ | _____ | _____ |
| Total Handle Time | _____ | _____ | _____ | _____ | _____ | _____ |
| Hang Time | _____ | _____ | _____ | _____ | _____ | _____ |
| Total | _____ | _____ | _____ | _____ | _____ | _____ |


**Fakes**

Diagrams:


**Punt – Pre-Game**

| # | _____ | Snapper (Snap) | _____ | _____ | _____ | _____ | _____ |
|---|---|---|---|---|---|---|---|
| # | _____ | | _____ | _____ | _____ | _____ | _____ |
| # | _____ | | _____ | _____ | _____ | _____ | _____ |
| # | _____ | Punter (Time) | _____ | _____ | _____ | _____ | _____ |
| # | _____ | | _____ | _____ | _____ | _____ | _____ |
| # | _____ | | _____ | _____ | _____ | _____ | _____ |
| | _____ | Total | _____ | _____ | _____ | _____ | _____ |

| # | _____ | Returners |
|---|---|---|
| # | _____ | |
| # | _____ | |
| # | _____ | |


| Punter | # | _____ | Punter | # | _____ | Punter | # | _____ |
|---|---|---|---|---|---|---|---|---|
| Depth | | _____ | Depth | | _____ | Depth | | _____ |
| Steps | | _____ | Steps | | _____ | Steps | | _____ |
| Hang Time | | _____ | Hang Time | | _____ | Hang Time | | _____ |
| Head Wind | | _____ | Head Wind | | _____ | Head Wind | | _____ |
| Tail Wind | | _____ | Tail Wind | | _____ | Tail Wind | | _____ |

Snapper Mannerisms:

# Extra Point/Field Goal – Film Study

Base Formation:

## Personnel

|  | # | Height | Weight | Grade |
|---|---|---|---|---|
| Center | _____ | _____ | _____ | _____ |
| Right Guard | _____ | _____ | _____ | _____ |
| Left Guard | _____ | _____ | _____ | _____ |
| Right Tackle | _____ | _____ | _____ | _____ |
| Left Tackle | _____ | _____ | _____ | _____ |
| Right End | _____ | _____ | _____ | _____ |
| Left End | _____ | _____ | _____ | _____ |
| Right Wing | _____ | _____ | _____ | _____ |
| Left Wing | _____ | _____ | _____ | _____ |
| Holder | _____ | _____ | _____ | _____ |
| Kicker | _____ | _____ | _____ | _____ |

Weakest Blocker(s) _____

Holder

    Depth _____

    Pass/Run Threat _____

    Hands _____

    Quickness _____

Kicker

    Soccer _____

    Straight On _____

    Height of Kick _____

Snapper Mannerisms:

## Time

Snap _____ Snap _____ Snap _____ Snap _____ Snap _____

Total _____ Total _____ Total _____ Total _____ Total _____

# Extra Point/Field Goal – Pre-Game

Kicker       #_____     #_____     #_____
Holder       #_____     #_____     #_____
Snapper     #_____     #_____     #_____

Depth of Holder      _____
Number of Steps     _____
Height of Kick       _____
Range of Kicker      _____
Head Wind         _____
Tail Wind          _____

## Time

Snap ____ Snap ____ Snap ____ Snap ____ Snap ____
Total ____ Total ____ Total ____ Total ____ Total ____

Snapper Mannerisms:

# Extra Point/Field Goal Defense – Film Study

## Basic Rush

Diagram:

Do they cover all eligibles?     _____
Most Dangerous Rusher       _____
Where can we fake it?        _____

# 11

# Special Teams Practice

Practice organization is usually the litmus test of whether a head coach truly believes that special teams play is a third of the game. Is he a true disciple of special teams play, or is he just paying lip service? Some coaches have a mistaken notion that to effectively prepare their special teams they must devote an exorbitant amount of their practice time to special teams play, and when this is not possible they become disillusioned and frustrated. What they should understand is that to have an outstanding kicking game they do not have to spend an excessive amount of practice time on special teams. The secret to effective special teams play is not necessarily the amount of time spent, but when to use the available time.

Most teams practice special teams either at the beginning or at the end of practice. The teams that practice special teams play at the beginning of practice usually foster a "let's get it over with so we can get into the real practice" attitude, while teams which wait until the end of practice to drill special teams play are faced with a "get it over with so we can go home" attitude. Pre-practice special teams drills can be looked upon as punishment. Players may say, "Why should I be out here before practice working, while most of my teammates are lounging around waiting for the real practice?"

Coaches are faced with the difficult task of balancing offensive, defensive, and special teams periods in a structured and effective manner. Planning and organizing allotted practice time is a key to successful, and effective, special teams play. Special teams play should be emphasized in pre-season camps. Special teams work can be combined with conditioning drills. Covering all aspects of special teams play before the first game is a must. Well-conditioned players and effective special teams preparation can serve to help win early games. The following progression can be used to implement special teams play:

- Find deep snappers, punters, kickers, and return men first. Coaches should have open tryouts to make sure that no one is overlooked.
- Coverage schemes (kickoff coverage and punt coverage)
- Return schemes (kickoff return and punt return)
- Field-goal and extra-point attempts
- Field-goal and extra-point defense

A basic and highly effective practice plan would include five stages or levels:
- Level 1 – Chalk-talk/walk-through mode (the scheme should be introduced in a chalk-talk or walk-through setting).
- Level 2 – Jog-through mode
- Level 3 – Half-speed run-through
- Level 4 – Full-speed
- Level 5 – Game-speed

Specialist periods that deal with players who handle the ball should be included in a comprehensive practice plan. Long snappers should team up with the punter and punt returners, short snappers with a holder and a kicker, while the kickoff returner should catch kickoffs. To conserve time (and improve timing), punters should always kick a ball snapped by a center. The punt returner should field the punt. Place kicks should be practiced together by the core players (snapper, holder, kicker). Care should be taken, however, as to when specialty periods take place; quality reps will not result if specialty players feel that these extra duties are a form of punishment. However, if a player does not play another position, he should be open to work at any point during or after practice.

Two schools in particular are known for their innovative approach to practice: Virginia Tech and Texas Tech. Virginia Tech, and Coach Beamer, are nationally known as leaders and trendsetters in regards to special teams play. Many teams have implemented many of Coach Beamer's innovative practice ideas and practice structures. He promotes a feeling of worth and purpose for each special teams unit. For example, Virginia Tech's punt team is referred to as the Pride Team. The punt block team is alluded to as the Pride and Joy Team. Another innovator of special teams play is Texas Tech's Manny Matsakis. Coach Matsakis uses musical themes in his special teams practices. Loudspeakers at the practice field broadcast a particular song during different phases of special teams practice. The following is a list of Tech's special teams units with its nickname and theme song:

- Punt Team – Bomb Squad – "Mission Impossible" theme.
- Kickoff Return – Showtime – "Start Me Up" (Rolling Stones).
- Kickoff Cover – Head Hunters – "Seek and Destroy" (Metallica).
- Punt Return – Sharks – "Jaws" Theme.
- Field Goal – Score – "Rock and Roll Part 2" (Gary Glitter).

The music gives each group an identity and "gets them keyed up." The music generates a "bunch of energy" and is a source of pride. Practice during special teams periods can be time well spent with the right amount of organization, motivation, and the use of the best players on the team. The time used can easily be converted into wins throughout the year.

Part of any game organization should include getting the various special teams units on and off the field at the appropriate time. Nothing is more embarrassing or damaging than having too many (or not enough) men on the field. Costly penalties and wasted timeouts can come back to haunt a team. A simple and effective way to practice getting special teams units on and off the field is to script special teams into scrimmages. The following are examples of scripts for full-speed kicking scrimmages, as well as an intra-squad situation.

# Intra-Squad Scrimmage

- Take a safety (-3)
- Safety kickoff (-20)
- Tight punt (-3)
- Spread punt (-30)
- Fake punt (50)
- Pooch punt (+30)
- Fair catch kick (+30)
- Field goal (+20)
- PAT (+3)
- Fake PAT (+3)
- Fire PAT (+3)

- PAT block (-3)
- Field-goal block (-20)
- Kickoff (-40)
- Onside kick (-40)
- Sky kick (-40)
- Kickoff return (-50)
- Hands team (-50)
- Punt return (50)
- Punt block (50)
- Safety return (+30)

# Kick Scrimmage Versus an Opponent

| Team A | Team B |
|---|---|
| Kickoff | Kickoff return |
| Punt return (+30) | Punt (-30) |
| Punt (50) | Punt return (50) |
| Punt block (+40) | Punt (-40) |
| Tight punt (-3) | Tight punt return |
| Field-goal block left hash (-15) | Field goal right hash (+15) |
| Kickoff return | Kickoff |
| Punt (pooch) (+35) | Punt return (pooch) (-35) |
| Tight punt return | Tight punt (-3) |
| Field goal – right hash (+15) | Field-goal block left hash (-15) |
| Safety kick (-20) | Safety return |
| Field-goal block right hash (-15) | Field goal left hash (+15) |
| Point after touchdown | Point after touchdown block |
| Point after touchdown block | Point after touchdown |
| Safety return | Safety kick (-20) |
| Punt (-30) | Punt return (+30) |
| Punt return (50) | Punt (50) |
| Field goal left hash (+15) | Field-goal block right hash (-15) |
| Punt (-40) | Punt block (+40) |
| Punt return – pooch (-35) | Punt (pooch) (+35) |

# 12

# Grading System for Special Teams

The following is an example of a grading scale, which can be used to grade game film, evaluate performances, and to keep a special team's goal and performance chart. This scale and chart could serve to motivate and grade special teams performance. Award winners can also be based upon this grading procedure.

## Kickoff Coverage

### Kicker

| | |
|---|---|
| Hang time of 4.0 seconds | 1 point |
| Correct location of directional kick | 1 point |
| Good special kick | 2 points |
| Touchback | 2 points |

### Coverage

| | |
|---|---|
| First man downfield (35-yard-line) | 1 point |
| Wedge buster eliminate more than one man | 2 points |

| | |
|---|---|
| Tackle the ball carrier inside the 20-yard-line | 2 points |
| Tackle the ball carrier inside the 10-yard-line | 3 points |
| Achieve goal of average starting yard line goal | 3 points |
| Great effort | 4 points |
| Big hit | 4 points |

# Kickoff Return

| | |
|---|---|
| Break a tackle | 2 points |
| Execute a good block | 2 points |
| Achieve average starting yard line for game | 3 points |
| Big return (+35 yards) | 3 points |
| Two blocks on one play | 4 points |
| Key block on long return | 4 points |
| Great effort | 4 points |

# Punt Protection and Coverage

Punter
| | |
|---|---|
| Hang time 4.0 | 1 point |
| Hang time better than 4.0 | 2 points |
| Good location of directional kick | 1 point |
| Punt inside 20-yard-line | 1 point |
| Punt inside 10-yard-line | 2 points |

## Snapper

| | |
|---|---|
| Good snap | 1 point |

## Coverage

| | |
|---|---|
| Wedge buster | 2 points |
| Tackle ball carrier inside 20-yard-line | 2 points |
| Tackle ball carrier inside 10-yard-line | 3 points |
| Achieve punting net goal | 3 points |
| Great effort | 4 points |

# Punt Return and Block

| | |
|---|---|
| Break tackle | 2 points |
| Key return | 3 points |
| Good block | 2 points |
| Force bad kick | 3 points |
| Achieve net goal for game | 3 points |
| Great effort | 4 points |

# Miscellaneous

| | |
|---|---|
| Good snap on PAT/FG | 1 point |
| Good hold on PAT/FG | 1 point |
| Force a miss on PAT/FG | 3 points |
| Safety | 2 points |
| Force a fumble | 6 points |
| Recover a fumble | 6 points |
| Block a punt | 6 points |
| Block PAT/FG | 6 points |
| Touchdown | 6 points |
| Field Goal | 3 points |
| PAT | 1 point |
| Solo tackle | 4 points |
| Second hit | 2 points |
| Hit on ball carrier | 1 point |

# 13

# Special Teams Drills

### Team Kickoff Return Drill

*Objective*: To enable two kickoff return units to get quality reps in a short amount of time.

*Description*: This drill involves two return teams and two service cover teams, for a total of 44 players. A kickoff team aligns on the kickoff line with a return team facing them. On the kickoff team's kickoff line, the number two return team huddles on the sideline. On the kickoff return team's alignment line, a second kickoff team huddles on the sideline. After the first kickoff team kicks, and the return team executes the called return, the number two return team and the number two kickoff team take the field. Also, if each unit huddles at the end of the field in the direction they are working, they can align and perform their assignment going in the opposite direction. This setup enables each return unit to get two quality reps in a short amount of time. Also, each return unit will get a rep going in either direction.

### Communication Drill

*Objective*: To establish and improve communication between the two halfbacks and deep returner on kickoff returns.

*Description*: The two halfbacks and deep returner align in their kickoff return positions. A jugs machine, or a coach who has good control and arm strength, places the ball in various areas between the halfbacks and the returner. The returner and the halfbacks should communicate who will field the ball. The returner is like a centerfielder in baseball. He will give "you" and "me" calls. The halfbacks should not back up to field a ball. The coach should mix in rolling balls, which simulates a squib kickoff.

## Kickoff Cover Drill

*Objective*: To provide cover men the experience of sprinting downfield and tackling the return man. They will learn to operate in space and defend a kickoff.

*Description*: Line up cover men in single file. On the other end of the field will be a line of returners. On command, the cover man will cover, and on a second command the return man will return. The defender will sprint downfield and come to balance five yards from the returner. The cover man should understand which leverage he should use. He should be instructed as to which shoulder to leverage the bal, and position himself to apply a two-handed tag below the waist on the returner. This drill can be done regardless of the attire used for that particular practice.

## Kickoff Cover Drill

*Objective*: To perfect coverage technique in the speed and contact zones.

*Description*: A kicker making his normal approach is used to simulate a kick. A returner will also be involved to give the coverage team a target. The use of a kicker serves to allow the cover men to polish takeoff skills. Groups of three cover men are used. The cover men are faced with two groups of three service personnel who use hand shields. This first line of resistance sets up 10 yards away. Cover men should outrun any block in this zone. Blocks should be beaten with speed and hands. Blocks should be avoided to the ball side, and cover men should not slow down. These blocks will be defeated with speed. The second line will set up 10 yards from the returner and try to shield block their assigned cover man as they near the contact zone. The cover men will engage the blocker. In the contact zone, blocks should be attacked and defeated while holding appropriate leverage, then disengage and front up the returner.

## Bad Snap Drill

*Objective*: To help the punter become more proficient in fielding errant snaps.

*Description*: The punter will field balls which are purposely short hopped, rolled, or off target. A coach will trigger the drill by under-handing the ball. The punter should field the ball and get the kick off. If a rusher is added, the punter should field the ball, elude the rusher, and launch the kick.

## Coffin Corner Punt Drill

*Objective*: To perfect out-of-bounds punts.

*Description*: The punter will launch punts from the right hash, from the left hash, and from points between the hashes. The punter will aim to the right on punts from the middle of the field to the right hash. A service person will serve as a shagger and target. The target will line up on the goal line. The punter will aim at the target and try to drive the ball out of bounds. The ball should sail out of bounds from near the goal line to the five-yard line. Balls kicked from the left side should be aimed at the target who will line up on the 10-yard line. This landmark should cause the ball to leave the field between the 10-yard line and the goal line.

## Drop Consistency Drill

*Objective*: To develop the mechanics of a consistent drop.

*Description*: The punter places his kicking leg on a yard line, takes his normal stride into the ball, and drops the ball on the line without kicking the ball. A proper drop should find the nose of the ball slightly in and down. A ball dropped with proper positioning will bounce back and slightly outside the line. If the ball bounces forward, it signals the ball was dropped with the back of the ball lower than the front of the ball. If the ball bounces backward toward the punter, it would signal that the front end struck the ground first.

## Buddy Drill

*Objective*: To work on the drop. The drill incorporates a drop and a kicking action.

*Description*: Two people are needed for the drill. The punter has a service person to assist him as he goes through his normal kicking steps and drops the ball. The buddy will catch the ball before it hits the kicker's foot. With the ball removed, the punter will follow through normally.

## Punt Cover Drill

*Objective*: To teach the punt cover team how to properly cover a punt.

*Description*: Launch a ball to a returner with a jugs machine, or by simply lobbing the ball. The returner fields the ball, runs forward, and then side-to-side. The cover team should start toward their landmarks, find the ball, and converge. They should shuffle to hold proper leverage with the ball. If the ball moves away, defenders should shuffle and overlap. They should keep their shoulders square to the ball, and gradually close down the running area. A second returner can be added to run a reverse. This drill should have only two or three changes of direction. Care must be taken that it does not turn into a conditioning drill. Gunners should run past the catch.

### Distraction Drill

*Objective*: To enhance the returner's concentration and focus.

*Description*: A man should shadow the returner, and when the ball descends, he will close to the returner and wave his arms and yell. Multiple shadows with shields can be used. These service people can bang the returner just after he has caught the ball.

### Punt Return Block Techniques Drill

*Objective*: To perfect blocking assignments used in the various punt return schemes.

*Description*: Split the return team into halves. Work on individual techniques for the left side independently from the right side. The drill then progresses to a half-line set-up. Once again, the right and left sides work independently. Splitting the unit into halves allows for more concentrated work. Finish with a full-unit scheme.

### Punt Pressure Drill

*Objective*: To benefit both punt blockers and the middlemen on the punt team. Rushers get a feel of blocking the punt at the launch point, while the snapper and punter perform under pressure.

*Description*: The center snaps the ball to the punter, who kicks the ball with no blocking or protection. The rusher has a free run at the punter, coming from either side of the center from a width of seven yards. The snap should be perfect, and the punter should punt quickly and on time.

### Basic Run-Through Drill

*Objective*: To teach kick blockers the basic get off and run-through.

*Description*: Cones (or an offensive play strip) should be used to simulate the line of scrimmage. Players should explode on ball movement and run through the spot of the punt. The spot may be identified with a cone, shirt, or painted mark. A coach will be near the spot and will toss a deflated football for the rusher to block. Correct hand placement should be used, with the thumbs touching. The rusher should turn his shoulders to the ball, serving to widen the blocking surface.

### Basic Layout Drill

*Objective*: To further teach the basic run-through technique. This drill adds a layout technique.

*Description*: Each rusher moves on ball movement. Two yards from the spot, he will get airborne. The airborne technique is not a jump. It is a lunge with the body parallel to the ground, arms extended, and thumbs touching. A mat can be used to soften the landing. The blocker will follow through by getting off of the ground, scooping the ball, and scoring.

## Full Speed Block Drill

*Objective*: To teach players the feel of blocking a punt.

*Description*: Line up players in two lines facing the coach. On ball movement, one side rushes the coach who is simulating the punter. Each player aims for the launch point, which is marked by a towel or shirt, explodes out of his stance, and works to the contact point. At the spot, he should extend his arms parallel to the ground, making sure they remain below helmet level. The thumbs should be touching. The coach will underhand the ball and allow the player to get a feel of running through the contact point and blocking the ball. The drill should end with the player scooping the ball and scoring. The coach can time each player to create a sense of competition.

## Horseshoe Drill

*Objective*: To allow field-goal kickers the opportunity to line up kicks from various angles.

*Description*: The kicker will kick at 10 different spots, which should be in the shape of a horseshoe. The kicker gets one kick from each spot.

## Placekicking Pressure Drill

*Objective*: To promote competition between a skeleton unit of the middle players on the field-goal or extra-point team, and a rusher who has a free run at the kick. The drill benefits the rush team as well as the field-goal/extra-point team.

*Description*: A rusher rushes the kick on the snap, using a run-through or layout technique at the kick spot. The middle players should perform flawlessly in order to get the kick off. The center should execute a good snap, while the holder receives the ball and executes a good placement.

## Place Kick Pressure Drill

*Objective*: To train edge rushers to effectively rush a place kick.

*Description*: Markers are used to simulate the tight end and wing on both sides. The edge rushers align in their respective slots. One man at a time will rush on ball movement. A mat will be placed with the launch point marked. Each rusher should come off low and hard on ball movement. False steps and rising up on the charge should be avoided. Each man should be coached to explode out of his stance and take the correct angle. At the spot, the rusher should drive through the block area with thumbs touching. If he leaves his feet, he should lay out parallel to the ground. The rusher should avoid any dive that is upward or vertical.

## Distance Snap Drill

*Objective*: To improve snap speed.

*Description*: The snapper places several balls around him, addressing each of the balls with the correct grip and stance. He will then snap each ball as straight and as far as he can. The main goal for each snap is distance.

## Goal Post Drill

*Objective*: To work on accuracy of long or short snaps.

*Description*: The snapper lines up sevens from the goal post to simulate a field-goal or extra-point attempt, snaps the ball, and tries to hit the goal post. The snapper then moves to a depth of 15 yards from the goal post, snaps the ball, and tries to hit the goal post from this distance.

## No Step Drill

*Objective*: To help the placekicker perfect body position at impact – probably the most important phase of a kick.

*Description*: The kicker places his plant foot even with, and six inches from, the ball with the toe pointed toward the goal post. From this position, the kicker simply swings his kicking leg and kicks the ball. Little momentum will occur, so the ball will not travel far. The drill is great for teaching the proper body position at contact. This drill also benefits the follow-through. The kicker should swing his leg hard but smooth and follow through down the target line. The leg should swing above the waist on the follow-through.

## Trajectory Drill

*Objective*: To improve the trajectory of a field-goal or extra-point attempt. Low trajectory is a prime reason for blocked kicks, and is a common problem for kickers who are moving from the high school level to the collegiate level.

*Description*: The kicker places the ball seven yards from the goal post. He tries to kick the ball up and over the goal post. The kicker will need to hit a spot that is a little lower on ball in order for it to cross the bar.

## Door Handle Drill

*Objective*: To teach proper follow-through on a field-goal or extra-point attempt. Many soccer-style kickers have poor follow-though habits.

*Description*: This drill is done off the field. The kicker will place his hand on a doorknob, countertop, or any surface that would serve to stabilize the kicker. From this position, the kicker simply swings his kicking leg as high as he can.

## Bad Snap Drill

*Objective*: To teach the kicker to kick a ball after a bad snap. Since every hold in a game is not perfect, this drill allows the kicker to get used to kicking a field goal or extra point with a less than perfect hold.

*Description*: The kicker places the ball on a kickoff tee in awkward positions. The ball can be placed with the laces facing the kicker, the ball tilted too far to the right, or the ball tilted to the left.

# About the Author

**Kenny Ratledge** is the defensive coordinator at Sevier County High School (5A) in Sevierville, Tennessee. Ratledge has published 26 articles about football in national publications, as well as two books, *Attacking Football's Wing T* and *Football's Attacking 46 Bear Defense*.

Ratledge previously coached at Doyle High School in Knoxville, TN, and Lenoir City (TN) High School. A defensive coordinator for 25 years, Ratledge has coached defensive line, inside linebackers, outside linebackers, secondary, and offensive line. During his career, he has also coached baseball and basketball. His defense led the state in scoring defense in 1997, as Sevier County went to the state semi-finals. Sevier County won the State 5A Championship in 1999, setting a state record with five interceptions in the championship game. From 1995 to 2000, Sevier County finished first or second in defense in the Big East Conference, which has four former state champions (one of those teams leads the state in all-time wins).

A graduate of the University of Tennessee (B.S., M.S.), Ratledge earned an Ed.S. degree from Lincoln Memorial University, and has attained a professional teaching rating of Career Ladder III (highest level). Ratledge also played baseball at Hiwassee College, and was named the AFLAC National Assistant Coach of the Year in 2002.